Every Split Second Counts

Martin Hines
with Richard Coomber

Every Split Second Counts

JOHN BLAKE

Published by John Blake Publishing Ltd,
3 Bramber Court, 2 Bramber Road,
London W14 9PB, UK

www.blake.co.uk

First published in hardback in 2008

ISBN: 978-1-84454-658-9

British Library Cataloguing-in-Publication Data:
A catalogue record for this book is available from the British Library.

Design by www.envydesign.co.uk

Printed in the UK by CPI William Clowes Beccles NR34 7TL

1 3 5 7 9 10 8 6 4 2

Text copyright © Martin Hines and Richard Coomber, 2008

Papers used by John Blake Publishing are natural, recyclable
products made from wood grown in sustainable forests.
The manufacturing processes conform to the environmental
regulations of the country of origin.

I dedicate this book to the memory of my daughter Kelly and to my Mother and Father who loved and supported me through thick and thin. My father was an incredible influence and an absolute inspiration in my life while my mother gave me the belief that nothing was impossible and there is no such word as can't. I am indeed so proud to have been the son of Mark and Maudie Hines.

This has been a fantastic journey over many decades and many wonderful people have touched my life in so many ways on the track, in the world of business and in life itself.

It would be easy to overlook an individual so in fear of doing this I would like to say a heartfelt global thank you to every single one of you, with special thanks going to my loyal team of staff at Zip Kart, my wife Tina, son Luke and daughter Tuesday, who all have to put up with me every day!

This indeed has been a testing experience for my memory and the stories I have told are exactly as my mind recalls them so any mistakes are down to my overstressed memory.

My thanks go to Richard Coomber, my ghost-writer, who made this story of my life an absolute pleasure to script. I have promised Richard we will not leave it so long before we start on the next book.

Also a big thank you to Rocky and Pam, because without them this book would never have happened.

We must not forget to mention all the photographers that we have used work from, they are all friends and I would not want to leave them out: Fred Scatley, Maureen McGee, Doug Rees,

Chris Dixon, Chris Walker, Mark Burgess and Erick Severe. My special thanks to Mark Burgess of Karting Magazine for supplying items from their archives that helped replenish my memory, likewise Eric Severe of Media Superkart.

Contents

Forewords

I don't remember when I first met Martin Hines but for sure it was several years after I first observed the 'King of Karting' round the many long circuit racetracks of the UK, places such as Donington Park and Silverstone. I would see the super-slick Zip Kart team and the permanently tanned Martin winning another GP plate.

He was like a hero figure to a young lad making his way up the junior formula and at that time I wanted nothing more from my career than to be like him. I didn't think about car racing or Formula One. Why would I when he appeared to have it all, winning races in the fastest 250cc superkarts and running a successful business producing karts for each formula below that?

As you can imagine from what I have written above, I was in awe of Martin and the way he ran his business. Therefore, you can also guess how it was finally to be introduced to him after a couple of years and then, a few more years down the line, to race for his Zip Kart team in Junior Britain through 1987 and 1988 and to win the championship for him.

A friendship was formed that has endured until today,

despite the fact that my career has taken me into car racing, leaving karting behind. But kart racers stick together like a big family, and it doesn't matter how long it is since you raced a kart, you still remember the innocent days of going racing wheel to wheel without the politics that exists in car racing.

I cannot think of anyone who has had so many drivers pass through his team and progress to success in car racing. And he always did it with a smile and without trying to take a percentage of the driver's future earnings. He did it because he believed in the talent and knew he had the facilities to help them achieve success and then assist them on their journey into professional careers in cars.

It is easy to put words down on paper that don't always accurately reflect the individual, because they can sound sycophantic; but, with my fingers held up and with the words 'cub's honour' on my lips, I swear that you will never find another like Martin Hines: a true gentleman, a hard racer and someone with an unusual willingness to be happy for others' success. He can also scare the hell out of you with a deathly look if you cross him, but, thankfully, I have never been on the end of that. The bottom line is, he is hard but extremely fair.

I never raced wheel to wheel with Martin and I am glad, because I know he would have won.

David Coulthard
Monaco, May 2008

first met Martin Hines together with his parents, Mark and Maude, at the Zip Kart factory in Hoddesdon when they invited me to join the early Young Guns team.

We won many championships and I particularly remember the Junior World Championship in West Germany. Martin produced a special kart for the event which later became the ubiquitous '935'. The tyres from Bridgestone were 1.5 seconds a lap quicker than our rivals' and as the distributor, Martin and his family donated a supply to the British team - just one of the examples of Martin, Mark and Maude's commitment and generosity to young British karting talent.

At 16, I entered the 135cc Series for Zip Kart, using the 935 and, at times, the A chassis using engines from Michael Schumacher's German Tuner and later AIME. These karts were utterly fantastic, so powerful, and I well remember Martin travelling to Jesolo and Parma in Italy bringing special tyres or chassis parts.

I will always remember with such fondness travelling to Zip from Newcastle to build new chassis using the factory's facilities, then going round the corner to test at Rye House Circuit. Martin's mum and dad were so supportive of me. I'll never forget how kind they were to me... My father has since told me Mark would give him the occasional £500 to help with expenses. It is commonplace in these politically correct days to speak well of all the people one comes across in their motorsport career. I don't give a shit for 'PC', which is why I hold the Hines family in such high regard. It was Martin who demonstrated how important image was in both in your equipment and your driver's race wear. It is also vital to consider how you promote yourself.

Yes, Martin is one of the good guys in motorsport and I am privileged to consider myself a friend. Indeed, he and his wife Tina were guests at my wedding. Long may he continue to hold his passion for karting and helping young kids live their dreams.

Jason Plato
Zip Kart works driver

After a successful start to my racing career, my father Denis and I quickly realised the importance of factory support and equipment, and how even at such an entry level this could create the right results.

In 1991, at the age of twelve, I was lucky enough to be given the chance to drive for the Zip Young Guns team in its infancy, in the Cadet 60cc class. At this time team owner Martin Hines was still racing himself in the 250E gearbox karts at World Championship level and was known in the UK as 'Mr Karting'. It was an important step for me, as this was the first time I would drive for a works team and be in direct competition with my teammates; and also for Martin himself, who was pioneering a new way in which 'Dad and lad' went racing. Needless to say, the team was a great success, and grew year by year to become almost unstoppable in the junior ranks of UK karting.

In 1993 I won my first serious championship, which in turn led to where I am today, and I will always be grateful to Martin and everybody at Zip Kart who helped me on my way to F1 in those early days.

Anthony Davidson

Chapter 1

You Never Forget Your First Time

She didn't realise it at the time, but Mum was about to say the nine words that would change my life for ever: 'You can have one of those if you like.'

I looked across at Dad and we grinned at each other. Fantastic! We were going karting.

The garage just round the corner from where we lived in Church Crescent, Finchley, mainly sold sports cars but they also stocked TAB karts, and, as soon as they opened the following morning, Dad did a deal to buy two. Our nearest track was Rye House, at Hoddesdon in the Lea Valley in Hertfordshire, about thirty miles away, and the next couple of days dragged by until we could get there to put them through their paces.

I remember the moment I first drove a kart as though it had happened this morning. I can still feel the vibration that rattled every bone in my body; can still hear the glorious roar as the engine responded to my foot on the pedal; and, most of all, can still see in my mind's eye exactly what I saw as I set off down the straight faster than I'd ever travelled solo. Straw bales were just a blur as I careered round corners that loomed up far more quickly than I expected and exerted forces on my body that I'd never experienced before.

Watching from the sidelines, I'd thought of karts as superior toy cars. It was only when I drove one that I realised they are so much more. Karts are an instant cure for constipation. When you're that low to the ground – in those days it was one or two inches; today it's half an inch – you see the world from a whole new perspective. You don't sit in a kart – you are part of it. The front wheels are an extension of your feet; the back wheels part of your shoulders. It's nothing like driving a car. You can't see as much, you have no suspension to smooth out the bumps and you don't have that solid shell protecting you from the wind, the rain and being hurtled through the air if you crash. The lower you are, the more sensation you have of speed, so, when you drive a kart at even 50 m.p.h., you feel like a worm with a rocket up its backside.

I was hooked.

Ironically, Mum had picked karting because she hoped to distract me from my dream of becoming a speedway rider. She'd worried about me ever since she had seen me practise my cornering technique while tearing round the back garden on a moped. In one spectacular slide I managed to put the bike and myself through a neighbour's fence. Mum's plan worked to an extent, because I never did race on a speedway track, but my love of living on the edge couldn't be stifled, and I've had some spectacular crashes in karts, some of which I was lucky to walk away from alive.

Karting was like a drug and I couldn't get enough. That day at Rye House was the tentative start of a career that lasted more than forty years and saw me pick up at least one major championship in every decade. I'm proud of the fact that I've won more titles than any other driver and that I've beaten guys who went on to become top names in Formula One. But my obsession went beyond driving. Within a few weeks of buying those TABs, Dad and I had started a business that became Zip Karts, and we've been at the sharp end as karting has developed from simple beginnings to being recognised by motorsport's governing body, the FIA, as one of their major formulas. We led the way in superkarts. I was the first driver to average over 100 m.p.h. around Silverstone in a kart and went round the world demonstrating that gearbox karts are as spectacular – and as fast – as most other machines on four wheels or two.

The business has been my passion for nearly half a century. It's earned me a good living, made me some good friends and one or two enemies – but the latter are mostly among people who found they couldn't keep up. The track at Rye House has also played a very important part in my life. Dad took over the lease soon after we started karting and in 1968 he packed the place for the only 100cc World Championship to be held in Britain. The Zip factory is still only a few minutes' drive from the track where I first spotted the talent of youngsters I have helped on the way to motorsport superstardom: top drivers such as David Coulthard, Lewis Hamilton, Gary Paffett, Anthony Davidson, Jason Plato, Oliver Rowland and my son Luke, who shook off the trauma of an accident that almost cost him his life to become a leading touring-car and GT driver. There are others who may not yet be household names but are on their way, people such as James Calado, now driving Formula Renault, Oliver Turvey, who is in Formula Three, and Mike Conway, the Formula Three champion of 2007.

People say that, if I had a 10 per cent share in the drivers I have helped launch, I could retire. But that's never been the aim. The goal has been to work with talented young drivers, get them in a Zip Kart and win everything there is to win.

It's fair to say karting took over my life. It has taken me to the heights while providing enough kicks in the pants to stop me getting too cocky. It helped me through personal tragedies I thought would destroy me. Because of karting I have travelled the world, got to know a lot of interesting people, including some exceptionally beautiful women, and even entertained a future king and his brother. The buzz that captivated a sixteen-year-old on his first drive has never left him. I guess I've gone through life with a rocket up my backside.

Chapter 2

I Start Racing – Pigeons

It's hard to believe your life is going to be ordinary when your birth is greeted by local church bells ringing for all they are worth. Of course, there are people who will tell you that the clamour outside the window of the maternity ward in Hampstead at precisely noon on 22 April 1946 was to mark the start of the annual fair, and that those bells had pealed like that on Easter Monday since the nineteenth century. But I prefer to believe they were a signal, telling me I was especially welcome into this world.

That was certainly the way my dad, Mark William Hines, once of Ipswich but by then a successful entrepreneur in Finchley, made me feel. And my mother, Maudie Lavinia Hines, saw me as a very special gift. She loved children and always said she wanted five or six, but she suffered several miscarriages and one son was stillborn, so I turned out to be her only child and was spoiled rotten by a very special mum.

They took me home to our large Victorian house at 26 Church Crescent, Finchley, where the council had moved them when their place in Long Lane was bombed during the war. By the time I was born, Dad had managed to raise a mortgage and bought the place for £2,250. Mum's parents, Alfred and Maude Cushing, lived on the second floor and we also shared the house with a series of dogs. I've always been a dog lover, which may explain why I've known a few of the two-legged variety over the years.

The house was just a few hundred yards from Dad's bike business and, as I grew up, the double-fronted shop next to a chemist's became one of the centres of my universe. Dad started the firm shortly after World War Two. He'd made a few bob when he came out of the army by buying vegetables and selling them from a big carrier on the front of his bike. Rationing was still in force and, as a sideline, he would also collect people's ration books and then go to the local grocer or butcher and negotiate a deal that meant everyone had their ration and he received a bit extra to sell on the side.

His best friend was Wally Green. They became mates in the army, where their sparky spirits often got them into and out of a variety of scrapes. At one stage, they were separated from their unit in a battle but managed to find their way back to their base, by now wearing bits and pieces of borrowed uniform. Parts of it had been cadged from officers, so the pair of them managed to pass themselves off in the officers' mess until someone realised their accents weren't quite pukka and had them slung out. Dad eventually left the army as a sergeant major first class, despite facing a court martial for pushing a local off a bridge in India after the guy had spat at the troops marching by. Dad was acquitted.

Dad and Uncle Wally – it was normal in those days for kids to call their parents' friends Uncle or Aunt, even if they weren't related – quickly built up the bike business and Hines & Green became renowned among serious riders as a place where the owners knew their stuff. The 1950s was the golden era of cycling. Only the wealthy could afford a car, so bikes were the most popular transport for ordinary people, and Dad and Wally sold a lot of standard machines such as Raleigh and Sunbeam. But their passion was for producing specialist models, crafted from lightweight materials, for racers. They were precision bikes, customised to the rider's personal taste and specification. Dad and Wally were very good at what they did and also produced frames for leading manufacturers such as Kitchener and Claud Butler.

I started to hang round the shop from a very early age. It was a treasure trove, packed with bikes, saddles, wheels and parts, every surface covered in chains, handlebars, puncture repair kits and all sorts of odd bits of strangely shaped metal that made sense only to someone who knew bikes. There was a workshop out the back where Dad would sit and 'true up' wheels that had been buckled during a race, while downstairs in the large basement Wally and Harold 'Pete' Peters would build chassis and make repairs. Our bikes were much sought-after and a Hines frame was the first by a British manufacturer to finish in the top three of the Tour de France. Among our customers were 'the forces' sweetheart' Vera Lynn, a massive singing star at the end of the war, and King Hussein of Jordan, who would turn up in his limo and send his chauffeur downstairs with a mauve velvet cushion on which sat the part he wanted replacing.

My first school was St Mary's in Finchley, halfway between home and the shop. My grandfather had been the school caretaker for thirty-five years, so we knew most of the teachers and they treated me well despite the fact I was a bit mischievous and used to chase the girls even in those days. School was OK but it quickly became obvious I was never going to be an academic, and, however hard the teachers tried, most of what they taught me went in one ear and out the other. I never seemed able to concentrate and most lessons had me staring out of the window, wishing I was at the shop. The only subjects I enjoyed were art and, especially, maths – I could work things out in my head more quickly than the other kids, a talent that has stood me in good stead in many negotiations since. Throughout my school career, maths teachers loved me while most of the others were glad to see the back of me.

As soon as the bell rang for the end of the day I would usually make for the shop. I'd pack the odd parcel and try to look useful, but mainly I just enjoyed the chance to chat to Dad and watch him work. I got to know him very well and we started to form a bond that lasted until he died. It was never the most tranquil of relationships. We often fell out and had titanic rows and I knew at those times Dad would contradict whatever I said and, of course, I'd argue black was white if it suited me. But our bust-ups never lasted long and we always knew that beneath it all we loved each other. I have a similar volatile relationship with my son Luke. I hate it when we fight and I sometimes wonder if Dad is somewhere watching us and laughing because Luke is putting me through the same frustrations I inflicted on him.

Dad was the man I admired above all others. He was only about 5 foot 7 inches tall but he was a big man in every other way and strikingly good-looking, something he has clearly passed on to his son. OK, so some people might argue with that but no one can doubt the massive influence he had on me.

He taught me almost everything I know and made me the man I am today. He was strong-willed – after years of smoking eighty to a hundred cigarettes a day, he just stopped at the age of sixty-four and never lit up again. He was smart and inventive, always looking for new angles, new ways to stay ahead of the competition, and later he encouraged me to do the same.

And he was honest. He ran his businesses as a sole trader

rather than a limited company because he didn't think it right that when things became tough you could bale out and let others take the losses, then set up again under another name. He told me, 'Your debts are your debts and you pay them. I stand by my business and I make sure I have the money to pay my bills.' I've always been a sole trader, too.

Dad made a good living from the shop but we were by no means wealthy; yet, when the time came that I needed to go to a private school, he somehow found the cash. It came about when I found that being good at maths wasn't enough to get me through the eleven-plus exam for the grammar school. Instead, I ended up at Alder School, a secondary modern in Finchley, and started to hang out with the wrong set. The whole area was full of gangs and I tacked myself on to one of them. I'd been at the school only about nine months when kids from a rival gang attacked me and split my head open with a steel ruler. I was lucky: three months before another boy had been stabbed and died from his wounds.

A split head was quite enough for Mum and Dad. They took me away from Alders and paid for me to go to Clark's College in Ballards Lane, Finchley. But money can't buy you love, and it can't buy you a love of books. I was already behind the other kids, so they put me in a class a year younger than I was. Some would have seen that as humiliating, but not me. It was brilliant. It meant I was bigger than the rest of my group and, together with John Golding, another lad who was older than the others, I found I could wield power.

John and I worked our way through school, always the biggest in the class and always able to get menial jobs such as homework and lines done for us. The only person who got the better of us was a rather attractive French teacher who caught us writing notes about what we would like to do to her. In a novel, of course, she would have been the flattered older woman who introduced us to the delights of sex. But this is non-fiction – and she put us in detention.

All in all, school took up valuable time I would rather have spent on other things, such as my pigeons or going speedway racing. I haven't a clue where my interest in pigeons came from, but, around the age of nine or ten, I suddenly decided there was nothing I would rather do than race pigeons. I persuaded my friend Geoff Barker to give me a hand building a small loft in the bottom left-hand corner of our garden.

Geoff and I were good mates and got up to all the normal things that small boys do, such as scrumping apples and hiding in the bushes on the golf course and nicking the balls ready to sell them back to the club shop. But this was a much grander project. Before long our pigeon loft stretched right across the bottom of the garden and was filled with birds. There was a corner of Petticoat Lane set aside for pets and we used to go up on a Sunday morning, using our 'expertise' to pick out what we thought looked like the quickest birds in the group. We didn't realise they had probably been rounded up from Trafalgar Square the day before and were as likely to end a race on top of Nelson's Column as back in my loft.

Even at that age I liked to win, and I gradually built up a reasonably competitive group of birds. I joined a local club and bought all the equipment you needed to clock the birds in at the end of races. I can still remember the thrill of taking the baskets to the station to send the pigeons on their way, then sitting impatiently with Geoff, scouring the skies for the first dot that signalled a bird returning from up North or across in France. But it wasn't all fun. Geoff read in a magazine that we had to check regularly for canker because if one bird went down it could spread throughout the loft. The article had some vivid pictures of what the symptoms looked like and, sure enough, after a few weeks I realised that one of my best birds had been struck down.

'You know you have to wring its neck, don't you?' Geoff said.

I was horrified. I mumbled, 'I've never done anything like that. I don't know if I can.'

'You have to or all of them will die.'

I knew he was right. I grabbed the sick bird with one hand, put my other on its neck, looked away, swallowed, squeezed its body and twisted and pulled on its neck as hard as I could. The pigeon's head came off in my hand. I felt sick but at least it wasn't going to spread canker in the loft.

Just as I can't recall how my interest in pigeon racing started, I can't remember when it came to an end or what happened to the loft and the birds. It's a puzzle, because you can't just open the door and let them fly away – they would just come back again! Possibly I passed them on to Geoff, because about a year ago out of the blue I received an email from him with an attachment containing an article from a pigeon-racing magazine. He's still picking up prizes for his birds and, asked in the article how he'd started, Geoff replied, 'I got into it through a school friend, Martin Hines. I went on to become a fireman and still race pigeons; he went into motorsport and became a millionaire.' Well, he was right about the motorsport.

My love of speedway is easier to explain. It was a family thing. Wally was a top rider for West Ham and England and runner-up in the 1950 World Championships. All the Hines family were fans. Of course, Dad couldn't be content with just watching: he had to be down in the pits helping Wally with his bikes, and he even began to sell some mopeds and motorbikes from the shop. Eventually he started to organise events for the ACU, motorcycle racing's governing body in the UK, and at one stage ran the High Beech track near Loughton, Essex, where speedway started in this country back in 1928. My memories tend to be of watching races with Mum, then going down to the pits with Dad and Wally.

Speedway is a fantastic family sport, as important to petrolheads as football is to deadheads. The setup is much the same, with clubs around the country competing against each other. Back then, the obligatory kit for followers of sport wasn't overpriced replica shirts but a home-knitted scarf, a bobble hat and a wooden rattle to cheer your team on. I've still got mine at home.

As a kid I loved everything about speedway: the great atmosphere under the floodlights that seemed to shut the rest of the world out in the darkness beyond, the courage of the riders, the thrill of the races and the shower of cinders that sandblasted you if you stood too close to a bend. Above all I was hooked on the night air laced with the unforgettable smell of burning Castrol R in those old Jap engines. As far as I'm concerned, you can keep snorting cocaine, just give me that distinctive Castrol R scent and I'm high. If Chanel could find a way of bottling that perfume, women would find it much easier to keep their men at home.

The highlight of the speedway year was always the world championships at Wembley, where the crowd's singing of 'We'll Meet Again' – as traditional as 'Abide with Me' at the FA Cup final – always made me tingle with anticipation. But that was nothing to the feeling I had when my first sporting hero, Jack Young, took me round the track on his bike.

Jack was an Australian superstar who came to this country in 1949 and, having won all six races in his first meeting, stayed on for ten years. In 1951 he became the first rider from a Second Division British club to win the World Championship and then became the first rider to retain the title. It was traditional for the World Champion to do a lap of honour before racing started the following year, and you can imagine the feelings of a seven-year-old when Jack lifted me up on to the kidney tank and took me round in the dazzling glare of the spotlight. I can remember looking out into the semi-darkness and glimpsing the crowd as they stood and applauded. It blew me away and I guess I've loved being the centre of attention every since.

Chapter 3
Skid Kids and Bingo

Speedway was the inspiration for one of the great ideas to come out of Dad's shop, one of many examples of his ability to think outside the box in a way that made people sit up and take notice. On my way home from school one day I smoked a surreptitious 'joystick' – a double-length cigarette you could buy individually – then went down to the basement, where Wally and Pete were trying to bend some piping in a vice. It was a shape that seemed somehow familiar but not the kind of thing they usually did.

'What're you making?' I asked.

'Can't tell you,' Wally said with a smile. 'It's top secret. Maybe we'll show you next week.'

It was worth the wait. They'd stripped down an old bike to its bare frame and fitted new, stronger wheels with knobbly tyres. The mudguards had been chopped back so they were only about 15 cm long. And, most dramatic of all, they had replaced the traditional handlebars with cow-horn bars just like a speedway bike. I was looking at a prototype skid kid's bike. It looked the business and, to our delight, Wally's son David and I were going to be the first people to try it out. I knew the ideal spot.

At the back of Mill Hill golf course there was a patch of trees with a stream running through it and an oval area where there were natural berms and bumps, just perfect for a bike like this. We went down the following Saturday and just tore the place up for hours. There had never been a bike like this and it didn't take long before cow-horn handlebars were all the rage and the shop was producing them as fast as they could for all the major manufacturers.

I guess that, by the time I was around fourteen or so, I was becoming what my friends would call confident and those on the other side of the argument might describe as cocky. I started to get my dad to drop me off for school where he couldn't see the gate, then I'd walk on by and spend my days in a local workmen's café playing the pinball machines, smoking and drinking enough coffee to make a corpse hyper. Before anyone starts to criticise, just realise that it would have all worked out fine if I'd been content with being a pinball wizard. Instead I had the illusion I could be a decent footballer and occasionally went back to school for games afternoons.

One day as we were making our way down to the pitch, this whiny little kid behind me kept saying he was going to tell the teachers that I played truant. Eventually I got pissed off and spun round to shut him up. I didn't mean to hurt him – well, not badly – but when I caught him with my swinging football boot it was harder than I'd intended. He was knocked out and taken to hospital. I was invited to leave school. I was shocked – I never expected to be expelled from a school I was paying to be at.

Dad was livid and knew exactly how to punish me. He signed me up for Wilsden Technical College. But any hopes he nurtured that I would become a scholar were soon dashed. I'm just not the kind of person who can sit down and absorb theory. I've never read a single instruction manual. If I take something out of the packing and can't make it work by common sense, I send it back because it must be faulty. Wilsden wanted to teach me the ins and outs of everything without ever letting me get my hands on anything. I survived nine months and then had to get out.

I may not have been good at school but I was never work shy. Dad made sure of that and set me a great example. He seemed to have endless energy and it never occurred to him not to be doing something. I knew all about the bike shop and his involvement in speedway, but I also became aware that he spent a couple of nights a week working in a hall at the top of Barnet Hill. Eventually, he took me with him and outside the main doors, amid the posters for popular jazz acts such as Kenny Ball and Acker Bilk, there was a notice advertising twice-weekly whist drives organised by Mark Hines. I have to admit seeing dozens of people sitting round playing cards all evening wasn't my idea of fun, but Dad assured me it was very popular and there was a reasonable profit left after paying for the hire of the hall and buying the prizes.

In fact, it must have been quite a good profit because soon afterwards he announced he had taken the lease on the Temperance Hall at Tally Ho Corner, a large, old, parquet-floored building that at the time was a failing snooker club. Dad tidied it up and put on his whist drives there for a number of years while he thought up his next bright idea.

I was at home one day when a guy delivered a steel frame, about 1.8 x 1 metre and 3 foot high. Like most people, we had a 'front room', which was used only on high days and holidays. Dad would occasionally turn it into a temporary workshop in the evenings to straighten out a bike wheel that was needed urgently, and that was where he put the frame, ready to start work. It was quickly followed by a board that slotted on top of the frame, bits of wire, small electrical switches and several sheets of glass about 15–20 cm square.

I was intrigued and one evening I poked my head round the door and found Dad screwing ninety switches on to the board. I couldn't contain my curiosity any more. 'What on earth are you up to?'

'Well, we're not getting the turnout for whist drives any more, so I'm going to change it into a bingo hall. You know, like the bingo at the seaside. But instead of prizes our players will win money.'

I thought he was nuts but over the next few weeks he continued to work on his new board. By the time he erected it on the stage at the Temperance Hall, it was connected up to light bulbs behind the glass panels, which had been painted alternately red and black and numbered 1 to 90.

'See,' he said, 'when you call a number, you flick a switch and it lights up so the punters can see it as well as hear it.'

It was a terrific idea and inevitably ripped off. Someone saw the board and asked Dad to make one for him. He did and within six months all the major companies had a similar setup in their halls. I'll never be able to prove they lifted the idea from us but I know what I think.

The changeover from whist to bingo saw the whole family working flat out and Dad sent me to help his brother. Uncle John was one of those guys who can turn their hands to anything: he could run a pub, do a bit of plumbing or even build you a house as long as you didn't require more than a year's guarantee. I found him in the shed he used as a workshop, welding steel tubing into simple seat frames. He raised his protective mask and pointed to a huge blue pile in the corner. It turned out to be squares of wood that had been covered with foam and then had PVC stretched over them, and I had to screw two on to each frame to make a seat and a back.

It was tedious, fiddly work and I had six hundred to do before the bingo hall could open.

I think it was the first commercial bingo hall in London and, when the opening night came, the queues stretched round the block. We started the first session an hour late because we hadn't anticipated the time it would take to get so many people into the hall and kitted out with bingo cards and pencils. But the waiting didn't put them off, and they clearly had a good time because they kept coming back.

The bingo crowd became an extension of our family. Bingo evenings were social events and everyone got to know each other – it was a bit like *EastEnders* in a Temperance Hall. Mum loved it. She would probably have described herself as 'just a housewife', yet she also did the secretarial work for the shop, kept all Dad's books and worked in the bingo hall. Mum was about 5 foot 9 inches tall with long legs. She had been a chorus girl in the 1940s, when that was considered not entirely proper, so she had learned to cut through hypocrisy and bullshit. She took people as she found them and was as comfortable with a cleaning lady as with a duchess.

She quickly befriended the bingo regulars, especially their kids, and I think it helped her a lot. She had been through some rough times – twice when she miscarried, she slumped into a severe depression and had to go into hospital. On one occasion the doctors kept her drugged for around six months. Dad wouldn't let me go to see her when she was very ill and, despite his and my grandparents' efforts, there was a big hole at home. Even when she was getting better, I can remember him taking me along to Knapsbury Hospital, a specialist mental unit, and I could hardly recognise the sad, tentative woman in front of me as the vibrant, lovely mother that I knew. Yet, when she eventually recovered, she would become her old self again and enjoyed nothing more than sitting in the kiosk on bingo night, selling people their sweets and cigarettes and having a chat.

Just like the Queen Vic in *EastEnders*, the bingo hall was always alive with gossip. At times it seemed there were as many tales as punters. None caused more of a stir than when one of our MCs disappeared. He was a lovely, gentle man, probably in his forties, with a smile and a joke for everyone. He and his wife seemed to have an idyllic existence, until one night he simply didn't turn up for work. No one has seen him since.

You can imagine how quickly the rumours started to fly around as people speculated what had happened to him. Among the suggestions I heard, he'd been kidnapped, murdered or wandered off into oblivion having lost his memory and was probably sleeping rough beneath the arches by the Embankment Underground station. In the end, the majority view was that he'd run off with a much younger woman. With examples like that, is it any wonder I had so much trouble holding down a relationship in my early years?

The family atmosphere of the bingo was summed up every Christmas when we threw a massive party, where we would hand out cake and drinks. The other young MCs and I used to don our round-necked, collarless suits and wigs and mime to Beatles records. Dad rounded off the evening with his rendition of 'White Christmas'. There wasn't a dry eye in the house and it would have been hard to find anyone who didn't reckon that 'our Mark's version was every bit as good as Bing Crosby's'.

The bingo hall was a big part of that community but bingo was ended by a few mindless idiots. I was woken up about three o'clock one morning by Dad shaking me. 'Quick, son, the club's on fire.' We raced up there but there was nothing we could do. We just stood and watched it burn, Dad with tears running down his cheeks. It was all so mindless. Vandals, out for a lark, had set light to it and ran off, leaving it engulfed in flames. The fire brigade did what they could and managed to save much of the shell but it was going to be a long time before there could ever be a bingo session again. Dad and Mum were devastated. It was not just that they had lost a business: they were concerned about what their customers were going to do, especially the elderly women for who bingo was their one bit of social life.

The financial implications became more grave a couple of weeks after the fire, when the woman who owned the building told Dad his insurance cover wasn't enough to rebuild the hall and he would have to make up the difference. He pointed out that he'd followed the letter of the lease as far as insurance was concerned, so any shortfall was her fault or that of the agent who had drawn up the agreement. I never did hear the full story of the negotiations, but Dad must have driven a hard bargain, because he ended up owning the freehold of the burnt-out shell.

It was time to call in Uncle John again. He and some of his mates, along with Dad and I started to rebuild the hall ourselves and, even if I do say so myself, we made a pretty good job of it. Once again, Dad was one step ahead of everyone else. Midway through the rebuilding, he announced that he was going to divide the hall in two. Bingo, he declared, was on its way down, while, thanks to TV coverage, snooker was on its way up again. They would be given equal billing in the new hall. By the time we completed the renovation, about nine months after the fire, Dad decided that bingo was out and the hall became a snooker club once more, only this time a successful one. Uncle John and his son David ran it and I sold it as a going concern a only couple of years ago.

While the bingo hall was a lot of fun and a big part of my

early teenage years, there were times when working there cramped my style, especially as I was becoming increasingly interested in girls.

Chapter 4

Low-cc but High-Octane Fun

My first girlfriend was Pamela Rowland. I was twelve or thirteen at the time and, if I'm honest, it was more of a crush than a romance. I'm not even sure Pamela was ever aware we were an item. But she certainly sparked my interest and from then on there were a series of flirtations that saw me grow more confident and knowledgeable about the difference between the sexes and how much fun that difference can be.

My pulling power improved as soon as I was sixteen and got my first motorbike. Dad had started to sell 99cc Garelli bikes from Italy, which were very popular because you didn't pay as much road tax on them. They looked fantastic with low handlebars, so you could tuck yourself down, making out you were riding a proper racing bike. With no helmets in those days it wasn't too hard to cut a dashing figure that girls seemed to find attractive.

Garellis were surprisingly nippy. I remember leaving the bingo hall in a hurry one night because I was late to meet a girl I'd been chatting up. I opened up the throttle and about a mile down the road I became aware of a flashing blue light in my mirror. I pulled over to let them pass but they stopped too and accused me of speeding. When I told the copper my name and address, he said. 'You're a lucky lad. Your dad looks after our bikes so I'll let you off with a warning this time, but don't you ever let me catch you speeding again.'

There was little chance of that because two months later the bike was a write-off. I was in West Hendon, stuck behind a Rolls-Royce tootling along aristocratically in the middle of the road. As soon as we reached a straight stretch, I pulled out to go by him but, without any indication, the Roller swung across me to turn right. Oh, shit!

I'd read somewhere that with motorbikes it's usually the machine that kills you, not the accident, and I had enough sense to drop the bike down, let go and get it out of the way. I hit the deck with a thud that shook me up but I escaped with a few grazes. The weight of the bike took it careering on under the car and it reappeared on the other side crushed and almost unrecognisable. If I'd hung on, that would have been my fate too.

That was the end of my motorcycling. I changed image and converted to a Mod. Out went the leather jacket, Chuck Berry and Brylcreem; in came the sharp Italian suits, trad jazz and a Vespa GS scooter with more mirrors than a Hollywood boudoir. But with Mods and Rockers deciding bank holidays were designed specifically for them to fight each other along seaside promenades, Dad decided I'd be safer giving up bikes altogether in case I felt the urge to join in. He tempted me with my first car, a Bond three-wheeler, which you were allowed to drive on a motorbike licence. In the hierarchy of production models following on from Lamborghini or Aston Martin, the Bond came a little below the Trotters' Reliant Robin but I loved that car with a passion. Neither Mods nor Rockers would have reckoned it was cool, but at least you didn't get wet when it rained and there was just about room to squeeze a girl in there with you.

After the Bond came a Ford Squire and a Triumph Herald, then my first car straight from the showroom, a dark-blue Vauxhall Viva HV, which I bought for £449. That was followed by a Sunbeam Stiletto and I've had a lot of cars since then, including E-type, BMW, a Lamborghini, two Porsches and my latest Merc E55 AMG. I got a kick out of most of them – but it's difficult to think of any that has given me as much fun as that old green-and-cream Bond with its 197-9F Villiers two-stroke engine.

It wasn't all plain sailing. Being a bit lairy, I fitted it with a Peco exhaust system that they used in motocross. It was perfect, giving the engine a deep, throaty roar so that, when I drove through Finchley, heads would turn thinking a Ferrari was coming. Sadly, I hadn't realised that the fumes were no longer being taken underneath the car and out the back but were now seeping through the dash and building up inside the cab. I noticed that it smelled a bit but didn't realise the full implications until I took my pal Johnny Burford out for a longer spin. We were cruising along happily until we passed out, overcome by carbon monoxide, and crashed into a hedge. We clambered out and spewed up all over the place. It was time for a rethink on the exhaust.

Johnny was also with me when we took the Bond sledging. We decided that a generous fall of snow would be the ideal conditions to take the car to the hill on Station Road and try a few handbrake turns. It was fantastic. We went spinning down the hill like something out of a mad-cap ice show. Until we hit the kerb. The Bond flipped over on to its roof and, from a car with rubber tyres, brakes and a steering wheel, it became a metal sledge, hurtling downhill with nothing to control it. As the friction started to wear away the roof, I could feel the top of my head becoming hotter and hotter. I was laughing because screaming would have been pointless, but I was also wondering what would happen when the roof finally wore away. Luckily, we came to a halt before we found out. We somehow scrambled out and I phoned Dad to come and help us.

It took five of us to get the Bond the right way up. Dad attached a tow line to his car. Unfortunately, the crash had done more damage than we'd realised and, when we stopped at traffic lights, I braked but nothing happened. The Bond slid elegantly into Dad's rear bumper. We eventually got it to the repair shop, where the guy admitted it was the first time he'd been asked to fix a car where the main damage was that the roof had been worn thin.

With all this expense, it was a good thing I was starting to earn some money. I'd had an interest in movies ever since my childhood, when Signet Films, who had a studio in a basement round the corner from Dad's shop, chose me as their juvenile lead in a couple of their productions. In the first I was the composer Handel as a small boy and was even allowed to pretend to play a harpsichord belonging to the Queen Mother. I was so brilliant in the role – or maybe it was because I was cheap – that I was selected to play the King of the Lilliputians in *Gulliver's Travels*, which required me to sit on a throne and use my sceptre to prod people who looked about a tenth of my size thanks to some artful work with mirrors.

I thoroughly enjoyed the experience and, as I got older, I guess I thought I had what it took to be a movie star, if only a producer would spot my moody good looks and sheer animal magnetism. I felt I was perfect to become a cowboy or a chisel-jawed war hero. I loved war epics, especially when the Brits were particularly heroic as in *The Bridge on the River Kwai* or *The Dam Busters*. I also enjoyed gangster films with Humphrey Bogart and James Cagney, and action movies. My all-time favourite was Audie Murphy in *To Hell and Back*, in which he starred in his own heroic life story. (If there are any producers out there who want the rights to *this* book, I do have quite a lot of experience in front of cameras and I could do my own stunts!)

I was also interested in the technical side of films. I had a small cine camera and enjoyed making home movies, so thought it would be a good way to make a living, at least until I was 'discovered'. I wasn't sure how to go about it until Dad reminded me that Wally, who had now left the bike shop, worked in the transport department for Samuelson Film Services. The company was run by four brothers – Sydney, David, Neville and Michael Samuelson – and had started when, as a young TV cameraman, Sydney discovered the BBC would pay him £10 just to use his camera when he didn't need it. A ten-week contract brought him a hundred quid and the brothers realised they had hit on a gap in the market. Samuelson's became one of the biggest names in the industry, providing equipment for film and TV companies as well as making programmes of their own.

Wally explained there was a problem getting into the technical side of the business: you couldn't get a job unless you were a member of the ACTT union and you couldn't join the union unless you had a job. Fortunately, when he introduced me to the Samuelson brothers they took to me and said they would sort out the union card and I could work as an apprentice under Mr Vickers, one of the country's leading camera technicians. This was a fantastic opportunity to learn a trade under the guidance of an expert. It was a rapidly growing industry that I was interested in and I would be with one of the top companies. Above all, it was the kind of hands-on, practical work that I enjoyed most.

My first serious assignment at Samuelson Film was to work

on the hit TV show *Candid Camera* which trapped the public in hilarious situations. This was the first edition starring Jonathan Routh and one of those things that you never forget in life! One of the first programmes I worked on was when we took a Bubble car into a petrol station at Hendon Central to fill it up with fuel. They would normally take about two gallons but, unknown to the public and the garage staff, the car was just one big petrol tank with a Bubble body on it. The other classic I worked on was when goldfish were being eaten straight from the bowl. There were plenty of horrified faces from people who didn't realise fish-shaped carrots were being consumed. Even with all this fun going on I still became restless and my dream job lasted less than a year.

I didn't like working under someone and having him tell me what to do. It wasn't Mr Vickers's fault – he was fine to me – and I wasn't being rebellious out of bloody-mindedness. I just came from a family that didn't have a boss and it didn't feel right. I needed to be my own boss and, by a stroke of great fortune, I was about to have the chance.

Chapter 5

A Member of the Warren Street Boys

With kids now starting competitive racing at eight years old, it seems incredible that I was sixteen before I even sat in a kart. But you have to remember the sport was still in its infancy. The very first kart was built in 1956 by Art Ingels, a hot-rodder and racing-car builder in the States. He and some mates brought their karts with them when they were based in England with the US Air Force and within a few weeks it had started to catch on over here. It was more a hobby than an organised sport, an adrenaline rush for people like Wally Green, who turned to karting after he packed in speedway.

It was while we were watching Wally that Mum decided I could try karting and we bought our first TABs. Dad worked on them when we got back to the shop and was impressed with the quality. These weren't toys: they were real little racing machines, albeit somewhat basic. He decided there could be a business in this growing craze. At the very least it might pay enough to cover the cost of our own karting, so we started buying and selling equipment and I had the chance to run the new company, imaginatively named Mart's Karts.

One of my first jobs was to go and see Micky Flynn, a

former American Air Force captain, who had remained in England after he was demobbed. He set up a company importing all those home comforts the Yanks who were still serving over here couldn't buy in England, including karting gear from the big US companies such as Homelite and McCullochs. He was supposed to supply only the US bases but it wasn't hard to persuade Micky to do a few deals for us too, just as long as we didn't let on where we were getting the stuff.

Micky was one of the pioneers of kart racing in Europe and we had a series of 'what a small world' moments concerning him a few years ago. The first was when we spent a family Christmas in La Manga Club in Spain. Luke came back from an evening on the town and announced, 'I was drinking with a girl who reckons you knew her grandfather. He helped start karting in England.' Sure enough, she was Micky's granddaughter. Some time later I was chatting to a guy in a bar over there who told me he had an affinity with karting because his grandfather had been involved and I was able to tell him, 'Not only did I know your granddad, my son knows your sister!' Eventually I met their mum, Micky's daughter, and since then her husband and I have done a bit of business, so it's gone full circle.

Dad always threw himself into every project wholeheartedly and quite soon Mart's Karts wasn't enough for him. He took on the lease at the Rye House track and within a few months had become chairman of the club. He decided this was going to be the HQ for our expanding kart business, so he and I knocked down the old wooden hut that stood near the track, dug out some foundations, mixed and laid the cement and erected a smart portable building to act as our new offices.

At first the business consisted mainly of selling bits and pieces off a trailer we used to tow behind the car to race meetings. At the time, most of the karts sold in this country came from two large manufacturers or were imported from Italy but that all changed when Dad got talking to a friend of his. Alec Bottoms was the plumbing half of building company Bottoms & Bartrup. He was also a motorsport enthusiast and he'd combined the two interests to produce a kart chassis he called the Zipper, which apparently was his nickname at school, though I don't dare imagine why. It was agreed that I would race his Zipper Mark II chassis and it went well, so Dad suggested we should sell them from our shop.

We did OK with them, but Alec didn't have time to build many himself, and, when he gave the job to a firm in Waltham Abbey, they too were slow in supplying us. Frustrated at losing sales, Dad approached Alec and persuaded him to sell us the jigs so we could take over the complete operation. Suddenly, Mart's Karts was a major manufacturer. I wasn't too keen on the name Zipper – although for a while we did use the slogan 'There's no flies on us, we've got a Zipper' – but thought Zip had the right image, so we changed the name of the karts and decided it made sense to change the name of the company at the same time.

We worked on the karts, modifying them from my experiences as a driver, and they started to become very popular. The business grew rapidly and after a while we had to build a factory on a site I found on an industrial estate at Hoddesdon. That quickly became too small, so we found another plot of land just down the road and had plans drawn up for a bigger unit. Dad arranged for the design to be in two stages, with an extension that could be added whenever we needed it, but, just before building work started, I was chatting with the contractor and found out the extension would cost twice as much if we waited as it would if we had it all built at once. With the rate we were growing it made sense to me to go for it now, so I told him to go ahead. I forgot to tell Dad of my decision and, a few weeks after work had started, he went to have a look round and came back very excited.

'The builders have made a mistake,' he said. 'They're building the whole thing at once. We're gonna get a bargain.'

I had to confess that I'd told them to go ahead, but he forgave me when he realised how much we would save in the long run.

I was excited about the business but, if I'm honest, at that stage it was more a way of earning enough money and creating the time so that I could drive. I had quickly realised there were two sorts of karting: one for the general public who just wanted to have some fun, and the other for a small, elite group of serious racers. I wanted to be in that set. They looked the part, they had the right overalls, the right kit and their karts went faster than others, including mine.

These boys were nearly all the sons of wealthy motor dealers and didn't seem to do a lot of work, spending most of their time hanging around a second-hand car showroom in Warren Street. The leader of the pack was Bobby Day, whose dad, Alan, had the biggest Mercedes dealership in the country. Bobby had film-star looks and the attitude to go with them, and his mates weren't too dusty, either. They included Mickey Allen; Bruno Ferrari, whose family connections meant he was never short of a bob or two; Buzz Ware, who earned his money making supermarket trolleys; and a lovable rogue, John J Ermelli. Buzz and Jon Jon were to become two of our first works drivers and we remain good friends to this day.

I knew I wasn't as good in a kart as they were, but I reasoned that, like them, I had two arms, two legs, two eyes and certainly as much bottle, so there must be a way I could catch them up. I had one great advantage: I had plenty of access to Rye House and, even with my aptitude for mental arithmetic, I can't begin to work out how many times I drove round that track, always trying to go a bit faster. It's interesting that some people are drawn to karting because they are engine junkies, never happier than when they have a spanner in their hand, tinkering with this bit or that. Sometimes I feel they enjoy that more than the driving. I like fiddling with engines but the thing that has always given me the biggest buzz is to have my kart go faster than everyone else's and, as the business progressed, I also wanted to sell more than the competition. Nothing gave me greater satisfaction than coming away from a meeting having driven the fastest lap of the day on one of our karts. Even when I lost a World Championship on the final lap one year, the disappointment was less because I'd driven the fastest lap.

I had a massive desire to succeed and, unlike some of the other kids who dropped by the wayside, I would not let myself be put off by setbacks. In those days I occasionally drove a gearbox kart with a 197-9F Villiers engine and, in one of my early races round Rye House, my engine blew when I was in second place. Back in the pits I realised the cylinder was going nowhere. Then I remembered that the trusty Bond had the same type of engine, so I worked frantically for the next hour and a half and transferred the Bond cylinder into the kart and raced it in the final. Unfortunately, that blew, too. I now had no kart and a car in bits and had to phone dad for a lift. We soon had both kart and car back in working condition and, despite the expense, he wasn't at all upset that I'd blown two engines; in fact I think he was quietly proud that I'd shown some initiative.

I've never been much of a believer in the theory that some people are born with a steering wheel in their hand. I think the most important ingredient for success in motorsport – and in life – is what goes on in the six inches between your ears, or, for us bigheads, seven inches. Of course, it helps if you have some natural talent and it can be impossible if you have a handicap that means some things are just physically beyond you. But for most of us the key is having the drive and determination to put in the work it takes to succeed and to learn from our mistakes.

The best example I've ever seen is Ayrton Senna, who I first met in those early karting days. I'm convinced that, if Ayrton had decided to be a tennis player, he would have won Wimbledon; if he'd chosen golf, he would have shot 60 round St Andrews. I remember him flying model helicopters for relaxation but still his mastery of them was just incredible. He could have been brilliant at anything he decided to do, because he had that mindset. Second was failure to him and he made sure he covered every angle to ensure he would succeed.

I was determined I would become a top kart driver. I would find out what time the good drivers were testing and slip out behind them, following them round, checking which lines they took, where they braked and when they hit the power. Then I'd go out on my own and try to replicate what I'd learned, always looking to shave a fraction of a second off my previous best. Finally, I knew I was ready to take them on.

It took me a couple of years to start winning but I eventually found myself accepted by the in-crowd. At last I enjoyed a taste of their glamorous lifestyle, joining up with and driving against the Warren Street Boys and their young pretenders, who included Glen Beer, Dave Ferris, Trevor Waite and a couple of guys – Barry Cox and Dave Salamone – who even went on to star as Mini-Cooper S drivers in the original *Italian Job* movie with Michael Caine. They claimed they were cast because of their good looks but if that had been the case, surely I'd have been chosen!

The reality was that Dave was acting as chauffeur to actor

Stanley Baker, who was one of the producers on the film, and Dave's dad had a dealership, so was able to provide the Minis. After filming was over Dave offered me one of the cars – 'just a few dents and scratches but only about a thousand miles on the clock' – for £500. I turned him down and still have sleepless nights thinking about how much it would be worth now. Later, he offered me a BMW M11 with the M11 number plate. He wanted about fifteen grand for that and, again, I said no thanks, thus throwing away a potential profit today of around £485,000.

Fortunately, my driving was better than my eye for a bargain and people started to notice I was winning races. Eventually, I was chosen as one of the seven-man team to represent England in Belgium, which meant I could wear the coveted green helmet with the red, white and blue stripes down the middle. I couldn't have been prouder.

Chapter 6

Crisps and a Silver Coke Bottle

I was always eager to learn, and my first trip as a member of the England team was another stage in my karting education. We were racing on a tight, twisty track that really tested our ability to focus, but I quickly realised one driver had mastered it better than the rest of us. This was the first time I saw François Goldstein, one of the greatest drivers of all time in any format. He went on to win five 100cc World Championships, a record that stood for many years until one of my factory drivers, Mike Wilson, went one better. I learned a lot by watching François race, especially about concentration. Over the years I noticed his parents would be in one particular place in the grandstand and every time he passed them he would give a brief signal. It had nothing to do with the race: it was just a discipline to ensure he was constantly thinking about what he had to do.

The weekend in Belgium went well and I thought I'd done enough to impress team manager Doug Jest and the rest of the RAC bigwigs. I enjoyed being an international but, as happens so often in my life, my habit of opening my mouth before engaging my brain threatened to get me thrown off the team.

On the ferry going out, we'd all stocked up with far more duty-free cigarettes than we were allowed so, when we packed up to go home, we stuffed them into toolboxes and put them in the truck underneath the karts, thinking no one would bother to look there. Wrong! We arrived in Dover and were waved to one side by a customs officer. We explained we had been racing for England, thinking that would impress him. It certainly aroused his interest because he emptied out the truck and, of course, found the fags in the toolboxes.

For some reason I appointed myself spokesman, stammering out the first thought that came into my head: 'Er, they belong to our team manager. He asked us to bring them back for him. We didn't realise we had too many.'

That cut no ice and he confiscated the cigarettes. I was too naïve to realise that some probably took them home and smoked them or flogged them to pals, and for weeks afterwards I was crapping myself, fearing Customs and Excise, as it was then called, would turn up at the RAC and say, 'We've got Mr Jest's cigarettes.'

Fortunately, they didn't, and I must have driven OK, because I remained part of the England team for about six years and was also selected in the four-man team to compete in the European and World Championships. It was a fantastic experience, travelling the world and competing against people such as Elio de Angelis, Eddie Cheever, future world champion Keke Rosberg, Andrea de Cesaris, who was already practising his crashing technique, Stefan Johansson and Alain Prost, all of who went on to become top Formula One drivers. It's strange, I suppose, but, whereas these days all the top young kart drivers are dreaming of moving into F1 or another top formula, it never crossed my mind. I was just thrilled to be karting.

Racing all round Europe gave the whole Hines family the chance to explore life outside Britain and inevitably there were a few culture clashes along the way. I especially remember a meal we had on the Champs-Élysées, which almost ended in our being arrested. Dad was a plain-food man – egg and chips was about as continental as he usually ventured but, from time to time, when he was feeling very cosmopolitan, he might have a fried tomato with it. He was always a bit unsure of foreign restaurants and this particular place was destined never to find its way into *The Mark Hines Good Food Guide*, no matter what the man from Michelin said. To start with, it had one of those French waiters who can be very friendly when you arrive but, as soon as there's a problem, decide they don't speak English. The problem on this occasion was Dad's meal. He ordered an omelette and chips and, while the omelette was perfect, instead of a plateful of big juicy chips, he received a handful of crisps.

He called the waiter over, waved a crisp at him and said '*Non*! What I want is chips – like those.' And he pointed to a plate on the next table.

The waiter made out he didn't understand, scampered off and never returned. If there was a prize for the master of the waiters' art of managing to avoid your eye when you try to catch their attention, this guy would have been world champion.

Dad finally gave up and just ate his omelette but when he went to pay the bill he made it clear he wasn't happy and wouldn't be paying for the crisps. 'And you can tell your mate there not to hold his breath if he expects a tip,' he added.

Instead of knocking a couple of francs off and calling it quits, the owner started to argue. Then the waiter weighed in with his two centimes' worth, having miraculously recovered his grasp of English. That pissed Dad off even more.

'You stay out of it,' he barked. 'You caused this trouble in the first place.'

The waiter put his arm round Dad's neck as if to lead him

away, at which I jumped on his back and all hell let loose. The skirmish didn't last long. A couple of hefty gendarmes appeared from nowhere and grabbed us. It looked as though we were destined for a night in the Bastille. Fortunately, as he was telling the police his tale, the waiter took his hand out of his pocket to gesticulate and a load of bank notes fluttered to the floor. It turned out that, when customers left cash payment on their table, he would pocket the money and tear up the bill. Suddenly, the owner was no longer interested in us. He had the police take the waiter away and then offered us a drink on the house.

'Thank you,' Dad said. 'I'd like a nice cup of tea.'

There was something about France that always seemed to mean trouble. Towards the end of the 1960s, Coca-Cola produced a silver trophy made in the world-famous shape of a Coke bottle and presented one to a different sport each year. This particular year, it was going to be for karting, and they chose the six-hour international kart race in Caen in Normandy. We fancied it would look pretty good in our trophy cabinet.

Even with guys taking it in turns to drive a forty-five-minute shift, a six-hour race with no suspension is a bit like being pummelled by a Sumo wrestler – your body aches and your arms feel too weak to lift them up, let alone fight the steering wheel round bends and over bumps. But John Stokes and I were pretty good at it and had already won the Shennington International six-hour race, so we were quite confident.

We blew the opposition away in Caen and were in a great mood when we set off for the presentation reception in the evening. The third-placed team, from France, went up and received a handsome trophy and a whole load of expensive goods, including portable TVs. We looked at each other. This was clearly a competition worth winning. The second team, also French, were given even more valuable prizes and a bigger trophy. I was just hoping our van was going to be big enough to carry all our prizes.

Our names were announced and we went on to the stage. Beaming, the official gave us a cup and a cheap battery-powered radio each. We'd been stuffed. Still, we thought, at least we'd won the silver Coke bottle. But we should have realised this was France. After another announcement, the second team went forward and held it aloft.

'I'm not having that,' Dad said and charged up on stage. This was daylight robbery and suddenly the *entente* was anything but *cordiale*. The organisers tried to persuade us that the Coca-Cola trophy was for the first French team in the race but Dad thrust the programme under their nose and said, 'It says here it's for the winners. It don't say anything about having to be born in a bloody beret or eating frogs' legs. We won, it's our trophy and if you don't hand it over we will sue you through the courts.' Eventually they had to agree and, even though we never received any of the other goodies, the silver Coke bottle still has pride of place alongside my other trophies.

John and I raced together many times and spent quite a lot of time in each other's company, either travelling round Europe or at the bar he opened just off the Bull Ring in Birmingham called Bogart's, a great name for a terrific bar. John had style and a silver tongue from which no woman, not even a nun, was safe. He was also one of the first guys to see the sense of opening a place that catered for all kinds of tastes in the same building: the latest music on the ground floor, bierkeller downstairs, and a smoochy couples bar with champagne, soft lights and sweet music upstairs. He and I also used to hang around the Steering Wheel Club in West Bromwich, which was owned by Sidney Taylor, who was to eventually nominate me for membership of the British Racing Drivers' Club (BRDC). Among Sidney's many barmaids there was one who was more friendly than others, so his club was the kind of place where you would pop in for a couple of hours and end up staying two days.

But, at the time we won the Coca-Cola trophy, those hedonistic times were still ahead of me. At that stage I was about to settle down and become a married man.

Chapter 7
A Nickel or Two in the Jukebox

When I first became one half of a serious relationship it seemed like a romantic idea to have a record we thought of as 'our song'. What I hadn't realised was that by the time I married my third and present wife, Tina, I would need a bloody jukebox to keep them all on.

The first Mrs Hines was Christine, who I met when I was about sixteen. In those infant days of pop music we always looked on Chuck Berry's 'Sweet Little Sixteen' and 'Dream Lover' sung by Bobby Darin as our special tunes. Christine and I just seemed to happen. What with karting and building the business, I guess I just became too busy to think about other girls and stopped looking. Eventually, we had been girlfriend and boyfriend so long that everyone expected us to get married, including us, so we drifted into our wedding day at the church up the road – me in my sharp new suit, Christine radiant in white, and Mum in a new hat specially bought for the occasion.

It was about ten days before it hit me what I had done. It wasn't Christine's fault: we'd just met far too young and I realised there was a lot of fruit I hadn't tasted and tons of wild oats I hadn't sown. I set about sowing them as fast as I could.

Every Split Second Counts

I was starting to do a lot of travelling, which provided plenty of opportunity to scatter a few seeds on foreign soil. Mostly it was here today, forgotten tomorrow, but then I met someone I found I couldn't put out of my mind quite so easily. It was time to load another record on the jukebox, this time Andy Williams's version of 'Strangers in the Night'.

It started on the ferry going over for a race in Paris with my mate Chris. We travelled on the Wednesday night, in time for testing on Thursday and Friday. Then Mum, Dad and Christine were going to join us on Saturday morning, in time for the qualifying and racing on Sunday. After a bite to eat on the ferry, Chris and I went to the bar for a drink and I spotted a very attractive girl sitting at a table on her own. I'd always been brought up to be polite, so, naturally, I went over to talk to her. We couldn't let the girl be lonely, could we?

She told us her name was Mary, that she was French-Canadian and on her way to Paris to live with her uncle's family for six months, experiencing the French way of life while working as an au pair. Then she would return home to marry her fiancé. Alarm bells clanged briefly – women will be unfaithful to their husbands but not usually their fiancés – but there was something about this girl that made me ignore the warning. She was not only beautiful and had a great body, but there was something in her eyes and her smile that made me want to get to know her better. A lot better.

After a couple of glasses of wine and a bit more chitchat, she accepted my offer of a lift to Paris. So far, so good. I decided to push a bit harder.

'Do you have to be in Paris tomorrow?' I asked.

'Not necessarily.'

Good reply. 'So you could spend a couple of days with us at the track. You'll love it.'

There was some hesitation, but after a little urging that glint returned to her eyes and she agreed.

Chris and I were booked to share a twin room at the Cheval Rouge hotel until the family came over, but luckily it wasn't too difficult to arrange a second room when we arrived. After a few drinks in the bar, I decided it was only professional for me to turn in early so I'd be in peak condition for testing the next day. I made sure I had both sets of keys and when we reached the first room I said, 'Mary, you're in there.' Then I threw the other key to Chris and said, 'You're over there.' With that I gently pushed Mary into the room and followed her in.

This could have been the moment when the best-laid schemes of a lecherous karter came to an embarrassing, face-slapping halt. Instead, it was not at all awkward and felt as though we had known each other for ages.

The next couple of days flew by, as near perfect as you could hope for. Testing went well and Mary and I went even better. It was one of those rare times in your life that you wish would last for ever, because it is just so idyllic. I had never felt so comfortable with a woman, or enjoyed having her with me every second of the day. By Friday night, of course, we had to draw up some contingency plans. I'd been completely honest with her and told her my wife was arriving on Saturday morning, but said I would put her on a train to Paris, and promised we would definitely meet again.

I don't know what time we eventually drifted off to sleep on Friday night but it was a far gentler process than our awakening. We were jolted upright at about 6.30 by one of the other drivers hammering on our door. I detected more than a hint of joy in his voice as he yelled, 'Martin, your mum and dad and Christine are down in reception! You're in the shit, mate.'

Looking back, I realised that what I should have done was to collect Mary's things together and put them and her in what had become Chris's room to give me time to sort things out. But even Einstein would have problems thinking clearly on being woken up with a lover before dawn by someone carrying the news that his wife is downstairs. Suddenly, I knew exactly how a hedgehog feels when it sees headlights approaching. My first instinct was to roll up into a ball, hoping for the best, but, as the panic levels subsided to mere crisis, I told Mary to collect her stuff together while I went down to stall them and figured out what to do.

The family were sitting in reception and definitely more pleased to see me than I was to see them. Dad told me he'd decided he might as well drive through the night and catch some kip on the ferry. Thanks, Dad. I explained that the rooms weren't ready yet but, if they had some breakfast, I'd sort it out. 'Just give me half an hour,' I said as I left them tucking into croissants in the dining room.

Taking the front or back doors was too risky. There was only one option: it had to be the window. It didn't look too difficult. All we had to do was to ease our way across a flattish roof, shimmy down on to a balcony, drop to the car park and make our way to the station. Hell, if James Bond could do it...

I explained the plan to Mary and instead of protesting, as most women would in that situation, she laughed and said, '*Pourquoi pas, mon cher?*' and led the way. Sliding her cases before us, feeling somewhat exposed yet very alive, we eventually made it.

By the time I got back from the station, I was feeling quite pleased with myself. Then I realised I had to climb back into the room the same way I'd come down. That was much harder and not achieved entirely elegantly, but the effort was rewarded when I found a pencilled note from Mary leaving me in no doubt how much those two days had meant to her. This was a woman I had to see again.

Meanwhile, I had to carry on with the rest of the weekend as though nothing had happened. The other drivers thought the whole escapade was hilarious and I'm sure Christine walked in on a number of conversations where the subject changed awkwardly when she arrived, but somehow we survived without her being any the wiser.

I knew I wouldn't be able to stay away from Mary long. I planned a 'business' trip to France and arranged to meet her under the Eiffel Tower. She managed to take a week off work but told me she wouldn't be able to meet me until midnight because she had to babysit while the family went to the opera. It was about ten minutes past when I eased my car to a halt under the Tower. In those pre-terrorist days you could park right underneath, and what could be more elegant under the world-renowned French landmark than an iconic, British, racing-green, E-type, 4.2-litre Mark II?

I sat there for about an hour with no sign of her. I thought maybe she had arrived at midnight and left before I turned up, or perhaps she'd changed her mind and wasn't coming. It seemed hopeless but I couldn't bring myself to leave and somehow dozed off, which is quite an achievement in an E-type when you are six foot tall. I was jerked out of a fitful sleep by rapping on the window. It was Mary, full of apologies, explaining that the family had gone on for a meal, so she wasn't able to get away.

'Don't worry about it, I'm just pleased to see you,' I said, and after a couple of minutes to become re-acquainted – and rub the cramp out of my legs – we set off for a fabulous few days' touring round France to a soundtrack of Andy Williams's *Love Songs* album on my eight-track cartridge player. As we drew into a service station, 'Strangers in the

Night' was playing. Mary said, 'That's what we were when we met on the ferry. This is our song.'

That was pretty much the pattern for the next few months. I worked my butt off to develop our business in France so I had an excuse to keep going over there, and Mary also joined me when I went to Denmark and Sweden. Sometimes, I would fly her to London so she could travel with us. It was intense and very special. We couldn't get enough of each other. But as the time went on there was a cloud building up on the horizon: she was due to go back to Canada to be married. A couple of weeks before she was booked to fly home, we spent four days together, talking about little else. It was a difficult, occasionally tearful time, which we knew would have a profound effect on the rest of our lives. I felt I was ready to leave Christine, and Mary said she would stay in England with me. It was a momentous decision but it felt right for us.

However, we were also aware we were just about to shatter a lot of other people's lives. And what if it didn't work out in the long run? After all, we were from different worlds and, while we had been magic together, we'd never spent more than a few days at a time in each other's company and never had to face up to the mundane hassles of everyday life that so often kill the romance in a relationship. We were reasonably sure we knew what we wanted but gave ourselves a while apart to make absolutely certain. Once again, Mary was different class. There were no hysterics or threats, just a simple plan.

She said, 'I will fly into Heathrow and I will wait half an hour. If you turn up we will be together. If you don't, I will catch my flight to Canada and get married.'

I didn't turn up.

I still don't know why and as it ticked past the moment I knew she would be boarding the plane to Canada, I ached with regret. I wondered how she felt. I don't know if she did wait – I have no idea what happened to her from that day to this. I would very much like to know and hope that life turned out well for her. Above all, I would like her to understand it was not a casual thing for me but something I look back on with great tenderness. In fact, I would go as far as to say that, while I have known a lot of women in my life, there have only ever been two that I truly loved: Tina and Mary. They say that the follies a man regrets most are those he didn't have the courage to commit, and, while I have few regrets about my life, I do occasionally wonder how different it would have been if I'd turned up at Heathrow.

Mary apart, most of my dalliances were casual affairs, the majority one-night stands, nothing that would distract from karting. I was working my way through the ranks as a driver and Dad decided it was time for him to become a major promoter. Typically, he started off in a big way.

There had never been a world championship in Britain and in 1968 he was given permission to stage it at Rye House, which is still the only time the 100cc title has been raced for in this country. Being the man he was, Dad went about it with enormous energy and style. He spent a lot of money advertising and promoting the event and ran coaches from London down to the track. There wasn't a parking spot to be had in Hoddesdon and that wasn't all that got clogged up. The only toilets at Rye House were buckets in little sheds and, with well over 10,000 people descending on the place, they were soon full! But it was a great occasion and Ronnie Nilsson emerged as a worthy champion.

I was too involved in helping Dad with the organising to race but the following year I came into my own and became the top driver in Europe.

Chapter 8

With Just a Spanner and a Hammer

Being tall, I'd always carried 4–5 kilos more than my rivals and, even in those early days, the extra weight could cost a couple of tenths of a second and make all the difference between winning and coming second. With the 1969 European Championships coming up, I was determined to overcome this hurdle and started to diet and exercise. Losing a few pounds made a big difference and the concentration I put into getting superfit made me much sharper mentally.

The championship was a team affair but everyone thought of the leading points scorer as the individual European champion, and I was determined I was going to be it. After the first two rounds in Jesolo, just outside Venice, and Copenhagen, the English team – Dave Ferris, Paul Fletcher, Roy Mortara and I – were three slender points ahead of Germany with the rest already out of sight. That didn't mean that some of the individual drivers, such as Keke Rosberg and François Goldstein, couldn't take valuable points off us in the final round. We also knew the Germans would have an advantage because we would be racing on their home territory and on a new track at Fulda, on which they had practised but which we hadn't seen before. We needed to put down an early marker and Dave Ferris and I sent out a clear message when we set the fastest times in practice.

I was on pole position in my first heat next to Hans Heyer. He was a brilliant driver who later became a folk hero in Germany when he won the Supercar World Championship for Porsche. He and I had several great tussles and, wearing his trademark Bavarian hat with a feather in the band, he still seems pleased to see me when I bump into him at GT championships. I managed to get ahead from the start but Hans and his teammate Wolfgang Kromer managed to trap me at a tight bend and I had to settle for second place. It was a similar story in the next two heats with the Germans working as a team trying to cut me out but I hung on to Hans's tail and took second again.

By the time of the final it had started to rain and the circuit was very slippery. This was going to be much trickier and the Germans would have even more advantage, having driven the circuit in the wet before. Dave Ferris and I were on the second row of the grid behind Goldstein and Heyer, with Kromer and another German, Karl-Heinz Peters, just behind us. If we could keep it like that, England would win the championship for the first time.

We all took it pretty carefully over the first few laps, then, with no team pressures on him, François showed his mastery of the conditions and began to put daylight between him and the rest of the field. It was tempting to chase him but it was more important to make sure we got round safely in front of at least one of the Germans. It was not to be. Dave's engine began to slow, allowing Kromer and Peters to sweep past him, and, even though I managed to keep them behind me for a few more laps, without Dave's help it was impossible and they eventually went past.

François won the race by some distance but, with Roy Mortara and Paul Fletcher having made up some places from their start, we still weren't sure who had won the title. Some of the Germans came over to congratulate us but when the results were finally totted up they had pipped us by just six points. Switzerland and Denmark were joint third, ninety-eight points further back. I was disappointed that we had lost the team event but chuffed that, when they added up the individual points, I was the top driver in Europe ahead of a number of guys I really admired.

The European Championships were Doug Jest's last event as team manager. He had done a lot for the sport, including building Rye House, and we were sad to see him go, although we still used to meet him around the circuits until he died a few years ago. My dad took over as junior team manager with Frank Jones in charge of the senior teams. Of our team, Roy Mortara died in a road accident a few years later; Paul Fletcher is still in the kart business and has his own track in Lincolnshire; and Dave Ferris went on to race Formula Ford and Formula Three. I believe he was destined to end up in F1 but he was involved in an accident at Snetterton when a stone went through the front of his helmet and injured him badly. He recovered but never appeared on the scene again.

It was a great team with terrific camaraderie, except of course when we were competing against each other, as Dave showed when we were rivals in the World Championships in Paris. I was driving a kart with fantastic BM engines, tuned by Franco Baroni, the number-one engine tuner in the world. I turned up in Paris ready to test and Franco said, 'What are you doing here? David's father told me you are sick and not coming, so I gave him the best engines.'

Even with second best, I still ended up on the front of the grid alongside Keke Rosberg in the final and thought I was in with a good chance until one of my Italian mechanics screwed up. There's something about Italians that makes them very jumpy when they are in with a chance of winning. We all have nerves but the Scandinavians and the English handle them better, which is probably why we have more world champions. This guy decided to change my spark plugs, 'just in case', even though we'd never had a problem with the plugs and, Sod's Law, this time we had a dud and the kart wouldn't start. We had to push it to one side, fix another plug, and, by the time I got away, I was already 200 yards behind the rest. I gave it a charge but there was too much ground to make up. After about ten laps my engine blew up, and so did my title hopes.

Despite that disappointment, 1969 had still been a very special year for me. Racing was very different back then from today and the times slower, but I still believe it was much harder. I remember talking to Keke Rosberg's son Niko and my son Luke when they were racing against each other a few years ago and the cheeky little sods were laughing at our era, saying it wasn't anything like as good as theirs.

I countered, 'When you look at the equipment we had, the driving was far better than now. We had a spanner and a hammer and that was it, none of your computer wizardry, yet races were still decided by tenths of seconds. And look at the tyres – you're going out with eight-inch tyres on the back and five-inch on the front, enough to hold a bloody jumbo jet on the track. Ours were four inches and three. If you two had been in those machines, Keke and I would have lapped you, maybe even twice.' They weren't convinced and we'll never know for sure, but you can bet Keke agrees with me.

The only regret I have about 1969 is that I lost a medal presented to me by the head of BM for being top driver in Europe. It was a silver shield with the letters BM in gold and red flashes on the B, and I was very proud of it. Somehow I lost it in a swimming pool and, even though I spent ages diving to try to recover it and asked the attendant to check the filters, it was never found.

After the year I'd had, I looked set to be one of the top drivers for some time to come but in fact that was the end of my 100cc career. I'd discovered gearbox karting and realised this was where I was most at home.

Chapter 9

Dented Pride Restored by Rocket Man

Elite kart drivers tended to be a bit sniffy about gearbox karting and I suppose I was, too, until the day I climbed into a machine with a 200cc Montessa engine. I'd done a bit with the Villiers engine but, when I took the Montessa out for a few laps, it was completely different.

I thought, 'Whoa! I like this. This is a bit grunty.'

I loved the extra power, the ability to use the gears to prise the maximum out of the kart, and the longer tracks with straights where you could achieve some serious speed. I had a lot to learn but, in an odd way, it proved to be to my advantage that I was racing against guys who had driven only the bigger karts. They had always used the gears and the greater horsepower to obtain the speed they wanted but ignored some of the finer points I'd learned on the 100cc machines. With only 16bhp and no gears, I'd had to master the intricacies of teasing the final bit of power out of my setup and tyres, and the absolute importance of driving smoothly.

When you come down a straight at 120 m.p.h. with your bum half an inch off the floor and unable to see round corners, you'd better have good technique. I mastered the braking very quickly and it didn't take long for me to realise I had to change my point of vision. On shorter courses you are never sitting back: you are fighting every split second for every inch of tarmac. There's always someone alongside you or bumping you from behind, so all the time your eyes are on your front wheels. There's never time to look up and see what's coming. I realised that on tracks that were less tight and twisting, and one and a half times longer, I needed to look further ahead and not become fixated by the few inches immediately in front of me. I learned as I came out of one corner to look up the track to the next, and that gave me the shortest possible line.

I took all the lessons from seven years at the top of 100cc competition and applied them to the new discipline: how to position a kart, how to get the maximum speed to the middle of corners then let the wheels find their own straightness as quickly as they can. A kart going in a straight line is going fast. As soon as you turn the steering wheel, even slightly, you are putting drag on the tyres. After forty years of racing, I still use the same technique on every corner, still talk my way through as though it were my first time: 'Brake here, get your entry right, turn in and set your front wheels where you want them before squeezing the power on, let it run loose on the way out, don't pull the kart in too tight; OK, another near-perfect corner.'

The technique worked and I soon started to win a lot of races. There was still the general feeling that this was karting for old men but – having been brought up by a dad who was always thinking one step ahead of the rest and a mum whose slogan was 'Nothing's impossible; there's no such word as *can't*' – I could see nothing but potential. I met a guy called Philip Hilton, who was playing about with a 250cc Suzuki two-cylinder engine on a kart, and it was stunningly quick, high-revving and sounded fantastic. This was a superkart and ideas tumbled in on each other faster than I could write them down about how we could make this *the* kart. If we put attractive bodywork on it and introduced some down force so it held the track better, this could be karting's equivalent of F1. And why not race it on top circuits such as Brands Hatch and Silverstone? This was the future and I wanted a part in creating it. It was also a fantastic opportunity for the company.

The Hines family were now becoming major players in the industry, starting trends that others followed, even those who objected when we first came up with them. Back then karts were very basic and, partly to try to make them better aerodynamically and partly because I was a bit flash, I introduced some bodywork on the front of my kart. When I turned up with it at the old Crystal Palace track, I was told it was illegal and I couldn't run with it.

I'd done my homework. 'Show me in the regulations where it says I can't have bodywork on my kart,' I said.

They delayed the meeting for at least an hour while they scoured the rule books but in the end they had to admit they were wrong. That pissed them off but not as much as the fact that I won the race by a distance. Suddenly everyone wanted a nose cone for their kart and knew where to obtain them.

As we developed the idea of superkarts, more and more people started to realise the potential of long-circuit racing and I was invited to take our karts to demonstrate just how exciting it could be. This was publicity you couldn't buy. All over the world the concept of gearbox karting was being linked with the name of Zip Karts. It was also monster fun for me and the team of drivers I took with me. We all paid our own way and we had a ball. It was amazing that we didn't get locked up at times, but what can you expect when you have a dozen or so testosterone-fuelled (and sometimes alcohol-fuelled) young men, travelling together and taking part in a sport that has been known to attract women with high hormone levels? Sorry, Vicar, don't think this is the weekend break for you.

The more traditional karting world was not entirely happy about our success but it also had an inkling it might work to its benefit. Ernest Buser, the Swiss guy at the top of karting's governing body, the CIK, had a love–hate relationship with me. He relished being in the limelight and wasn't entirely happy that, when superkarts were around, people wanted to talk to me as much as him. But he recognised that, while the media had shown little interest in what they considered go-karts, they quickly took notice when a madman started to hare round circuits at 150 m.p.h. on what was little more than a tea tray. That caught their imagination and we started to see plenty of photos in the papers and clips on TV.

I realised that if I was smart I could use this publicity to my advantage and managed to secure my first major sponsorship deal with Duckhams Oil. They had sponsored Van Diemen's Formula Ford team for about twenty years and were one of the leading oil manufacturers in motorsport racing, so I approached their head of motor sport/racing, Ron Carnell, to see if he could help me. I showed him the kind of press coverage we were receiving, told him about the trips we were taking round the world and sold him the idea of how it could help promote Duckhams. Somewhat to my surprise, he quickly agreed. It wasn't a deal that brought me in big bucks – most of the support was in the form of products – but you should have seen people's faces when I turned up with my kart kitted out in distinctive blue and yellow with 'Duckhams' emblazoned all over it and wearing overalls to match. It was another first for Zip Karts and added to our growing reputation as the sport's trendsetters.

My success at raising sponsorship has sometimes caused a bit of envy in other teams and I've been accused of being a bit hard-nosed and self-centred when it comes to business. But I learned early on that motorsport is a cut-throat business and the only person you can trust one hundred per cent is yourself. It was on one of our promotional trips to Finland that it was brought home to me that, no matter how much you think someone is your mate, you can never be quite sure.

Terry Donoghue was one of our regular drivers – never that competitive in a kart but good fun to be with and, like me, usually successful at finding female company to help pass the time when we weren't driving. So it was on this trip. After testing, he and I went out on the town and hooked up with a couple of attractive girls, who helped warm the next couple of cold Finnish nights. Testing went well. There was plenty of media interest with Zip Karts given more than its fair share of attention. All seemed cool until Terry came to see me the day before we were due to start racing, looking concerned. He said, 'I've got real trouble at home, mate. I need to fly back but I haven't enough money for the ticket. Can you help me?'

He seemed really cut up so I told him not to worry, I'd sort out the cash. He caught his flight and we carried on with the racing.

It was only when I returned home a couple of days later that I discovered that the 'real trouble' he had concerned my wife Christine. I arrived to an empty house and a note saying that Terry had told her how I slept around when I was away and that she had therefore gone off with him. It seemed clear that Terry and Christine may have been having an affair for many months, as she was not the type just to drop everything and run. She was perhaps attracted to his playboy image and maybe Terry had used our escapades in Finland to tip her over the edge and persuade her to run away with him. I tried to track them down and at one stage there was a bit of a car chase through London, but I didn't catch him, which was fortunate, because I'd probably have done something I would have regretted – such as throttling the two-faced bastard.

I was devastated that she had left me for Terry. Initially, I wanted to get her back and certainly sort Terry out. I was hurt that someone I'd thought of as a mate had let me down. And, worst of all, I'd lent him the money to do it. Was it love I'd lost or just that my pride had taken a severe battering? I certainly realised I had made a mistake when I hadn't turned up at Heathrow Airport to meet Mary.

If I'm honest, the biggest blow was that I had recently moved to Roselands Avenue in Hoddesdon to be near work, so I was now living out in the sticks in what to me was relatively unknown 'hunting' territory, rattling round the house on my own, something I'm not particularly good at. My own company is OK for a few days but I prefer to have someone with me, preferably a beautiful woman.

I needed to get out and about and, after a bit of scouting, I discovered Woodside Country Club. From the outside it looked weird. It was an old mansion in the middle of nowhere, like something out of a 1960s, black-and-white, horror B-movie. It was dingy and dark with only a 60-watt light over the door to let you know where the entrance was. It wasn't much brighter when you finally found your way to the bar, but the music was good, there was buzz about the place and, as your eyes adjusted to the gloom, it was clear that this was where the local talent hung out.

I perched myself on a stool and looked around. I quickly focused on a girl at the other end of the bar. She was about 5 foot 9 inches tall, a proper shape, with blonde hair that cascaded over her shoulders and down her back. She was a dead ringer for *Charlie's Angels* star Farah Fawcett-Majors, whose photo in a red swimsuit sold 8 million posters and caused young boys all over the world to have disturbed sleep patterns. The lookalike in the Woodside was chatting to a fella but I also had the impression she kept glancing over at me. I wasn't sure what signals she was sending out, so, when he went to the gents, I eased over and asked if she was with anyone.

She knew I knew, but still smiled and said, 'Yes.' Then after the briefest of significant pauses, added, 'My brother.'

I want you to imagine for a moment how a guy manages to sit calmly sipping a drink, trying to look cool, while inside every fibre of his being he is punching the air and yelling '*Yesss!*' It was fortunate that I was a professional athlete with nerves of steel and so managed to restrict my ecstatic reaction to a smile and a tinkling of the ice against my glass as I raised it slightly in a toast. Here's to lust.

She told me her name was Lindy. We started to dance and Elton John's 'Rocket Man' found its way on to the Hines jukebox. She insisted on going home with her brother that night but agreed to meet me the following day at Chalk Farm station. It was a warm summer evening and she turned up wonderfully understated in sprayed-on pants and a lemon top that left nothing to the imagination. After a pleasant meal, she ended up back at Roselands Avenue and it was a long time before she moved out.

It was a fiery relationship almost from day one. We were either madly in love and couldn't take our hands off each other or we hated each other with equal passion. Lindy came to many of the kart events but, as the success of the superkart roadshows grew, I spent more and more time away from home, so we were able to get a breather from each other.

We drove the karts all over Europe and we flew them to South Africa, Australia and America, where we raced round the magnificent Daytona track. Quite often, a few expats with karts would turn up and join in, so there were some quite crowded grids. We were driving on the same tracks as motorcycles and cars, and the fans who had thought karting was for kids were suddenly aware that this was a bit different. Superkarts could shift, and the competition was intense. This was real motorsport and they wanted more. The growth was phenomenal and everywhere we went I would be doing deals that ensured Zip Karts stayed at number one. I also honed my driving technique to make sure Martin Hines kept ahead of the rest.

I used my growing contacts book to ensure I got as much track time as possible. I'd become friendly with Colin Chapman and the Lotus guys and on their test days, I'd toss a few quid in the team's drink fund and they would let me slip out between runs and put the kart through its paces, looking for anything that might save me a few tenths of a second. Hiring a track for a day can cost several grand, and, when you add the expense of mechanics, tyres and parts, it can soon become prohibitively expensive.

I didn't have that kind of spare cash but wanted as much time behind the wheel as I could get, so I came up with the idea of the Central Kart Club. I would rent a track and then charge drivers £30 a day to test, hoping I'd attract a hundred or so along to cover my costs and give me free track time. It didn't always work out. Often I was out of pocket, but I drove more miles in a superkart than anyone else and as with everything else in life, the more you do something, the better you become. I was soon to prove I was getting better than most of the rest.

There was one guy who could always give me a good race. Reg Gange had been 100cc British Champion in 1971 and won the blue-riband gearbox event, the World Cup, at Morecambe in 1973. We were always opponents, never enemies, but in 1976 we became fierce rivals for the British Championship. I was in good form, having won the open championship at Knockhill the previous weekend, but could take nothing for granted against Reg. It all came down to the last lap of the last race at Oulton Park. It was a case of winner take all.

Reg made his move as we went into Foster's. He tried to dive under me. The karts locked for a split second and we were both in danger of crashing out. I gripped my steering wheel, determined to hold my line. It worked. He bounced off, bending his axle in the process and had to retire. I powered on, just managing to hold off a charge by Derek Rodgers, and took the chequered flag.

It was only when I got back into the *parc fermé* and on to the scales ready to be weighed that I realised just how lucky I'd been. As I climbed out of the kart there was a bang and the outside rim of the back wheel came off, taking all the air out of the tyre. It had split when Reg whacked me and normally you would have expected it to go within a couple of hundred yards but somehow it had hung on and I'd picked up my first major gearbox title. We filled the trophy with champagne and I called Reg over to share it.

My Goodyear Blue Streak tyres had played a big part in my first British Championship. They were the best in the business. Or they were until the following year, when I did a deal that put them in the shade.

Chapter 10
What Were my Times Like?

One of the reasons Zip has managed to maintain its place as the leading kart company is that we have always been on the lookout for deals that will benefit our customers. As well as working on our own innovations to whet the appetite of karters, we have agents and contacts in all the main countries making sure we find out before our competitors about developments elsewhere. My philosophy has always been that it's worth the price of a plane ticket to see if we can do a deal that will keep us as number one. This was how our long and extraordinary partnership with Bridgestone started in 1977.

The tyre revolution began seven years before that. I first became aware something was going on when I was a member of the Scottish team in the World Championships under my team manager Bruno 'Mac' Ferrari. We'd both fallen out with our national team management and decided we would pledge allegiance to St Andrew, put a tartan band on our helmets and head off to Turin with the skirl of the pipes in our ears. We drew the line, however, at driving in kilts.

I was chatting to a guy from Norway in the pit lane when I

noticed the tyres on his kart. They were fucking monsters. We were all used to driving on 10-cm tyres but these beauties were 6.5 inches, with the words 'Goodyear Blue Streak' emblazoned all over them. They were the latest thing from America and they were hot. I *had* to have a set of these babies. There were only around twenty-five sets available, but I managed to get my hands on one, which I shared with Terry Fullerton, a young Zip driver, who was in his first Junior World Championship. The tyres were a second or so quicker than the ones we'd been using and it was noticeable that all the karts lined up for the finals were kitted out with Blue Streak. The impact was instant. Even after Terry and I had raced in them all weekend, I was able to sell our set for twice what I'd paid for them.

It took the other manufacturers a while to react but then the Italian company Sirio produced a superb tyre, the same size as Goodyear but with a softer rubber compound and softer side wall. Dunlop came out with something similar. The new tyres were definitely quicker but there was a snag: whereas a set of Goodyears would cost you about £60 and last half a season, the new, softer tyres set you back £200 and, if you were lucky, they survived two meetings.

I was talking about the problem to Tom Hanawa, who runs the Le Mans Company in Tokyo, and he said he'd heard Yokohama might be interested in becoming involved in karting and suggested I go over and meet them. It was a bit of a long shot and I knew it would not be a cheap trip. In those days the Japanese economy was upside down – it cost less to buy a large colour television than a meal in a restaurant, and hotels were incredibly expensive. Still, if I could persuade them to make a cheaper version of the Sirio tyres, it would be money well spent. I bought a ticket and flew out.

Tokyo is one of those cities where you feel a surge of energy as soon as you step off the plane. In lots of ways it is like most of the busy cities in the West, but it also has the power to stop you dead in your tracks with its unfamiliarity. Unlike in, say, America or most of Europe, you are always aware in Japan that you are in a foreign country with a very different culture and it is much harder to gauge the way negotiations are going. It's a cliché to say that the Japanese are enigmatic, but I certainly wouldn't want to play poker against them.

As it turned out, I never had the chance to talk to Yokohama – they simply said they were not interested. It looked as though I'd wasted my time and cash but Tom said I should stay on another couple of days to see if we could set up a meeting with Bridgestone. Why not? It would be better than going home with nothing.

Bridgestone had started out making rubber soles for shoes. One day, in the 1930s, the chairman decided it was time they made rubber soles for cars, and they built up one of the biggest tyre-manufacturing companies in the world. In the early seventies they were just dipping their toe into motorbike racing, so I hoped I could persuade them to follow that with specialist tyres for karts. They admitted they knew nothing at all about the sport but agreed to meet me and they listened politely as we explained how fast the karting market was growing. Tom and I spent several hours talking to them about the kind of product we required, emphasising the need for a good price and a tyre that was hardwearing. At the end of our discussion they asked if we could go back the next day. 'There are some other people we would like you to meet,' they said.

The next two or three days followed a very similar pattern, each day moving up through the Bridgestone hierarchy until we finally met the directors. We told our story again and this time the response was, 'Please send us some of the tyres that you are using at the moment and we will see what we can do.'

I flew home not really sure if it had been a worthwhile trip. I bundled up a selection of tyres and posted them off, then put the whole thing out of my mind. About three months later a box arrived marked for my attention. It was full of plain black tyres with no markings. They were different from anything I'd ever seen before. They had a bit of a radius on the top edge and the corners were quite round. The side walls were very soft, almost like balloons. They looked good but I was disappointed because they didn't seem to be what I had asked for. I reckoned they would hardly last two laps, let alone two months. I shoved them back in the box, slid it under my desk and got on with more urgent things.

The tyres sat there for about three months, until Mike Wilson came down to test a new chassis ahead of the start of the season. Mike was one of the all-time great kart drivers, winning the world championship six times. If anyone could give a new product a thorough test, he could. He put the chassis through its paces on Goodyear and went well, then I put a set of the Bridgestones on his kart.

I said, 'Mike, these are brand-new tyres, never tested before, so take it easy. I'm not sure how strong they are and how long they'll last. They're also a bit bigger than the Goodyears so they'll unbalance the kart and upset the gearing, but I don't think they're going to amount to much, so we won't bother changing it. Just take a lap to get the feel of them, then do two or three more to see how they go.'

He did a tentative lap, then put his foot down. As he came across the line, I clicked my stopwatch. I looked across at my mechanic and said, 'I didn't change positions, did I?' I couldn't believe what I was seeing. Mike looked really uncomfortable but by my watch he had just lapped Rye House half a second faster than we'd ever been round there before. I watched him do another circuit and noticed he was having problems on the corners. He was trying to flick the back of the kart out as he usually would on Goodyears, but now the kart was bucking. He still finished the lap three-quarters of a second better than ever before. I called him in and asked him what he thought.

'They're crap. Horrible. You can't slide them, you can't do anything with them. What were my times like?'

He obviously didn't realise how quick he was going and I wanted him to tell me what he was feeling without influencing him one way or another.

'Don't worry about that,' I said. 'Look, I want you to go out again, and this time don't flick the back out on the corners. When you come up to a bend, I want you to brake as late as possible, turn in, set the front wheels right, and then put on the power.'

'But it ain't gonna be quick,' he complained.

'You won't know until you try. Just try to drive as smoothly as you possibly can.'

He still wasn't happy but he did what I asked and we were now a second faster and still the gearing wasn't right.

'How was it that time?' he asked, clearly curious as to why were going to all this bother for useless tyres.

I nodded. 'It ain't bad. Let's adjust the gearing and see how you go.' By the end of the day we had done what I thought was pretty well impossible – we had shaved a full second and a half off our best time and we were still on the first set of tyres. They hadn't blown.

I wanted to try them out under race conditions. The regulations said that tyres had to be a recognised make, so we arranged for an engraver to put Zip on the side and filled it in with gold paint. As far as anyone was concerned they were now Zip tyres. Mike took them back to his home in Barnsley in Yorkshire and, with strict orders to say nothing to anyone, raced them at Wombwell. He phoned me that night and I could hear the excitement in his voice: 'These tyres are something else. I not only won, I lapped everyone.'

A few weeks later we sent him to a major European race at Jesolo in Italy. All the factory teams were there with their motor homes and big entourages while Mike turned up with his van, a tent, two chassis, two engines and the new Zip tyres. He was a boy against men but he qualified at the front of the grid for the final and would have won, but the Italians drove him off the track at the first corner and damaged his kart. He still managed to recover and finished third.

The next day I was on the phone: 'Tom, I'll be in Tokyo tomorrow. Fix up for us to meet the top man at Bridgestone. We have to sort out a deal.'

Chapter 11

Just Sit at Woodcote and Watch

On the plane back to Tokyo, I worked out my strategy and by the time I walked into Bridgestone's offices I knew exactly what I wanted. Tom and I sat opposite three of their senior executives and I put my cards on the table. Well, most of them – no point in wasting their time with all the details of how fast we'd gone.

I said, 'We tried out the tyres you sent me and they are quite good. I think we could sell quite a lot. I'd like you to make them as Zip tyres and we'll sell them all round the world.'

'I'm sorry, Mr Hines. We cannot do that. We already have agreements in countries that don't allow us to give you what you want.'

Time for Plan B. 'Can you sell them as Bridgestone tyres?'

'Yes, we can do that.'

'OK. You don't do anything in karting, so I will be your world distributor for karting.'

'I'm sorry, Mr Hines. We cannot do that, either. We have distributors in many countries who sell all our products. We could, however, let you have rights in Britain and Ireland.'

This wasn't what I had planned. These tyres were a bit

special and I'd sell a lot in the UK, but I wanted a bigger slice of the cake. I let Tom do some talking while I recalculated.

'How many could you produce?' I asked.

There was some chat between them in Japanese, a quick telephone call, some jottings on a pad, some more chat and three heads nodded in agreement.

'We think we could make three thousand this year, the same the next year and then four thousand in the third year. After that, whatever you want.'

I went into my briefcase, took out a pad and wrote an order for ten thousand Bridgestone kart tyres to be delivered over the next three years. I passed it across the desk.

'That's my order.'

The top guy looked surprised. 'So soon?' Then he read it and smiled. 'Ah, I see.'

I smiled back. 'I've just bought your first three years' production. You don't have to advertise or market them, just make them. OK?'

They chatted for thirty seconds or so, then said, 'OK, you have a deal.'

I was taking a huge risk, committing well over a hundred and fifty grand, but I've never been afraid to back my hunches and this one proved to be solid gold. It was the start of a relationship that is still going today, which I think says a lot for both companies. Bridgestone went into a market they knew nothing about and with a company they didn't know much about, but over the next two or three years we changed the karting world. Everyone was switching to Bridgestones and they are still the leading manufacturer. Of course, we trod on a few toes and upset a few people, but that goes with the territory.

Many legends grew up in the industry about Zip and Bridgestone, most of which are just fanciful, but a couple are true. One incident that gave me most satisfaction was at the

European Championships in Estoril. All the drivers were clamouring for these new tyres, so, to be fair, I let them all buy the same number of sets. I thought I was being more than kind to the Italian teams, who, when we had been using their engines in the past, usually gave us the worst engines and charged us top dollar. But they obviously didn't think so. On the Friday night a very well-known Italian engine tuner came to me and said, 'Martin, we need three more sets of tyres.'

'Sorry, no can do. I've been fair to everyone and I can't change the rules for you.'

'Martin, be reasonable. What do you want for three sets? You want a new car? Just name the make. You know the people behind me, they won't let you down.'

I knew he was right. In the past the same company had provided an Alpha Romeo in return for favours, but, much as it hurt, I couldn't do it. Especially not for the teams that had been so difficult with us in the past.

In contrast, I was happy to let a German, George Beloff, have a lot of tyres. I knew him because his two sons, George Jr and Stefan, drove Zip Karts. George ran an unbelievable body shop in Germany for Mercedes where you could take your smashed-up car in the morning, put it on the conveyor belt, and when you got back in the evening it had been through the whole process and come out the other end as good as new. George wanted some Bridgestone tyres to distribute and I swapped him for a white, right-hand-drive Mercedes 450SEL.

I rang my local Customs and Excise office and confirmed a story I'd heard that, because I was out of the country a lot, I could keep the German plates on for six months, then import the car as second-hand and pay less tax. It would probably have all worked as smooth as the Merc's engine, except there was another scam going on – this one illegal and run by gangs in Europe. They were stealing top-of-the-range motors, taking them on the ferry from Calais to Dover, then driving them to Southampton, where they were loaded into containers for the Middle East and a fat profit.

The week before I picked up my lovely new 450SEL, the BBC ran a TV investigation into this illegal trade, so the guys at the ports were more on their toes than usual when I purred into customs without a care in the world, looking forward to my first rip up the motorway in my new motor.

'Excuse me, sir, is this your car?'

'Yes, why?' I hadn't seen the programme but I could tell from his voice this wasn't going to be a quick job.

'I would like you to pull over into that compound. I'll hold your passport.'

Two sharp-suited blokes came out of the office, looking like Bodie and Doyle out of *The Professionals*. They took me into a room 'to chat about your car, sir. Won't take long.'

They lied. They grilled me for more than two hours, wanting to know why an Englishman was driving a car with German plates. Where had I been? Where was I going? They went over the same ground time and time again, checking and rechecking my story. I showed them the documentation, but they still didn't believe me. They said that if I was importing the car I was going about it the wrong way, and they believed I was a link in the chain of stolen vehicles. They also surprised me by producing a sheet that told them how often I'd been out of the country and where I'd been in the last six months. So much for privacy – and that was before the sophisticated computers they have today! In the end they said they were confiscating the car and warned me they would be handing over the file to the police.

I had to phone Dad to come and pick me up and the next day I reported to the local police station. After a lot of toing and froing, I was taken to court by Customs and Excise for illegally importing a car. Apparently, that particular tax dodge worked only if you spent more than 180 days a year out of the country, and I'd been away less than that. To be fair, the local customs guy I had asked for advice was dead straight – he testified that I had checked with him and to his credit admitted that he had probably misled me by not telling me about the 180-day rule. Nevertheless, they fined me £500 and gave me back my Merc – once I'd paid full duty on it.

I was also being accused of skulduggery by karters who claimed the only way you could get your hands on a set of Bridgestones was to buy a Zip kart with the tyres already fitted. It is true that in the early years the demand was so great that I couldn't keep everyone happy and naturally I kept a quota aside for my own use. There would have been a lot of unhappy customers if I'd been selling my own karts with inferior tyres when I was the Bridgestone distributor. But, to put the record straight, I know of only two people who bought a kart simply to have the tyres.

Bridgestone were fantastic to deal with: punctual with deliveries, never dropping their quality and always doing exactly what they promised. After three years, we renewed our deal and, while I could no longer hope to corner the market, they listened to what I had to say about distributors worldwide. They revolutionised the business in the way Goodyear had all those years ago, but they also kept ahead of the game. Whenever another manufacturer started to catch up, Bridgestone came up with an innovation that set a new standard. Only once did we have a failure, and even then they eventually sorted it out.

It came in the early 1980s and was dangerous. The rubber round the bead of a tyre has four or five steel rings moulded into it to hold the bead in place. In karting you have only a 12.7-cm wheel, so, at 140 m.p.h., that wheel is making a lot of revs per minute and the tyre is getting very hot. If you don't hold it in place properly, it will pop off the rim with disastrous results. These tyres had originally been developed for 100cc karts, but we were now using them on superkarts that were twice the weight and certainly twice as quick. We had also developed bodywork that was creating solid down force and, with cornering speeds going up, this was putting more strain on the tyre. Sure enough, we started to suffer catastrophic tyre failures. They would occur when the tyre and driver were under the most stress, such as going flat out through Woodcote, the sweeping right-hander at Silverstone, which we would take at 130 m.p.h. Nine times out of ten, it happened when I was driving because I was always on the ragged edge between heroism and stupidity and those extra couple of miles an hour created even more G-force. It cost me at least one European Championship and one World title, not to mention a few scary crashes and many sleepless nights.

I couldn't figure out what was happening. By the time the kart came to a halt, the wheel was so mangled there wasn't enough evidence left to give any clue as to what was causing the problem. Faxes flew to and from Tokyo and, to be fair to Bridgestone, they were as anxious as I was to sort it out. They certainly didn't want someone badly hurt because one of their tyres had blown at speed. They tried all kinds of solutions but none of them seemed to do any good.

Then the penny dropped: I realised their technicians probably still had a picture in their mind of 100cc karts. They didn't realise how much hammer their tyres were subject to and the kinds of force that were being generated. I phoned and said, 'I want your top technicians to come over and we'll try to recreate the situation in front of them.'

I hired Silverstone for the day. It was expensive but this was serious. Lives could be at risk, and it was a track that would put more pressure on the tyres than any other. I knew I had to drive a tyre to destruction, which meant crashing, so we rigged up a little trolley wheel on the back so the kart wouldn't dig into the ground and throw me out when the tyre blew. It would still be like trying to control a runaway horse with a cotton rein, but was better than nothing.

I took the kart out for a couple of warm-up laps to get everything up to speed, including me. As I drove by the pits I looked to see where the Bridgestone technicians were, but there was no sign of them. The next lap I came in to check tyre pressures and temperatures, only to see them sitting on chairs in the pit lane, too far away from the corners to see or experience anything.

I pulled in and said, 'You're no use there. You can't see enough. Come with me.' And I took the head guy and his chair and sat him about a foot from the edge of the track at Woodcote.

I climbed back into the kart and set off. As I approached where he was sitting I squeezed the throttle, the engine roared and I flashed past him at just over 130 m.p.h. He dived off his seat slightly faster than that. But give him his due: by the time I came back round he and his mates were right there, obviously fascinated by what they were seeing. About four laps later the tyre burst right in front of them. I'd had so many go by that time that I could recognise the signs – there was a millisecond when there was a slight vibration and a rumble – and I was able to put it on the opposite lock and catch it. The trolley wheel hit the ground and we roared up the straight with sparks flying from my rear end and the Bridgestone guys sprinting behind me.

They immediately started to examine what was left of they tyre, jabbering away in Japanese. They admitted they hadn't realised the forces the tyres were under and they would have to take the bits back to Tokyo. Two weeks later, a new batch arrived and we haven't had a failure since. They wrote and thanked me, saying that they had been able to take what they learned and apply it to F1 tyres, where similar accidents might have happened at 200 m.p.h.

I've always found Bridgestone to be scrupulous people to deal with and only once saw them deliberately break the rules. All CIK championships specify the tyre rubber compound for a season to stop manufacturers coming out with something new each month and forcing the poor old drivers into forking out to keep up. At this particular World Championship the recognised tyres were from the Italian manufacturer Vega and from Bridgestone. As we approached the final round, it was noticeable that Vega, which had been slower, was suddenly the quicker tyre. Vega denied they had changed the compound but, when we tested the new ones against the old, they were clearly much quicker.

Bridgestone approached the CIK and said, 'If you don't enforce your own rules effectively, we will produce our own new tyre for this one event.' There was no change, so, as good as their word, Bridgestone produced special new compound tyres, YBNs, and blew the opposition away. Some people realised what was happening and snapped up as many tyres as they could in order to sell them on – I know one guy who sold a set for £400. But eventually we killed the market because we knew the batch numbers and banned them from competition.

That was the only time I have known them do anything that wasn't 100 per cent correct. It has been a fantastic relationship and has been of great benefit to drivers. It's worth remembering that, thirty years on, tyres are light years better than they were and they still only cost £120 per set, cheaper than some of those early tyre-war prices.

I was delighted to be invited to a special tour of Bridgestone when Luke and I were in Suzuka for a CIK championship race in 1992. They treated us royally. The tour finished with a visit to their impressive museum and, as we walked round, I said to the director who was acting as our guide, 'But you don't have any kart tyres.'

He shook his head. 'No, it is sad; we have spent many years looking for the first kart tyres.'

'Why didn't you ask me? It was me you made them for.'

'Really? I didn't know. In 1977 I was sweeping the factory floor. You are not told much when you do that job.'

I said, 'I have one set left at home. As long as you put a notice on saying these were made for Zip Karts, I'll send you half a set, and I'll keep half a set.'

Of course, not all my ideas have been historic breakthroughs ending up in a museum. Some finished in the scrapyard.

Chapter 12

Pose for the Cameras, Pick up the Dosh

One of my first motorsport heroes was the 'Super Swede', Ronnie Petersen. He came from a karting background and made his Formula One name at March, where his brilliant driving earned him second place in the World Championship to Jackie Stewart in 1971. He had panache, skill, courage and incredible integrity. The way he continued to obey orders and trail in behind Mario Andretti in the ground effect Lotus – even though he knew he was due to leave the team at the end of the year – was something you are unlikely to see in modern F1. When he was killed at Imola, everyone agreed Ronnie was one of the greatest drivers never to win the world championship.

As I followed Ronnie's career, I wanted to understand exactly how the 'skirt' on the Lotus made it so competitive, wondering whether, if we added something similar to a kart, we might shave a few tenths of a second off our performance. I picked the brains of everyone I knew, going into great detail about exactly the shape and design I needed for maximum impact. I spent about six months and a lot of money developing the prototype of what I hoped would be a revolutionary new kart and in great secrecy finally took it out to test at Cadwell Park.

It was a disaster. It felt as if I were driving a lump of lead. The skirt worked far too well. Sure, the kart was solid on the track but it had lost its sharpness and it accelerated with all the agility of a Trabant up to its axles in mud. We had created so much down force that the grip was overpowering the engine. Fortunately, I'd had the foresight to design it so I could bolt back areas of flat tray to reduce the effect. Throughout the day, I attached them one at a time until I had completely eliminated the down force and I was left with an ordinary kart. But, as Dad used to say, there is no such thing as failure. At least I'd found out what didn't work. We applied that policy to all kinds of things. If someone came up with a new exhaust or a different body shape, we would try it out to see if it worked for us. If not, we would abandon it but at least we weren't left thinking, I wonder if...

I'm glad to say that most of our experiments were more successful than the skirt and we continued to dominate the karting world, especially in superkarts. We also kept ahead of the rest in sponsorship. I still receive letters every day asking for advice on how to go about raising money from sponsors. It's dead simple: all you need is hard work and a lot of luck. Sponsors usually turn out to be people you know or have met and got on well with, someone who has a soft spot for the sport and has a company that spends a reasonable amount on advertising and promotion. Then you just have to work your butt off to make sure they get value for money because, if they don't, they won't come back no matter how much they like you.

As a rule of thumb, I put at least half the money I receive into making sure the sponsor is given publicity through TV programmes or race meetings covered by TV. A lot of the time I would arrange for Brian Kreisky to put the programmes together and let the TV companies have them on the cheap. Brian was a friend of mine who made a fortune out of promoting motorsport and syndicating races for television. Tragically, he was killed, along with several other members of his family, when their light aircraft crashed soon after taking off from Blackbushe Airport in Hampshire in 2003.

The other key to keeping sponsors happy is to involve them all the time. Marketing people will produce all kinds of graphs showing the number of TV seconds they've achieved and conduct research to show increase in product awareness, but the aspect people enjoy most from their sponsorship is meeting the drivers, being able to wander around places they wouldn't normally be allowed to go, and being right up close where they can smell the fumes and feel the atmosphere. These guys spend most of their time in suits behind desks, so they love being in the pits and getting their hands dirty.

Our big breakthrough in sponsorship came when we teamed up with Hermetite, the leading maker of engine sealants, who already sponsored Isle of Man TT rider Alex George, sports car driver John Fitzpatrick and the young Tom Walkinshaw, who was bound for even greater things. They were clearly into motorsport in a big way, so I decided to try to woo them over to karting. I sent their MD, Harry Werrell, a folder I'd put together, showing how much coverage Duckhams had enjoyed from their involvement with Zip Karts. I posted the letter in October and had completely given up on it by February, when my phone rang.

'This is Harry Werrell. You wrote to me about sponsorship. Don't know what happened but I've only just found the letter. Can you come and see me?'

I jumped straight into my car and broke several speed limits on my way to West Drayton, rehearsing in my head all the reasons he should sponsor me.

Harry wasn't big on small talk. 'What are you going to offer me?' he asked.

I liked his approach. This wasn't someone you could bullshit but you also knew he wouldn't mess you about. I played it very straight, going through the Duckhams folder to show how we had achieved coverage all over the world. I didn't make any outrageous claims and by the time I'd finished I could sense he was interested. Time for the pitch.

'I know karting's new to you and I know I have to be sensible and prove myself to you,' I said. 'All I'm asking for is five hundred pounds' worth of product that I can use or sell. Then I want to come back in a year's time and, if I've done a good job for you, I want you to give me ten times that in cash.'

He shook my hand. 'You've got a deal.'

That was the start of a thirteen-year-relationship that was tremendous for both companies. My final three-year deal with Hermetite was for £35,000 a year and the partnership ended only because they were taken over and the new owners didn't want to spend that much. I didn't want to sell myself short, so we went our separate ways. Meanwhile, it had been a hell of a ride. As I'd guessed, Harry was fully committed from day one. His PR and design team came up with layouts for a complete livery that knocked everyone's socks off. The silver Hermetite Zip Kart became as recognisable in karting as a red Ferrari in F1. I knew that, if we handled it properly, we had potentially hit the big time and I put myself about to ensure the Hermetite name was always visible.

Rule One of successful sponsorship: you have to get off your backside. If a TV company say they want you at Land's End in two days to film a sequence, you don't argue or ask how much: you jump in your van and you drive to the tip of Cornwall. And you make sure they get the coverage they want. This way they come back for more, your sponsor is happy and he also comes back for more.

Rule Two is that you learn how to maximise every opportunity to help your sponsors' business, which is not as unselfish as it sounds because it usually means promoting yourself. I've always made sure my drivers mix with the guests on race days. At first they see it as a bit of chore, but they soon realise they are building up a lot of useful contacts. Many of the most important numbers in my phonebook came from meeting people in the Hermetite marquee at race meetings. It's not enough to be a quick but retiring driver. When asked, I'd go up on stage, crack a few jokes and tell the punters a few 'insider' stories about motorsport so they felt they were part of the scene. It must have worked, because Harry told me the demand for visits to karting was always bigger than for any other events, including Wimbledon. Three years after I linked up with Hermetite, they dropped most of their other motorsport sponsorship but they continued with Zip because it was providing them with great exposure around the globe.

I stress to my drivers that their rivals aren't competing against them only on the track but also for a share of the sponsorship cake, so they had better learn some of the tricks of the trade if they want to cash in. Calvin Fish, who is now one of the top commentators on IndyCar and NASCAR in the States, was one of the first to take the lessons on board. Or, rather, his dad, Roy, did.

Calvin was one of the drivers I took to Folembray, a circuit built in the middle of woodland just south of Calais, when we were invited to put on a superkart demo for French TV. Local F1 hero Patrick Depailler was invited along and quickly took to the karts. His endorsement meant we were likely to get a big audience when the programme went out on the Sunday, so we needed to put on a great show. The producer came to me and said they wanted to film a couple of staged laps with lots of passing and repassing to transmit during the week as a thirty-second trailer. No problem, we'd done it thousands of times.

When I was briefing the drivers before the laps, there was a bit of banter with the guys saying, 'If it's gonna be on TV, Hinesey'll be out front all the time!' They soon learned they were wrong. When I found myself in front for a while, I'd go out wide at a corner just enough to let the others dive under me. Then I'd swoop back through and overtake. Several of the lads were impressed, thinking I'd done really well by them, until they saw the trailer on TV that night. The whole thirty seconds was either of me in the lead, or of me retaking the lead.

The next day, while we were waiting to practise some starts, Roy said to me, 'How the hell did you do that?'

'It's easy,' I replied. 'Before we began I noticed where the cameras were placed and made sure we were out of sight of them when I fell behind, but when we approached a camera I saw to it I was either in front or overtaking.'

'You need to teach Calvin these tricks. For instance, I'm always the last to climb into my kart on the grid before a race. That's for the photographers. They want something more interesting to shoot than a rank of karts with people sitting in them with their faces covered by visors.

'Snappers want interesting shots and I ensure they get them. I try to find out who the two or three key photographers are and I deliberately pose so they have chance to take a picture of me just as I'm about to pull the helmet down over my face. That way, if I win they have a good shot for their editor and if I'm in an accident they've got the last photo of me where you can see my eyes.'

I indicated a photographer with a long lens up on the roof of a building looking right down the grid. 'I bet he's already taken several shots but I'm going to give him another one now.' I turned to face the camera, looking back down the row of karts with the drivers sitting in them, and posed for a split second as I slipped my helmet on. (Sure enough, that was the picture in the paper the next day.)

Roy shook his head. 'And I thought it was just about driving fast,' he said.

I assured him that came into it as well. Over the weekend I took two-tenths of a second off the lap record previously held by an F1 car, which also gave the papers another story and picture of me and my Hermetite kart.

The first major event to which we took the iconic silver Hermetite kart was the 1977 European Championship in Jyllands-Ringen in Denmark. It's one of the few circuits that run anticlockwise, which gives you whole new set of forces to cope with. It was the first full FIA–CIK championship, a one-off event and I knew my greatest competition was going to come from my two British teammates Reg Gange and Dave Buttigieg. This was also the first big race where I was going to use Bridgestone tyres. I gave the other two the option of buying a few sets but they decided to stick with their Goodyear Blue Streaks, their first wrong move of the meeting.

My preparation couldn't have gone much better. I had a Yamaha TD3 engine prepared by Tony Smith, a motorcycle rider back in the days when BSA were kings of the track. He and I worked for hours to make sure the engines were perfect. They were set to the very limit. We got so much detonation on the piston, it would eat the top away – a piston that would normally last two or three meetings on a motorbike lasted us one heat. It was a fine balancing act but we had it dead right.

In the first heat I broke the track record; in the second I went out and extended it; and in the third heat I went faster still. In the final I was in pole alongside Butty. I won a lot of races in the first lap because I made sure I had my racing head on as soon as I sat in the kart, while some of the others didn't lock on until the lights changed. If I could snatch a second or so advantage on the field in the first lap, I would usually back myself to defend it just by driving consistently.

I could tell from Butty's body language that he wanted this as badly as I did. The starts are always a battle of nerves and with four of us on the front row there would be an immense tussle as we vied for the lead. As the lights flickered, I was gone. I managed to fight off the opposition to take the lead at the first corner and I was able to stay in front until the flag signalled I was European champion. What happened to Butty? He stalled on the line. Nerves can do that.

After the race a friend of mine suggested I should stroll down to the *parc fermé* and check out one of my rival's kart. 'Take a look at the petrol lines,' he said.

To avoid surging when the tank gets low, we always have two outlets from the petrol tank, one on the left and one on the right, linked together so there will always be fuel on one side or the other getting into the fuel line.

'Go and look at that kart and tell me why you think he has one fuel line going to the engine and the other along the chassis rails and taped on to his back bumper, pointing out the back of his kart. If I was a suspicious person, I'd wonder if he was aiming to get the jump on you then turn the left tank tap on and spray you,' he said.

If he was right, it would have been disastrous, because the two-stroke fuel had oil in it, which would have smeared my visor and taken the grip out of my tyres. I had no reason to believe my mate was making it up – you never know what might happen when there are titles on the line – but nothing had come of it and I was so delighted to be European champion that I didn't follow it up.

Pose for the Cameras, Pick up the Dosh

When I got home, Anglia TV phoned and asked if I would go to Snetterton to record an interview for their local news programme. A shy-looking young guy came up and introduced himself. 'Hi, I'm Steve Rider. I ought to tell you this is the first time they've let me out of the studio on my own, so I'm a lot more nervous than you are.' He was clearly a motorsport fan and after the interview asked if he could take a kart out. He adapted very quickly and we had a hell of a job to get him back in. We finally had to wave a petrol can at him to persuade him to call it a day. He's obviously still in love with the sport and enjoying covering F1 for ITV. I wonder if he's persuaded anyone to let him have a drive in one of those babies.

Being European champion was a great feeling, but not as great as the one I was about to experience.

Chapter 13

100 m.p.h. Average Wins over 'Mr Silverstone'

It was partly thanks to my connections with Hermetite that superkarts made one of their biggest breakthroughs. Harry Werrell was a good customer at Silverstone and he managed to persuade the owner, Jim Brown, to allow us to put on a kart demonstration before the British Motorcycle Grand Prix. There has always been an affinity between karts and motorbikes – we both wear leathers, use the same engines, tend to be down-to-earth people and find it astonishing when outsiders say we are nuts to put our lives on the line with a machine that affords the same kind of protection as a straw hat in a monsoon.

Jim, or as he appears in the official documents, James Wilson Brown, was the farmer who in 1948 took a disused airfield and turned it into a Grand Prix circuit in two months. He was Mr Silverstone. He continued to live in his beautiful farm house in the middle of the circuit and was justly proud of having created one of the most famous racetracks in the world. Woodcote, Maggots, Becketts, Hangar Straight, Stowe, Club and Abbey may not sound like poetry to some people but motorsport fans talk about them with the same reverence as a nun reciting a rosary. Jim was another man who wasn't afraid to let you know where you stood. A few years after I got to know him, he asked me to look after his son Hamish's karts, adding, 'If you kill him, you'll have me to answer to.'

To me, Silverstone is the best circuit in the world, though my chances of driving it seemed slim when Jim said, 'I'm not having bloody go-karts around my track. Silly little things.' It took a lot of persuading to change his mind. Harry assured him they were more spectacular than he thought; Hamish added an enthusiastic endorsement; and I promised a show that would excite the punters. Eventually he gave in.

I asked Malcolm Turner to come with me. He was a great driver who had taken part in plenty of demos around the world and knew how to make them memorable. We worked on the machines all week in the build-up because I wanted them to be 100 per cent right, but I was more keyed up than I'd been for years when we pulled off the A43 towards the circuit. My butterflies weren't exactly settled when Hamish told us his dad hadn't put aside any time for testing. I protested that we didn't know the circuit but the best he could offer was to take us round in one of the course cars when he went out to check the track. It was better than nothing and he did his best to be helpful with tips such as, 'At this corner you hit the apex at the third cone.'

I replied, 'That's great, Hamish, but with my bum half an inch off the ground I won't even *see* the bloody cones.'

I memorised what I could of the track but, in reality, we would be driving blind. Still, the show must go on and there wasn't much riding on this – just the future of superkarting. And what the hell, there were only about 100,000 people watching.

I shouldn't have worried. As soon as I nosed the kart out on to that legendary track I felt comfortable. All the nerves were swallowed up in a spurt of adrenaline and the nagging doubts drowned out by the sweet sound of a finely tuned engine. It was a drivers' circuit and by the time I went through Abbey on the run down to Woodcote for the first time – no chicane there for bikes and karts – I was flying. The trouble was that no one saw me! Even with my height, my shoulders are only about 53 cm from the ground on a kart, so to the people sitting in the grandstand, accustomed to seeing bikes fly by at about 4 feet (1.2 metre), I was down below the wall. But they knew something had happened because they heard the roar go past as if some phantom racer were tearing up the circuit, and the next time I came round I could see they were all standing and I could hear the cheer above the scream of my Yamaha engine.

The Tannoy kept the crowd informed of the lap times and there was a massive roar after my fifth circuit when they announced, 'Martin Hines has just completed a lap at an average speed of one hundred and two miles per hour.'

Karting had won some more converts. I spent the rest of the day signing autographs and talking about karts. I was on a high that no drug could ever give you. Motorsport crowds tend to be knowledgeable and they realised they had seen something special. Even Jim was quietly impressed, though when I suggested we should have a Superkart Grand Prix at Silverstone his first reaction was, 'No way!'

However, it was clear he thought we were on to something because he let us stage another demo, this time at the British F1 Grand Prix. Once again it was a tremendous hit and incidentally produced one of the top souvenirs in my collection. During the Grand Prix, Gilles Villeneuve crashed in a karting-style accident at the chicane at Woodcote. The following week, *Autosport*'s legendary cartoonist Barry Foley had a drawing of two guys talking:

'How did you enjoy the Grand Prix?'

'Fantastic. Just fantastic. I especially enjoyed that exciting display of karting.'

'Whose, Martin Hines' or Gilles Villeneuve's?'

I'd not only been in a Foley cartoon, I'd been mentioned in the same breath as Gilles Villeneuve, and, to top it all, Barry gave me the original drawing.

Jim was finally convinced, and in July 1978 we were back at Silverstone for the first British Kart Grand Prix sponsored by Hermetite and the *Daily Express*. There were 150 superkarts, plus as many again in the various other classes. There were nine heats for superkarts alone. I'd worked with the guys at the factory to modify the bodywork on my kart to suit the track, and the improved airflow and stability worked terrifically well. I won my first heat by 0.1 second in an immense battle with Steve Styrin, but Steve had his revenge in our next heat, charging to the front from the back of the grid and, though I got near him, I couldn't close the gap. It went pear-shaped for both of us in the final heat. Steve wiped out at Copse and suffered concussion, so missing out on the final. I went off at Woodcote but luckily was unhurt. Unfortunately, the same couldn't be said for the kart, and we had to do a major rebuilding job before the final on Sunday.

I'd still done enough to make the front of the grid alongside another Hermetite Zip driver, Paul Elmore, just ahead of Martin Poole, Dave Buttigieg and fifty-six others, all dreaming of winning the first Silverstone GP. I had a disastrous start, struggling with a misfire as the rest roared past me. Eventually, the engine recovered and I set off in pursuit of the frontrunners, where Paul was in a titanic battle with his brother Steve and Butty. I worked my way through the field until there were just the three in front of me. Dave had to drop out with a puncture, Steve lost top gear and I was able to swoop past him, but I couldn't quite overhaul Paul. Still, second from such a poor start was pretty good and it was fantastic to have Hermetite Zip one and two.

It had been a very special day and was the start of a long tradition of memorable events. The British Grand Prix became the biggest day in the karting calendar with people coming from all over the world just to be there. I remember having dinner with Eddie Irvine's mum and dad in the McLaren hospitality marquee and they said that, even though Eddie never raced karts, the whole family used to camp in the field at Silverstone for the kart GP.

My joy at getting the event off the ground was diminished by the death of Albert Carrera when he crashed in the race. Albert was a good friend and I'd built his kart for that weekend, so I was shattered by his death. My sorrow turned to fury when the next issue of one of the leading magazines alleged that, while everyone was mourning Albert's death, I was more interested in briefing Paul Elmore about what to say when he was on the podium. In fact, hardly anyone knew at that stage that Albert was dead. Jim Brown had told me because he knew I was a close friend, but there were only a handful of us who were aware of the tragedy. This particular magazine had often taken a pop at me and Zip Kart before, but this was going too far, and I vowed to hurt them as much as they'd hurt me. I'm not a great believer in suing people – that just gives money to lawyers – so I decided to hit them where it hurts.

We immediately withdrew our advertising, which wasn't inconsiderable, and I set about putting a team together to start a rival magazine. I hired Chris Lamden as editor. He did a fantastic job and is now one of the top motorsport publishers in Australia. His brief was to give karting the magazine it deserved. I'd felt for some time that the sport was worth more than the rather ordinary black-and-white publications with the occasional spot colour that were currently being served up. Now was my chance to show what I meant.

The first decision was to use good-quality paper and full-colour printing. Then Chris and I sat down with our favourite magazine, *Autosport*, and lifted all the best bits, just inserting karts where they would have cars. We published the same kind of features and gossipy news items in the same layouts, and we even managed to persuade Barry Foley to draw cartoons for us as well. We kept *Kart and Superkart* running for thirteen years and I closed it only after my dad died and I could no longer cram everything I needed to do into a twenty-four-hour day. Something had to go and it was the magazine, which was, anyway, costing me a small fortune to keep running. Over the years, our relationship with the other magazine healed and we now get on well, but I'd made my point.

Chapter 14

Beware Kiwi Bottle Shops – You Can Lose Your Shirt

Despite our volatile relationship, Lindy and I got married. It was a second marriage for both of us, which just goes to show that even the wisest people don't always learn from their mistakes. But, to be fair, we were reasonably happy in the early years and the marriage wasn't a complete disaster. Her dad, Allan, owned a nursery that had seen better days but it was close to the factory so ideal when he gave us half the land, which already had planning permission, for a three-bedroomed bungalow. The word bungalow smacked too much of retirement to my mind so I put in new plans for an ultra-modern, 1970s style house, which in hindsight was something of a monstrosity and certainly completely out of keeping with the neighbourhood. Planning committees being what they are, they gave us the go-ahead. The house, which included a one-bedroomed flat for Allan, was completed in the exceptionally hot summer of 1976. It was great to have the extra space and especially the swimming pool we'd had built out the back.

That same summer, 12 May to be precise, our daughter Kelly was born. I know all dads say this but she really was perfect – she even slept through the night as a baby and didn't

99

make too much fuss even through the teething process. She grew into a wonderful blonde-haired, blue-eyed child. Life seemed fine for a while. On the outside we were a happy family – mum, dad, daughter and two dogs – but even the love of my daughter could not stop the cracks appearing in our marriage. As the months passed, things grew steadily worse and it needed only an excuse for me to make up my mind to leave – and that excuse came along wearing leathers.

I met a woman who raced superkarts and we just clicked – the fact that we mostly saw each other in racing gear probably had something to do with our mutual attraction. One thing led to another and I decided it was time for me to move out of the family home. I packed a bag, slipped away and spent the next week or so in a hotel with my new lover. Maybe it was the lack of leathers, or the fact there was no engine noise in the background, or perhaps just that we were spending time together when we weren't high on adrenaline, but it soon became obvious this relationship wasn't going to work out, either. She went back to her partner and I thought I'd try again with Lindy. My good intentions ran out after a few months. Much as I wanted to be around Kelly while she grew up, I couldn't face the lifestyle that went with it. I would have ended up resenting her, and that would have been worse than being apart.

It was time to find somewhere new to live. Friends of mine from New Zealand, Russell and Barbara, had come to England for six months and were doing some work for me in between their sightseeing and exploring. They were living at Wormleybury House, an eighteenth-century estate near Hoddesdon, and told me there were some vacant apartments there. I was impressed by the place as soon as I drove up. Not only was it one of those stunning old buildings that England does so well, but there was a fantastic-looking woman in shorts and a T-shirt washing a car outside. She had the kind of body that looked as though it was used to being stared at, so I obliged. I smiled at her as I went in and grinned when Russell told me this vision was Barbara's daughter, Angela. Well, what kind of friend would I have been if I hadn't taken her out to dinner that night? It was meant to be. After all she was a Leo.

I first became interested in the way star signs can affect relationships when I was on a plane, going to America. The inflight magazine had an article by astrologer Linda Goodman and as I glanced through the section on Taurus, I thought, Bloody hell! This woman has been reading my mail. It was uncanny how accurate she was and what made me even more convinced she was on to something was that she said that a Taurean born in May (my dad) would be a home bird, happy to be around the house or in the garden, while one born in April (me) would have no interest in those things. How bloody true! I know a lot of people scoff at astrology, and I don't pretend to believe what my stars say in the papers every day, but I do think that the star sign you are born under has an effect on your personality.

I read a bit about it and found that Taurean men should steer clear of Aries women because they are hard to live with. If only I'd read that before I married Lindy! However, it suggested that, while Taurean men and Leo women are not suited as long-term partners, they do have one thing in common: they both like sex. A lot! I can vouch for that. I have always had a thing about Leo women, with their flowing hair and their ability to turn heads just by their presence when they enter the room. Angela certainly had that. I have a bit of a jealous streak and there were times when I felt other men were showing just a bit too much interest in her, and that I was ready to take them all outside.

Angela and I had nine incredible months together, travelling all over Europe, seldom apart. We seemed perfect for each other, but there were two snags. She was a lot younger than I was and I was worried that it might become a problem later on. I was also feeling guilty about walking out on Kelly. I felt I owed it to her to patch things up with Lindy and try to make our marriage work for our daughter's sake. Angela wasn't concerned about the age difference and, while she understood my feelings about Kelly, she didn't want our relationship to end. She decided the only way out would be for her to make a complete break and fly back to New Zealand so we could both make a fresh start.

Our last weekend was spent at a kart meeting in Portugal, but we didn't spend much time alone together. We were at the track all day Saturday and Sunday and on the Saturday night we were down the road from our hotel having dinner with the people from Bridgestone. By the time I came to pay my hotel bill on the Sunday night, I was tired and starting to feel depressed at what was about to happen to my love life. My mood wasn't helped when I saw there was a £240 bill for a dinner on my tab. Someone from our party, who had managed to forge my signature very convincingly, had thought it would be funny to charge what was then a hugely expensive meal to my room. We've all pulled strokes like that but you don't do it to mates, so I refused to pay. It took a while to resolve and only when the guilty party realised the police were about to be called and I was willing for us to miss our flight, did he sheepishly hand over his credit card.

The flight home was miserable. For the first time since we met, Angela and I didn't find conversation easy. There was nothing left to talk about, yet there was so much that needed saying. It was too late to change our decision and yet every bit of me ached just to say, 'Please don't go.' I said nothing. The next day, she flew out of Heathrow and, as I thought, out of my life.

Tiptoeing round a woman you no longer have feelings for while your gut is aching because you can't be with someone else is probably not the ideal formula for patching up a marriage. The miracle was that this reconciliation lasted all of ten days. I tried to make it work for Kelly's sake. She was a special girl, very self-aware and into fashion from an early age. Mum and Dad used to bring her racing most weekends and she lapped up the kart scene and was always confident around racing people. She would wander off talking to the riders and mechanics, and I remember when we had a meeting alongside the Superbike Championships, we found her chatting away to Barry Sheene while he worked on his bike. 'Oh, she's yours, Martin,' Barry said. 'I might have guessed.'

I loved being around her, but, much as I wanted to stay in the relationship with Lindy, I knew it was no good. There was a real sense of failure as I packed my bags again and left her for the last time. It was just before Christmas and I decided that not only did I have an urge to go away, but I needed to see Angela again. I wanted her back and if that meant flying round the world then that was what I would do. Fortunately she felt the same way. We agreed I would go to Auckland for the holiday and then she would come back to England with me.

The reunion was great. I met the rest of her family, including her grandmother, who was an incredible ninety-year-old delinquent. Angela introduced me to her friends, including two of the campest and nicest gay guys I've ever met. They gave me a tour of Auckland money can't buy – sightseeing peppered with their bitchy spats that were more entertaining than anything you'll see at the Palladium. It was Graham Norton meets Julian Clary on a bad-hair day and for me the memories of Aotea Square Market, Underwater World, Mission Bay and North Head will always have a soundtrack of my guides' brief but intense tiffs.

After spending Christmas with the family, Angela and I set off to drive to Ninety Mile Beach at the northern tip of New Zealand, with a warning from the hire company not to get their car caught in the quicksand. It's a long trek, so we booked into a motel on the way up and I stopped in a nearby town to pick up a couple of bottles of wine for the evening. Being a shy, retiring kind of bloke, I was wearing a grey Hermetite Zip T-shirt with a big picture of the kart and my name emblazoned across the front. As I plonked a bottle of red and bottle of white on the counter to pay, the owner took one look at my shirt and scurried into the backroom. Good job it didn't have my face on, too!

Seconds later, he reappeared holding a magazine. 'You are Martin Hines,' he said. 'I don't believe it. I've just been sitting back there reading this article in *Car and Car Conversions* about you and Derek Warwick in a track comparison test between his F3 and your kart at Donington.'

I didn't believe it myself. I was 11,500 miles from home, in a wine shop on the way to nowhere, and I'd found a fan.

'I love all motorsport but it takes ages for the magazines to come over here so I'm always a bit behind the times. Will you autograph this, please?' he said. 'And I don't suppose I could have your T-shirt?'

I signed his magazine and said, 'If I can have these two bottles of wine, pal, you can have my T-shirt.'

With that, we swapped and Angela gave me a strange look as I returned to the car bare-chested, a bottle of wine in each hand and a big grin on my face. I think for a moment she wondered what else I'd learned on my sightseeing tour.

We had five or six really good days before making our way back to Auckland, but this time the trip wasn't as highly charged as the flight from Portugal had been. Things had changed. We'd had a great time but it didn't feel the same as it had been before. Angela had decided she wasn't going to come back to England with me and I was quite relieved.

There was no point in hanging about. We said our goodbyes and I decided that, having come this far, I might as well go and see Peter Dell in Sydney. I'd got to know him when he raced in England, and he'd always said that if I was passing the end of his road...

Chapter 15

No, Thanks – I'd Rather Watch a Horror Film

Sydney was a good town to get over being unlucky in love. I booked into a hotel, phoned Peter and that night we hit the bars and got falling-down drunk. When I staggered into the lift to go back to my room about three in the morning, four guys got in with me. Even in my condition they looked remarkably like the people smiling out from the poster on the lift wall and being the worse for drink, I slurred, 'You are the Four Tops. Come on, sing me a song.' And to my surprise they gave me a quick chorus of 'It's All in the Game'. A truer word has seldom been sung.

The next thing I remember it was about seven o'clock and a maid woke me as she came into my room.

'Sorry, I'll come back later,' she said.

'No, it's OK. You carry on.'

My head was thumping and I wasn't quite focusing, but she looked OK, so, when she came out of the bathroom with the dirty towels, I said, 'Look, I've only just arrived in Sydney. It's my first trip. Why don't you show me around tonight?'

I can't have been looking my best, so I was a bit surprised when she said yes. She told me her name was Rosemary and explained that officially she wasn't allowed to go out with guests, so she would meet me at King's Cross station across the road at seven. My broken heart was on the mend again.

I spent the day with Peter who told me that he'd booked us into an Italian restaurant with some old friends that night.

'There might be one more,' I said, explaining what had happened. 'But I'm a bit worried. I can't really remember what she looks like and I can't help wondering how desperate she must be if she agreed to a date after seeing me in that state this morning. Let's meet in a bar, then if she turns out to be a bit rough we'll give her a quick drink, say we have to go off to a business meeting and give her the cab fare home.'

Peter was amazed that I'd found time to chat up a girl in the short while we'd been apart and reckoned the odds against her being anything but a one-eyed granny were pretty high. Throughout the day he would crack jokes like, 'Do you think we should buy a collar and lead in case?'

I went to meet her that evening, convinced Peter was right and I'd made a huge mistake. There was a long corridor leading out of the station between some shops, and there were crowds of people milling about. I looked around for a grey-haired old dear with a walking stick. One girl stood out from the crowd. I did a double take. Just like Lindy all those years ago, she had skin-tight pants and a lemon, see-through top. It was obvious, even to someone as naïve and innocent as I was, that she wasn't wearing a bra. Her colouring was the opposite of Lindy – this girl had flowing satin-black hair and a tan straight off Copacabana beach via Bondai – but the stirring I felt when I saw her was very similar. If only, I thought, wondering who the lucky guy was that she was smiling at behind me. Then I realised: it was me.

'Martin,' she said. 'You came.'

Being a cool kind of guy and especially as I was in the home of smooth-talking Aussie fellas, I greeted her with one of my more sophisticated lines.

'Rosemary? Fuck me, you are beautiful.'

I took her across to the bar and introduced her to Peter. It was he who now needed the collar and lead – to hold him back. He whispered to me, 'You pommy bastard. You've only been here five minutes and you've pulled the best-looking bird in Sydney. The only way I will forgive you is if you let me have her number when you leave.'

We went to the Italian restaurant, where I introduced Rosemary to the rest of the party. The men all seemed pleased to see her, their girlfriends less so. Sitting opposite me in a colourful shirt was a guy called Barry Beckman, who had once been my agent in Sydney. He'd ended up owing me about four thousand pounds when one of his businesses went under. It was a lot of money back then but I'd written it off and put it out of my mind as one of those things that happen in business. I knew he'd been unlucky and not dishonest, so I was genuinely pleased to see him and we greeted each other as friends. He leaned across the table, gave me an envelope and said, 'Before I forget, let me give you this. Don't open it now. Wait until you get back to your hotel.' And he turned his attention to chatting to Rosemary. Hang on, buddy: four grand was one thing, this woman was something else. Hands off!

We had a great evening and eventually Rosemary and I went back to my room, where I found better things for her to do than tidy up the towels. I ended up staying two weeks instead of two days and was having so much fun that I forgot to open Barry's envelope for several days. When I did, I found every penny that he owed me. He'd always said he would repay me but I never thought he'd be in a position to do so. I was very impressed and phoned him to tell him so.

Some of my friends say I should sell my treatment for broken hearts to Papworth hospital because it works so well. I arrived back in England recovering from two great romances, and within two days I'd met Tina.

I had seen her before I went to New Zealand when Russell and I had a night on the town and ended up in a pub called Masseys, where the girls behind the bar were known as Masseys' Lassies. It struck me that I would have enjoyed being the guy who hired them, as they were all good-looking girls with big personalities. Before the night was out I took a chance and asked Tina to join Russell and me for a meal but she threw me a bit of a curve.

'No thanks,' she said. 'I'm going home to watch a horror movie.'

It was time to try again and in the end, Chris Short, who worked for me and was an old schoolfriend of Tina's, set us up and I became a regular at Masseys. It was a friendly bar. You know the type: 'where everybody knows your name'. And it had a tradition that, at chucking-out time, they would play Barry White singing 'Don't Go Changing'. I have to tell you that the Last Night of the Proms can offer nothing to match the gang in Masseys, their arms around one another, admittedly after a drink or two, singing 'Don't go changing to try to please me', in seemingly perfect harmony. And on the nights when we persuaded Pete the landlord to play it twice, it was even better. It became 'our song' for Tina and me.

And that, my friends, was that. From that day to this – something like twenty-eight years – I've been a one-girl man, although I do sometimes wonder what would have happened to my life if Tina had reacted differently the first time I took her racing.

Chapter 16
The Nero of Silkeborg

We went to Lydden Hill in Kent for a meeting of karts and motorbikes. Gary Parkes, my engineer, had the karts in the Mercedes 508 transporter and I was following in a typically understated Hines motor – a metallic-blue BMW with racing stripes. Doodling along behind a truck in a BMW can be a bit boring and over the years Gary got used to keeping an eye in his mirror because I would practise taking the inside lane on him at roundabouts just to add a bit of spice. This day, we'd gone only as far as Tottenham when I went up on his inside, mounting the pavement, confident that Gary wouldn't cut across me. But this time he forgot to check and wiped out the front of my BMW. It was still driveable, so we carried on, but Tina went quiet on me for a few miles.

The meeting was great fun. Roy Fish was there with his son Calvin and his mate Micky, a tiny guy who could hardly see over the wheel of the Rolls-Royce he'd managed to buy out of selling foam rubber to market stalls. Roy and Micky were a double act – Ant and Dec with oily fingers and speaking English instead of Geordie. We also met Steve Eaton, a hillbilly racer in black overalls and with a real biker look, who was there for the 250 national single-cylinder races. He was OK and instantly became a member of the gang, and that night it all got a bit rowdy in the hotel bar. Tina and I decided not to stay up drinking all night and took our leave early, only to be woken in the early hours by a rumpus and the sound of police sirens outside the window. We went out on the balcony in time to see Roy being carted off to the nick for the night. Apparently he had sprayed the barman with a soda siphon when the guy decided he couldn't put up with any more of their drunken revelries. We bailed him out on the way to the track the next day.

It was one of those meetings where one thing leads to another and this one gradually got a bit silly. We found it was possible to spray Swarfega, that green slime you use to clean your hands, through a pump we usually used to wash down bearings on back axles with petrol. Our new friend Steve was the first to be caught, his 'hard-man' black leathers suddenly looking like a demented Teletubbies outfit. That kicked off a major war between karters and bikers. I managed to squeeze an ice-cream cornet under Steve's visor as he sat on the grid and by the end of the day the missiles had deteriorated to hot dogs with lashings of tomato sauce. It was pretty dirty. Bikers fancy themselves as the kings of high jinks, but that day even *they* had to give way to the karters.

It was all taken in the right spirit and, as we drove away from Lydden, we spotted Steve's Dormobile outside a transport café and pulled in to join him. This was no ordinary Dormobile: it had the large windows down the side and, with its matt-black finish, was thirty years ahead of its time. We had a fry-up and Tina was impressed with my 'new man' credentials when I asked the waitress if I could buy a tray of eggs to take away. 'I'd forgotten we were out,' she said, pleased to see at least one semblance of domesticity on this crazy trip.

The Nero of Silkeborg

It took a couple of miles to catch Steve up and, as we went past, I opened the sunroof and started lobbing eggs at him. A couple landed on his windscreen and the prat turned on his wipers. I have to tell you, that's a great way to make an omelette but all it did for Steve was block his vision with smeared yoke. Once more the man in black looked like something out of the circus and, as he pulled over to the hard shoulder, we sped away. Amazingly, Steve forgave us and went on to become a good friend, even though he reckoned it took him two weeks to clear the last of the egg off the bodywork.

Roy and Micky were also involved in one of the most bizarre incidents I can recall; in fact, Micky caused it. He had taken his Roller to Silkeborg in Denmark, where we were due to race. I flew out late and he and Roy met me at the airport at 11 p.m. and took me back to the Hotel Dania. With nowhere else to park, Micky perched his car on the pavement in front of the hotel and told me to dump my bags because we were going out on the town. We finally returned in the early hours and as I opened the door to my room, the whole back wall was a mass of orange flame. I slammed the door shut and raced down the corridor banging on doors and shouting 'Fire!' The reaction of some people to my alarm was like something out of Buster Keaton movie.

Our team manager, Bert Hesketh, opened his door, stark naked, and told me to shut up because he was trying to sleep. I managed to persuade him that this was real and he needed to cover up and get out.

Wyatt Stanley decided his suitcase was too heavy to carry downstairs but he didn't want to leave it in his room, so he tossed it from his fifth-floor window, yelling, 'Catch this, someone.' No one did. It burst open and his clothes dispersed into the night.

Most of the racing people were staying at the hotel and there was a mad panic with guys in various stages of undress tripping over one another in their rush to move the trucks containing about 600 gallons of race fuel from the car park.

Eventually everyone was outside in the road and we witnessed the most stylish reaction of all. I noticed a bloke come out of a luxurious house opposite the hotel, wearing a very expensive leather trench coat. He had a word with some of the staff and the next thing we knew they were scurrying back into the building, some returning with chairs, others with crates of beer and wine.

The guy said: 'Ladies and gentlemen, if you will all take a seat, we can have a drink while we watch my hotel burn down.'

As it turned out there were only about half a dozen rooms damaged before the fire brigade got things under control, so we didn't have to find another hotel for the weekend. It turned out the blaze had been started deliberately by a guy who had issues with people with money. When he saw Micky's Roller on the pavement he decided it was time to strike back.

I will always remember the hotel owner's calm in the face of a major crisis and I had been equally impressed with how Tina had coped with the mayhem of our first weekend together. I can only imagine she decided it couldn't get much crazier, so she might as well stay. Unlike most of my other relationships, which started perfectly and then went downhill, this one was often tricky in the early stages. I remember more than one rocky spell when I thought it wasn't going to work out because there seemed no way we could find a compromise to allow both of us to be happy at the same time. Tina hated to be in the limelight, and didn't even want to walk into a restaurant first. I was dead opposite. I'd learned early on that motorsport is not for wallflowers. You have to be at the front when they are taking photos so, when a camera appeared, I would be pushing forward and Tina would be pulling back.

Above: MH just a twinkle in their eye! Above left, Maudie Lavinia Hines and above right Mark William Hines.

Below left: Racing was always in Dad's blood.

Below right: A rare picture of MWH and MH on the beach.

Top: The Hines family.

Above left: Hines Of Finchley, 17 Hendon Lane, where it all began.

Above right: Best man for my mate Jeff.

Right: Bingo hall, Christmas party night, wishing happy 80th to our oldest customer.

Above left: Wally Green: my first boyhood hero.

Above right: The very first picture of me in my first Tab Kart/Clinton E65.

Below: A family affair: bingo hall kiosk with my grandparents and Mum and Dad.

Above: England v France 1967: Buzz Ware, MH, Glenn Beer, David Ferris and kneeling Roy Mortara, Ken Owen and Bruno Ferrari.

Below: Zip Kart moves to Rye House, the home of karting.

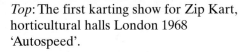

Top: The first karting show for Zip Kart, horticultural halls London 1968 'Autospeed'.

Above left: MH leads Keke Rosberg in the CIK/FIA European Championships.

Above right: The Shennington International six-hour winning team: MH and John Stokes with Mark Hines and Jeff May in the middle.

Right: Terry Fullerton and MH (Who's trying to look like who?). My last 100cc kart race in the Hong Kong Grand Prix.

Can you believe this? Racing on Boulogne Docks, late 1960s. Glen Beer and Dave Salamone (*The Italian Job*) crash as Roger Mills and Hines (10) take advantage.

Above left: At 17 years and 5 days, I passed my test in my loved Ford Squire. Why a Squire? Because you could get a kart in the back.

Above right: MH puts a move on Buzz Ware at Rye House, or is it Buzz puts a move on MH?

Bottom left: My first major win, the BP cup at Morecambe. The late, great Dave Leslie, seen kneeling here, pushed me all the way to the flag.

Bottom right: I even won Miss BP title at the banquet from Kelvin Hesketh and Harry Rolf. Lindy was seeing a different side of me.

Panel 1: HOW DID YOU ENJOY THE GRAND PRIX?

Panel 2: FANTASTIC, JUST FANTASTIC, I ESPECIALLY ENJOYED THAT EXCITING DISPLAY OF KARTING.

Panel 3: WHOSE, MARTIN HINES' OR GILLES VILLENEUVE'S?

Top: Ligier F1 driver Patrick Depailler tested a MH Kart at Folembray in France for French TV.

Centre: The Barry Foley cartoon in Autosport heralded the first kart Grand Prix in 1978.

Below left: The Silverstone GP was always a family affair with Mum, Dad, Kelly and my lovely Aunt Vi, Dad's sister.

Below right: The 1978 British GP: first Paul Elemore, second MH, third Malcolm Turner, as Lindy crowns Paul.

For once I was shaken as well as stirred and not sure what to do. She was so different from every other woman I had known. There was certainly a massive spark between us but we had to work harder than I'd ever worked to keep things going. I had a race coming up in Italy and said, 'We'll see how we feel after a week apart.' I think I expected I would make up my mind to end it. Instead, I thought about her all the time I was away and decided she was the woman I wanted to be with. It made no sense: I was thirty-four, she was twenty-one, so the age gap was greater than between Angela and me, and there were lots of things other girls would do that she simply refused. But we were very easy with each other and it felt right. The things that pushed us apart seemed much less important than the things that kept us together. Instead of ending it, I committed to it.

We moved in together and a couple of years later, on 4 May 1982, Luke was born. Having failed twice – and paid a big price emotionally and financially – I was reluctant to get married again, but, when she fell pregnant again, I left Tina a note pointing out that I'd never lived with a woman as old as twenty-five without being married, so we had better tie the knot. She said yes and my pregnant girlfriend and I became Mr and Mrs Hines in July 1985 and our daughter Tuesday arrived eight weeks early on 9 September.

It had been a special three years, made even more spectacular by the little matter of a World Championship.

Chapter 17
Beating the Odds -
Indoors and Out

If you stand still in business, you will go backwards as others overtake you, so I'm always on the lookout for ways to keep Zip Karts ahead of the field, even if some people in the sport don't approve. That is why I was happy to talk to Bob Pope and Martin Howell when they came to see me in the early 1980s.

I'd first met them when they were running a scheme in south London aimed at stopping kids from joyriding. They provided car-mad youngsters with an alternative to nicking motors by letting them work on engines and drive around a piece of waste land that the council allowed them to use. To keep within their budget, Bob and Martin bought some second-hand karts for the kids to work on and they often came to me for cheap spares. As so often with positive ideas, some politician decided there was another priority that would attract a few more votes, so the council pulled the plug on funding and, what's more, they wanted their land back.

To be fair, they did let Bob and Martin have a disused bus station to store their gear until they could dispose of it, an offer that turned out to be the start of a major new industry. It was a cavernous old building with a solid concrete floor, black from years of foot scuffing and oil spills. One day the guys got the karts out from under the dustsheets and raced round a makeshift track. They found it was terrific fun and fairly soon their mates were joining them and paying a few quid each towards the cost of fuel and wear and tear. That was when they came to see me.

'We think we could build this into a little business but at the moment the karts are too noisy and too smoky. Have you any ideas?' they asked.

As it happened, shortly before this Rover Cars had asked us to design some basic fun karts in their cream and maroon colours, which they put into senior schools in kit form for pupils to assemble. They also encouraged each group of youngsters to design some new features, such as bumpers and mud guards. The scheme gave schools a chance to provide practical lessons while Rover might be able to spot some bright young kids to who they could offer apprenticeships.

The karts had a Honda engine like those on a cement mixer and I thought they would be ideal for racing indoors, nippy without being too powerful, not too noisy and hardly any fumes. We built one up and let the guys try it out at Clapham.

Within a week, Bob phoned me: 'The kart's fantastic. We need six more. There's only one snag: we don't have any money.'

'Don't worry,' I said. 'I think it's a great idea. We'll supply the karts and you can pay us when you start making money.'

That was the start of indoor karting. The business took off much faster than any of us anticipated. Within weeks, you had to book well in advance to get a drive and, before the year was out, I'd been paid for the karts and the lads were driving round south London in flash new motors. Soon there was an indoor track at Shildon in County Durham and another near Heathrow Airport, and then they started springing up all over the place. But the bus station at Clapham remained one of the best indoor layouts. It was simple with fast sections, slow bits, easy parts where anyone could get a bit of a move on and tricky bits that could catch you out and where the better drivers came to the fore.

Of course, we received a lot of stick for being involved. Just as when we launched superkarts, the purists looked down their noses. Rival manufacturers started to put round stories that Zip Karts was no longer in the serious business of racing having 'sold out' to fun karts for kids. I knew it was bollocks and ignored them. Indoor karts were keeping us busy and as I expected it wasn't long before most of our competitors were also entering the market.

I've never understood why most people's automatic response to anything new is 'no'. Instead of seeing an opportunity, they see a threat. Indoor karting was never going to damage outdoor racing. On the contrary, it increased interest in the sport. It was ideal for TV and received extensive coverage. It gave thousands of people a lot of fun and, just as the weekend golfer loves to go and watch the pros at the big tournaments, many fun karters became hooked on top racing.

It's a bit frustrating when you have to battle so hard to establish any new idea but in a way it makes it sweeter when you are proved right. One of the most satisfying moments was when Ernest Buser said, 'You have superkart drivers all round the world. You have a Grand Prix at Silverstone. What you need now is a World Championship.'

He was willing to grant it full FIA–CIK backing, which would give the winner status alongside all the other FIA world champions from F1 to rallying. It was what I had dreamed about for thirteen years since switching to superkarts.

The new event, sponsored by Bridgestone, would be run on the same three-round format as the established 100cc kart world championship. Qualifying would give you your position in the heats, in which you would score points to give you your starting place in the first of two finals. World Championship points would be won in the pre-final and the final, with the first race determining where you started in the second. So the title would depend on the points you picked up in six finals. In the case of a tie, the driver with the most wins would take the trophy.

The first championship round was held at Jyllands-Ringen in June 1983 and I couldn't have made a better start. I had been driving well all season, winning races at Snetterton, Cadwell and Brands Hatch, and the kart was going perfectly. There was a massive entry in Denmark and we each had to drive three heats for our grid position in the final. I picked up two firsts and a second, shattering the lap record to a new 44.45 seconds in the process, to take pole in the pre-final, which I won after taking the lead on lap eight. The second final was one of those rare races where I didn't have to pass a single driver – I led from start to finish, picking up a maximum fifteen points. The weekend was topped off by hearing that Terry Fullerton had won the European 100cc title for Zip.

I was full of confidence going into the second round at Silverstone. I knew the circuit better than probably all the other drivers and loved it, but I hadn't factored in the misfortunes of a one-eyed starter and a track marshal. It was all going so well. My great rival Lennart Bohlin was pushing me hard in the pre-final but then went out with a puncture, leaving me to ease home and take pole in the final.

We were all on the grid, engines revving ready to leap off as soon as the light changed. But, instead of a clean break, there was chaos because the lights flickered just before going green. Half the field went, half hesitated. Back markers jumped the gun and shot through. The hesitating half waited no more and shot off. Except me. I sat still.

I had no choice, there was a marshal still standing in front of my kart. If I'd gone with the rest he would have been badly injured, maybe even killed. It turned out the starter had only one eye and my marshal was in his blind spot, so he started the race before the grid was clear!

The chaos at the start meant the karts were more bunched than usual going into the first corner and Copse became littered with broken machines, at least ten of which couldn't get started again. By the time I'd manoeuvred round pedestrians and broken karts, I was down in twentieth but managed to claw my way back through the field over the next couple of laps and got up to fifth. Two laps later I was in the lead and held it until my tyre burst with just a lap to go and I piled into the catch netting at 100 m.p.h. The only consolation was that I'd had the fastest lap and that guy never started another Silverstone kart GP.

I went into the final round at Le Mans in second place, seven points behind Torgjer Kleppe and only three in front of Steve Styrin, Poul Petersen and Chris Lambden. If I could win both finals and Torgjer finished outside the top three, I could still do it.

I was fastest in qualifying, 0.15 second ahead of Brian Heery, so on pole for my heats. My first heat was a tremendous tussle with Lennart Bohlin, who just pipped me in the final straight, but the second was a disaster: a primary gear let go and wrecked the engine. There was a lot of work to do before Sunday's pre-final and I would be twenty-second on the grid. The only good news was that Torgjer was also having problems and would start forty-fifth. We were still working on the kart during practice the next morning and hardly noticed the time. All weekend there had been trouble with the jobsworths controlling the gates to the pits. They were sticklers for locking up five minutes before the start, and, if you were on the wrong side, you were out of the race. We scrambled through with seconds to spare. Just behind us, Reg Gange had to push the guy to one side and shove the gate open to scrape in.

I threw caution to the wind in the pre-final and by the end of the first lap had climbed to fifth. It was a gruelling drive with an engine not quite 100 per cent and I was able to pull only one more place back, but at least I was still in with a chance as we went into the final, because Torgjer had failed to finish.

I got a flying start, storming into an early lead. The main challenge was coming from Lennart Bohlin and Brian Heery, who had shot through the pack from the back of the grid. It was nip and tuck but on the sixth lap they came out of my slip stream at the Blue S-bends and went past. Lennart started to open up a bit of a lead while Brian and I had a fantastic battle behind him. I had the better of him in a straight line but his kart was a bit quicker through the corners, so we each managed to pass the other in a series of darting manoeuvres. There was little between us, but Brian just managed to poke his nose in front of mine and I had to settle for third.

Back in the pit, everyone was going mad. Kleppe was down the field and they were confident I was champion. Dad was hugging anyone who came in range and Mum was drinking champagne straight from the bottle. I just stood there grinning. The adrenaline was still pumping and all I could think was, I've done it! I've bloody done it!

If you can imagine how it would feel to be in a lift plunging out of control from the top of the Empire State Building, you will have some idea of how I felt when the official result sheet came out and showed Torgjer was ninth, picking up enough points to make him champion. Everyone was talking at once but no one was saying anything that made sense. We were all reeling. Then I heard Dad's voice break through the cacophony: 'Hang on, they've missed off Roger Goff. Roger finished fifth but he's not on the list.' He rushed over to Roger who confirmed that he had indeed finished the race. Dad took him to the officials, who double-checked their lap charts. It was the longest fifteen minutes I can remember, but they finally confirmed that Roger was fifth, Torgjer tenth.

But still the drama was not over because that meant Torgjer had picked up three points and he and I were level on twenty-five points each. The officials scrambled for their rulebooks and finally decided I was champion because my next best score after my win was third while Torgjer's was seventh. I was champion by the narrowest of margins, but I was bloody champion.

It was a great feeling, especially when I found out that my fastest lap in the wet – 114.81 m.p.h. – was faster than any of the Formula 3000 cars that had been racing alongside us. It was another landmark in the acceptance of superkarts by motorsport enthusiasts and led to my being selected for a very different kind of competition.

Chapter 18

Can't Swim, Can't Run, but What a Rower!

Winning the world championship put me even more in the spotlight and I was asked to take part in the BBC *Superstars* programme. The show consisted of a number of high-profile competitors from different sports taking part in a series of events ranging from really tough gym tests, such as squats and dips, to target golf and from swimming to bike riding. It was an incredibly popular prime-time programme that ran for eleven years, and images of Kevin Keegan coming off his bike at top speed or Brian Jacks displaying incredible strength in the gym are burned on the memory of my generation.

Each series went out over several weeks but what the viewers didn't know was that the whole lot was filmed in one gruelling ten-day period. We were at it from six in the morning to eight at night, when most of the teams collapsed on their beds just hoping to recover enough for filming the next day. The only exception was the rugby team, who just showered, went out on the town and got pissed but were still ready to go the next day after about two hours' sleep.

Despite the gruelling schedule, it was enjoyable to be part of and a great opportunity to meet up with people from other sports. I particularly liked the boxers who included Dave 'Boy' Green and John Conteh, two down-to-earth guys. And Brian Jacks, the undoubted star of the show, was especially helpful, giving up his practice session to help me with my basketball when it was clear I was a complete novice. I was part of the motorsport team that included Derek Bell and Superbike champion Roger Marshall, with Stirling Moss as our team manager. I wasn't exactly ideal material for the show: I can't swim and running has always bored me – I puffed in last in the cross-country, despite some encouragement from the rugby team. The one discipline I fancied I could do well – I'd done a bit of training in the build-up – was in the gym. I reckoned I could do forty or fifty press-ups without too much bother but Belly claimed he could do more and the silly bugger lost.

Our best event was the Canadian longboats, even though none of us had ever rowed before. If you are not disciplined in motorsport you can be killed. It's not as dangerous if you mess up at rowing, but our discipline helped us quickly become a well-oiled machine and we broke the record for the series.

I've always realised the value of TV exposure and went out of my way to help whenever I was asked. Word got round that, if you wanted to feature karts, Martin was your man and I was on all kinds of programmes – *Runaround*, *Crackerjack*, *Get Fresh* and the daddy of them all, *Jim'll Fix It*. I still have my 'Fix It' badge at home.

I quickly sussed out what programme makers were looking for. They didn't want someone being earnest and dull: they wanted to present karting as exciting and fun. 'If you look as though you are enjoying yourself, Martin, the kids will want to do it too,' one producer told me.

I had a phone call one day from a Channel 4 researcher who said he was working on a new show that was going to be taken

126

round the Butlin's holiday camps. They were going to bring in teams of kids to compete in several different disciplines such as frisbee throwing, skating and quad bike racing. Each week, one of the sports would have an expert along to show the kids how to do it.

'And we would like you to bring along some karts, set up a mini track with some bales of straw and tyres and oversee kart racing,' he said.

'Sounds good; you'd better come and see me.'

That's how I met Jonathan Ross. He bounced into the office, not much more than a boy, but full of energy and enthusiasm, a much younger version of the way he is today, come to think of it. We hit it off straight away The series was fun to do – I remember being awestruck at the frisbee expert, who managed to land one of those tiny discs smack on a target at the other end of the field – and the kart racing proved very popular. I did get into hot water with the authorities because there was a crash in one race and a kid's helmet came off. That is a big no-no in the sport and obviously we should have made sure they all had their straps done up properly before racing. I hoped no one from karting would see it, but of course the producer thought it was great telly and ran the crash as a promo each week. I got more than a few caustic remarks from officialdom for a while, but sod 'em! Even with the odd clanger, I was doing more to promote the sport than all of them put together.

For the final programme, they decided to have a special event with the presenters going through their paces. But they had six sports and only five presenters, so Jonathan was called upon to make his first appearance on TV. He stole the show. He had to roller-skate down a tunnel, which he did very badly, but his patter and his expressions had everyone in hysterics. He was a natural and I for one was not at all surprised that within eighteen months he had his own series and went on to become a superstar.

Another guy I had a lot of fun working with on TV was Timmy Mallett. We did a fantastic series together but sadly it is still sitting in cans somewhere in the Midlands, having never been seen the light of day.

I'd done a programme for Central TV with Jimmy Greaves – embarrassing myself by asking the recovering-alcoholic ex-footballer if he wanted a drink – and got chatting with the producer Harry King about karting and the potential for a race series for kids. About six months later, he came back to me and said he'd been thinking about what I'd said and would like to put together a show. He'd been working on a series called *BMX Beat* and thought we could do something similar with karts, but he warned me, 'I've had loads of problems with temperamental kids and pushy parents, so, if there's any of that, I'll pull the plug. I want no committees and no arguments – you arrange it all and I deal only with you.' That suited me fine.

The show was to be called *Kartbeat*. We decided on a six round championship for eight- to twelve-year-olds, and Harry came up with the brilliant idea of having Timmy as the presenter. He was one of the biggest names on TV at the time following his success in *Wacaday* and *Wide Awake Club* and there was hardly a kid in the country who wasn't aware of Mallett's mallet or Magic the parrot.

I put a lot of effort into the planning. I chose the track at Rowrah in the Lake District because it was a natural bowl where the kids would get a good view of the action and it would provide good pictures for TV. I hired Peter Cooper, the top RAC official, and made him 'the Ruler' along the lines of Stuart Hall in *It's a Knockout*. We called all the drivers and their families together and told them we were on a tight schedule, so we didn't want any grief. I said, 'Whatever Peter says goes. If he says you are disqualified, you are disqualified, no disputes, no tantrums. If you aren't happy with the rules, walk away now because once we start there'll be no chance to change anything.' With Peter's quiet authority and a great attitude from all the parents and kids we didn't have a moment's bother. They all stayed in local B&Bs or camped near the track and thoroughly enjoyed themselves.

I'd worked out that, if we ran a tight ship, we could film the whole series in a week, but, even with that short schedule, Central weren't willing to meet all the costs. We needed a sponsor to the tune of about £10,000. I wasn't going to let all that work go for the sake of ten grand and said, 'Harry, I'll find us a sponsor and if I can't I'll put the cash up myself.' That's what I ended up doing.

One of the drivers I chose to include in the racing was Dougie Bell, who later went on to drive Formula Ford. His dad, Doug, was a second-hand car dealer and a bit of a 'Del Boy' character, and he and I had a history of winding each other up. A week before we were due to start filming, Doug phoned me.

'You've booked me into the hotel with you, haven't you, Martin?'

I explained I hadn't been able to because I'd taken over the whole of the Old Trout at Cockermouth for the TV crew and people connected with the programme. The place was full.

'But, Martin, you must get me in. Tell 'em I'm the doctor. You'll have to have a doctor.'

I rang the hotel and finally managed to work out how we could shuffle things around so there was a room for the 'doctor' and his son. I rang him back.

'Doug, you owe me big time. And don't you dare let me down. If the hotel management find out you're not the doctor after the work I've put them to, they'll string me up by my family jewels.'

129

All week, Doug acted the part to perfection. He was so convincing that I was almost ready to let him take my appendix out. You couldn't have asked for a more restrained and dignified chap and I helped the image along with the odd, 'Please give Dr Bell a drink.'

But the urge to put one over on him became too much. On the final night, I went to see the receptionist and asked if she could do me a favour: I needed an elderly member of staff to help me with a project. She found a lady in the accounts department who was willing to assist, and I explained what I wanted. Then I went back and joined the others in the dining room. A few minutes later, the waitress gave me the thumbs-up and the receptionist came rushing in and, with a performance that Angela Lansbury would have been proud of, cried, 'Dr Bell, Dr Bell, please come quickly, there's an emergency. One of our ladies has passed out on the front step. I think it's serious, she's turning blue.'

I jumped up: 'The poor woman. Quick, Doug, grab your bag. Thank goodness we brought a doctor with us.'

Doug looked at me, his mouth open, his panic-filled eyes beseeching me to save him.

'You'd better go, Dr Bell,' I said, relishing his discomfort.

He knelt down by the woman, who looked out for the count. I could see he didn't have a clue what to do next. Fortunately, he was saved further agony by his 'patient', who couldn't hold back her giggles any more.

By this time, I'd told everyone what was happening and, as Doug came back into the bar, they greeted him with a round of applause.

He looked at me. 'You bastard,' he said. Then he laughed and I know he has enjoyed the funny side ever since. It was certainly one of those special moments in my life.

Filming went like a dream. We ferried in kids from different schools each day to provide a crowd, and they loved it, shouting and screaming from the start to finish of every race. Timmy Mallett was the ultimate professional. I'd imagined from his TV image that he'd be a bit zany and off the wall. Instead he turned out to be quiet and laid back, enjoying nothing more than a stroll round the garden looking at the flowers. But, as soon as the cameras were on him, he snapped into character. He conducted interviews with the drivers just as if it were a proper Grand Prix and he was always on hand to maintain high energy levels and enthusiasm. During races, he and I would be in the commentators' booth – I was James Hunt to his Murray Walker. Off the cuff, he gave all the drivers nicknames – Silver Knight, Black Knight, and a kid from Yorkshire who was carrying a bit of extra weight was immediately dubbed Yorkshire Pudding – and he remembered them perfectly in his commentary.

We got all six programmes in the can by the end of the week and I received a call to say Central was very pleased with the rushes. Harry thought that, if the first series went well, there was a good chance there would be more to come, maybe even a five-year deal. It never happened. There was a change in the ITV contracts and Central was told it could have no extra children's programmes. *Kartbeat* was shelved and my ten grand is still sitting on a shelf somewhere.

Ah, well, chalk it down to experience and move on. In my case, it was time to return to driving and sorting out more problems with Doug Bell.

Chapter 19

I Was That Gangster

Doug was one of those guys you know are rogues but you can't help liking them. He'd swear blind a car had done only 10,000 miles and, even though you knew in your water it must be ten times that, you'd still end up buying it. The first car I bought off him was a black Lamborghini with a sports exhaust, which made it roar like an F1 car. It was the business – I could leave my house and the noise of the engine would alert the staff at my factory 1.8 miles away. I had to do a lot of fast talking to persuade Dad it was worth its not inconsiderable price tag, especially when he heard I had to pay extra to import it from California, but he was impressed by my foresight when over the next few years the value shot up and it was worth over £100,000. The trouble was that even though I used it only for big events like Silverstone or a Make A Wish visit – in total, I only drove it about six or seven hundred miles – I couldn't bear to part with it and when I did eventually let it go, the market had cooled and I only got £30,000.

I kept in touch with Doug and he was very useful when I bought my favourite number plate. I'd always liked the idea of a personalised plate and once bought 1UPA from a mate to put on my Porsche and get one up on the rest. I used to look through the adverts in the *Sunday Times* to see if anything relevant was on offer, but didn't do anything about it until I spotted MWH1 and thought it would be perfect for Dad, Mark William Hines.

I'm usually good at negotiating a decent price for things. I try never to want or need a deal so badly – buying or selling – that I can't walk away and leave the other guy guessing, but in this case my heart ruled my head and I paid top dollar. The owner lived in the North and agreed to drive down to pass over the plate and sort out the paperwork. I had it registered to Dad's brown 300SE Mercedes in mid-December and gave him the plates on Christmas morning. He was thrilled and immediately grabbed a screwdriver and fitted them.

'How did you find them?' he asked.

'I bought them from an advert in the paper.'

'It's just that I saw this number on a car a few weeks back and thought how much I'd like to have it.'

In an amazing coincidence Dad had found himself driving behind the guy on the day he was selling me the plates. He'd even suggested to Mum that he was going to pull him over and try to buy the number. Luckily for me, she talked him out of it.

By the time the H-prefix registrations were issued in 1990, the Driver and Vehicle Licensing Agency had a series of hotlines where you could phone to buy a special plate. I decided I wanted H1NES and arranged for a whole series of mates to try to phone in and buy it. I also contacted a car dealer friend of mine in Scotland, Bert McNish, whose son Allan drove an Audi to victory in the 2008 Le Mans twenty-four-hour race, and said to him that if he could purchase the plate he could put it on any BMW he liked and I would buy it. I did the same deal with the local Mercedes dealer. But despite all my efforts none of us got through in time and I missed out.

About six months later it appeared for sale in the paper and when I rang up the guy wanted £35,000 for it. I beat him down substantially but still not enough and said I'd think about it. It was time to contact Doug again. I persuaded him and another mate in the trade, Gary, to ring and offer silly money – a couple of grand or so – saying that the bottom had dropped out of the market. They kept up the pressure over the next few months and obviously persuaded the guy his asset was losing money fast because, when I was at the British Grand Prix at Silverstone, I received a call on my mobile, offering the plate for ten grand.

'It's near but not quite near enough,' I said. 'But if you change your mind you know where I am.'

Apparently, he phoned Doug and Gary, who said they felt it wasn't worth anything like £10,000 and before the end of the day he had sold it to me for £8,500, which included the brand-new Vespa scooter that it was on. The number is still on my motor home eighteen years later.

I owed the boys a drink for that one. I wish I could say the same about the biggest deal I did with Doug. Soon after I bought the Lamborghini he approached me with another offer, one I couldn't resist when I heard what was involved. When the Toleman race team ran into trouble, Ted Toleman went to live in Switzerland and told two of his associates to sell off the cars. It was only later I learned one of the people involved was my old mate Barry Lee. Always busy, Doug got involved as middle man and offered them to me. There were five cars, including Brian Henton's BP F2 machine, in which he'd won the European Championship, and, best of all, Ayrton Senna's No. 19 Segafredo .83B, the car he used in his first four Grands Prix and was driving when he picked up his first championship point for finishing sixth in the German GP, despite losing a nose cone.

I'd bought the lot before I even thought about where I was going to keep them. There was no room at the factory but Doug said not to worry, he had a pal with a lock-up where they would be safe. I was a bit concerned but he assured me there was CCTV coverage and the whole place was completely secure. I took masses of photos for my records, arranged special insurance and hoped he was right.

A couple of years later, I decided to sell two of the cars. I told Doug I'd cleared space at my factory and asked him to arrange delivery so I could check them over before putting them on the market. They didn't arrive. In the end I had to involve my solicitor and even then only two of the cars turned up. The others were apparently being 'looked after' by a friend of Doug's who, maybe unknown to Doug, had gone away for while – and I don't think it was on holiday.

One turned up later at an auction, bought by two farmers, who were then dismayed to learn it belonged to me. In the end we did a deal that meant they kept the car and I got my money back. Then I was approached by the police. They had recovered two F1 cars and wanted to know if they belonged to me. Sure enough, they turned out to be the two missing cars, including Senna's No. 19. I was not the only one laying claim to them but fortunately I had all the paperwork and was able to prove they were mine. My beloved Senna car was passed on to a friend of mine, Nigel Albon, who has just finished restoring it to its former glory.

A few years later I met Barry Lee in Birmingham. He's a former hotrod champion, who looks big enough to handle himself in a tight situation. He and I first met when Ayrton Senna drove for the Toleman Team; now we were featuring in a live show at the NEC. It was a motorsport spectacular presented by Jeremy Clarkson and Tiff Needel. Barry performed stunts in his big V8 saloon car while I zipped around (excuse the pun) in clouds of tyre smoke at ridiculous speeds in my superkart. The whole show was an hour long and was performed three or four times a day. One night, relaxing at the bar after a gruelling day of live shows, I told Barry the 'Dr Bell' story. 'Don't mention that guy's name to me,' he said. 'I was involved in selling him some F1 cars. He was flogging them on to some East End gangster who found a crack in one of the cylinders. This bastard threatened to blow Doug's family away and then come and sort me out, so the two of us had to pay out five grand for a new block. I've never been so scared in my life.'

I played him along for a while, coaxing out of him more lurid details of this gangster and his knee-capping, murderous gang of thugs, and eventually said, 'You daft bugger, that was me.'

Barry didn't know whether to be angry or see the funny side but in the end we both ended up laughing. Since then, he has teamed up again with Alex Hawkridge, the former team principle of Toleman, and they are looking after Barry's son Freddie, who is a chip off the old block and, if he can drive better than his old man, might just have a chance. I haven't seen Doug for about fourteen years. I heard he was living in Spain or the States and still ducking and diving. It would be nice to meet up for a drink one day, just to see if he has any deals on the go.

The years following my World Championship win were the most successful of my career. I was driving out of my skin – British champion for four years in a row and at the same time winning the FIA World Cup in 1985, and topping that with the World Enduro and European championships the following year. In between there were several 'near misses' with technical problems or shunts costing me, sometimes on the very last lap.

The Enduro championship was held at Daytona International in Florida and was unfinished business as far as I was concerned. We'd taken our Superkarts Road Show over there and, like everyone else who sees this world famous circuit, I was seriously impressed. I'd seen it on TV and read about the banking in magazines, but it is only when you stand at the bottom of the wall as it towers above you and realise you couldn't even crawl up the 31-degree slope on your hands and knees that you start to appreciate just how different this track is. On my first visit, I'd had problems with the American fuel, my engine and getting used to the banking, so had managed to finish only second. I knew I should have won, so there was no hesitation when I received an invitation to try my hand against the American superkarts.

Of course, the Yanks have to do things differently from the rest of the world. Instead of the usual twenty minutes for a race, this was twice as long, and they had a Le Mans-style start in which you have to run over to your kart, start your engine, jump in and go. With packed fields, it was chaotic and very dangerous. I got away about fiftieth but by the end of the first lap I was up to tenth and worked my way through the field to win comfortably. One of the American drivers came up to me afterwards and said, 'I have to take my hat off to you. I was starting to brake at the end of the straight and you came past me changing up. That's never happened to me before.'

The old saying 'no pain, no gain' was never truer for me than when I won the British title in 1986. I'd had a shunt in France and when I arrived for the final championship round at Snetterton my ribs were still very sore. That's the worst injury you can have in karting because the lack of suspension means every bump jars your ribcage and the pain shoots through you like an electric shock. Matters weren't improved when I had a tyre burst in the pre-final. I hit the kerb, flew out of the kart and, as surely as toast always falls butter side down, I landed on my damaged ribs. The pain was so fierce I didn't even want to breathe in case it hurt all over again.

My crew picked me up. They wanted to take me to the medical centre but I knew that, if the medics saw me, they wouldn't let me race again that day.

I said, 'Forget it. I can still win the championship. I don't even have to push myself too hard because all I have to do is finish in the top fifteen. I just have to get the kart round. How hard can that be?'

Bloody hard, as it turned out.

We found a flat piece of wood and in the motor home, away from prying eyes, we strapped it to my side with duct tape and pulled my leathers over it. Usually I would stride to the grid, put my helmet on and be the last to climb into the kart, but this day I drove down gingerly and hoped my rivals wouldn't realise the delicate state I was in.

Every second of that race was painful and, the longer it went on, the more my ribs hurt. The last three laps were torture. The pain seared through me like a flame. It was like a medieval version of hell and seemed to last an eternity. The worst bit was as the track drops down to the famous Bomb Hole, where the combination of going downhill and to your right at the same time creates G-forces that squeeze your body like a bear hug. Each time I went through, I clamped my teeth together but still couldn't stop a yelp escaping. But success sets the endorphins going and I hardly noticed the pain on the final lap. I knew I was champion and that made it all worthwhile. I found out later that I had pulled the muscles around the ribs and would have been better off if I had broken the bones. It was a long and painful trip home, but I couldn't wipe the smile off my face.

If you are going to race karts, you have to expect to be

involved in crashes from time to time. Even careful drivers can be taken out by somebody else's mistake and, if you are challenging for titles, the difference between winning and being wiped out can be down to a few millimetres. I've certainly had my fair share of shunts and a couple of spectacular crashes but, amazingly, I've never broken any bones – so far.

Chapter 20

Concussion and Confrontation

I have had my fair share of shunts over the years but perhaps the most frightening was not on the track but on the road and it was my experience driving karts that prevented it becoming a much bigger disaster. In the late sixties I had a British racing green 4.2 E Type Jaguar. I had been racing in Europe and was driving back early on Monday morning through Germany. It was one of those very misty mornings which was made more treacherous by heavy rain. To be honest I was travelling too fast for the conditions, especially as I had my kart strapped to the roof rack. I was pushing hard in a downhill section that had a right-hand curve to it. Although the rain had stopped by this time, the road was still wet. Not the ideal conditions to suffer a rear-tyre blow-out. Fortunately my racing instincts kicked in. I held the car for several hundred yards before finally launching off the Armco barrier in the central reservation and coming to rest perched on some branches high up in the trees on the other side. The police were amazed that I had managed to control the car for so long which obviously reduced the speed dramatically before I took off and they were impressed with the low-level flying skills that would later come in handy while testing a McLaren.

Superkart drivers realise there's no room for games when you have four or five karts within a few inches of each other at speeds of over 100 m.p.h. While there is a lot of bumping and boring in the direct-drive 100cc categories, superkart drivers realise that, when you have four or five karts within a few inches of each other at speeds over 100 m.p.h., there's no room for games. Anyone who gets up to tricks tends not to last very long. The other big advantage compared with car racing is that you are not strapped into a kart, so you are thrown clear in a crash. You are not stuck in the kart when it bends in on itself and, because it happens so quickly, you don't have time to tense up, so mostly you escape with a few bumps and bruises.

No matter how often you have crashed, the next one is always unexpected; even if you have a long slide and you know you are going to hit a wall, it's still a surprise when it finally happens. And contrary to what you are led to believe in the movies, where everything goes into slow motion, crashes happen in nanoseconds. There's no time to make a bargain with God if he (or she) lets you off hurting yourself. Most surprising of all is that it never hurts at the moment of impact. There are always a few moments before the pain reaches the brain.

The most embarrassing prangs are after you have won. This happened to me twice – in Belgium and Denmark. I took the chequered flag, started my lap of honour chuffed as hell with myself, the brain switched off and at 130 m.p.h. or so I forgot the braking point and ended up in the gravel, wrecking my kart and feeling like a right prat.

My first serious crash came in the early days of my 100cc international career in a six-hour international event in Paris. It was the kart equivalent of the Le Mans twenty-four-hour race, with a team of guys driving for an hour at a time. At one stage, I was tucked in behind race leader Mickey Allen as we approached the chicane leading to the pit straight, hoping to use his slipstream to shoot me through any gap he left. I was concerned about a back marker who was just in front of us and, sure enough, as we came into the chicane he hit a straw bale and spun into the middle of the track. Mickey's reflexes were lightning quick. He flicked his kart to the left and missed him by inches. That left me with nowhere to go. I hit him full chat and went up into the air and came down on my head.

They rushed both of us off to hospital but after a quick check-over I was allowed to go back to the track, where the race was still going on. It was a weird, almost out-of-body experience. I thought, What's all this noise? What's going on out there? What am I doing here? My dad came up to ask if I was OK. I was aware that I knew him but I didn't have a clue who he was. Who were any of these people who were talking to me as though they were my mates? The next thing I remember is waking up again in hospital several hours later and gradually recalling what had happened. It was very scary but, compared with the other lad, I got off lightly. He had immediately been taken into the operating theatre and never walked again.

My luckiest escape was when the World Cup was held at Morecambe. The cliff-top track was one of the hairiest to drive and even Nigel Mansell ended up in hospital after wiping out there in his youth. It was a great circuit for spectators because you could stand at the top of the hill and see the whole track spread out below you. Races started off uphill, then you turned at the top and were faced with a steep downhill straight that you took flat out even though it looked as though you were driving straight off the edge of the cliff and into the sea below. Instead, you came to a tight hairpin bend, which you inevitably hit too fast and put enormous strains on your kart and body.

Some drivers never made it, so on the outside of the hairpin there was a run-off area at the back of which were straw bales and then a wall made of railway sleepers. Because this was the slowest part of the course they put the caravan containing the lap scorers behind this wall.

This particular day I came honking down the hill and that was when my right-hand sub-axle decided to give up the ghost. I happened to be into a left-hand bend at the time, so it was not immediately obvious my wheel was flapping about and that, to all intents and purposes, I was cruising along at 90 m.p.h. on three wheels. It soon became apparent. I stamped on the brake and that was when I realised I'd lost a wheel and all my brake fluid. Nothing happened. Or, rather, nothing that was *supposed* to happen happened.

If I'm honest, I have very little recollection of the next few seconds but my friends later filled in the picture for me. I went across the run-off and, brushing aside the bales, I hit the sleepers, which disintegrated like matchwood. The kart dived under the caravan and the wreckage – with me still in the middle of it clutching the steering wheel – came to a halt just before we emerged from the other side.

'The noise', a friend told me, 'was horrific. And it was followed by a deathly hush, as though everyone was holding their breath at the same time. We all thought you must be dead.'

I'm not sure at what stage I came round but apparently I was conscious enough to say, as a gang hoisted the caravan so they could slide me out, 'How's my kart? Can we repair it for the next race?'

Fortunately, they ignored me and whipped me off to hospital, where I spent four or five hours being examined and X-rayed. Amazingly, I was largely only battered and bruised. The only serious injury was some damage to my Achilles tendon. They put a plaster on up to my thigh and sent me home with orders to rest for six weeks.

Concussion and Confrontation

No chance. I had a British Championship race in two weeks and I needed to be there. Someone told me that the England football physio Fred Street had a clinic nearby, so I went to see him and explained the situation. He cut off the plaster, examined me and said, 'I need to see you every day for physiotherapy and we'll see what we can do.' Two weeks later, I raced again, losing the final by a split second to Dave Buttigieg.

I guess it's the mentality that makes us become race drivers in the first place that persuades us we are immortal. I have lost close friends in racing accidents, yet I've never felt afraid to drive in case I'm killed. There's no logic to it. I rate Ayrton Senna as the greatest driver who ever lived, so, if he can be killed, we mere mortals certainly can. His death in 1994 was the biggest single tragedy in motorsport and affected a lot of people for many years. Everyone in the sport can remember where they were when they heard the news. Yet it never occurred to me that, if Ayrton can die on the track, so could I.

The safest drivers are those who can win while driving at 95 per cent of their capacity, still keeping enough in reserve to handle a crisis. But you can never cater for the accident caused by mechanical failure or where someone in front of you does something and you can't get out of the way. You just don't allow yourself to think about it. If I'm racing and a mate of mine crashes and is taken to hospital, I don't want to know anything about it until I have finished racing. It's not that I don't care but I can't let my mind dwell on negatives all the time I have to drive. I don't want to go out on the track thinking about accidents; no driver does.

Afterwards, I'll go and see him and talk to him about it and, if there are lessons to be learned to make driving safer, I'm always keen to learn them, even if it means another tangle with authority. I remember a European Championship race in Germany where conditions were so bad that no one should have even thought of racing. It was a big open track with no barriers around it to protect the spectators, and beyond them there were old planes in an airfield, so, if anyone went off, the results could have been disastrous. The straights were concrete runways where we could reach speeds of more than 120 m.p.h. but they were deadly because in places they would drop by 50 mm, and they snapped more than one back axle that weekend. The meeting should have been called off but the TV cameras were there and the officials didn't want to look stupid – it wasn't their bodies on the line – so they said we had to go ahead. I refused and pretty soon a lot of other drivers joined me. Eventually, a compromise was agreed: the event would go ahead but it would no longer be for the European title so that those drivers who didn't want to race wouldn't miss out. Dave Buttigieg won it and – lo and behold! – they presented him with the trophy and named him as champion.

The officials had obviously marked me down as a troublemaker who needed bringing down a peg or two and a few weeks later summoned me to a tribunal in London, threatening to take away my licence. There were witnesses for both sides but the difference was that mine were all drivers – including some of the guys who had raced – and they agreed the circuit had been too dangerous. I won the case and two members of the tribunal came up to me afterwards and said I'd been right and they were sorry it had ever been called.

Everyone in racing accepts accidents – even fatal accidents – as part of the sport. You grieve but you keep going and you console yourself with the knowledge that every single driver, if told he had to die young, would choose to die racing. I can come to terms with that. But what happened to me over the next few years was something I have never learned to live with and I don't think I ever will.

Above left: MH with Alex George, the start of an incredible 13-year partnership with Hermetite for MH.

Above right: The first Kart GP programme of 1978. There were over 150 superkarts entered from all over the world!

Below: I was always delighted to give time to the fans..

Top left: My lovely Kelly was always on hand and went to every race.

Top right: Barry Sheene: what a star he was in every way. He refused a go in my superkart one day, claiming that I was totally mad. I pointed out at least I had four wheels and could not fall off it.

Below: The team with our own guest superstar – singer, writer, composer Ronnie Foster all the way from California. The line-up was MH, Gary Parks, Ronnie Foster, Dave Buttiegieg, Carolyn Grant Sale and Russell Anderson.

Inset: *Kart and Superkart* was another major part of my career, but this time as a publisher. Few karting magazines ever pictured my racing hero Ayrton Senna on the front. Whenever we got the chance, we did: four times in all.

Above left: My first British GP win at Silverstone 1980. A very proud dad watches on as Kelly enjoys the limelight.

Above right: This was it 1983 and I was world champion – life gets no better than it is. *Kart and Superkart* cover with Brian Hearey, Leonart Bohlin and me.

Below: Russell Anderson, Steve Eaton and the World Champ – who is fully aware if it had not been for Russell and Steve it may never have happened.

Inset: My mum knew how to celebrate this fantastic day in our lives. What a great picture! What a great day!

Top left: Time to relax and collect the trophy. They say it's third time lucky – well, it was for me with Tina, the third Mrs Hines.

Top right: Mr and Mrs Steve Eaton get the surprise of their life and shed a tear or two.

Centre: *Kart Beat*, the Central TV series, with Timmy Mallett and myself. A six-part series that was made in 1989. While everyone agreed it was fantastic, through a TV political situation it was never shown. Timmy was a real character and perhaps Central TV will get it out of the archives one day.

Inset: Enter Jonathan Ross – programme researcher. We had great laughs on the *Track Trix* programme. This is where Jonathan made his very first TV appearance in the last show of the series. Tina and I both said he would be a star. Well, you can't be right all the time...

Above left: There was a new kid on the block – Luke. I wonder what he will do when he grows up?

Above right: Time to make it legal as Tina and I cut the cake and Kelly grabs the limelight.

Centre: Luke had already decided the type of motorsport he was destined for as he leans against Derek Bell's Porsche.

Left: Dad was always on hand and he loved every minute of it. Now I know just how he felt as I watch Luke.

GO HARRY *GO*

Top left: Jason Plato and his dad Tim after winning the British Championships for Zip. Another great motor sport dad and lad team.

Top right: Luke hits the track in the Comer Cadet formula – a breeding ground for the world's motorsport stars. No 42 rides again!

Centre: Princess Diana and William and Harry join the Zip Young Guns, where the young royals showed great promise and a very competitive streak.

Right: MH tentatively asks his Royal Highness about the knighthood.

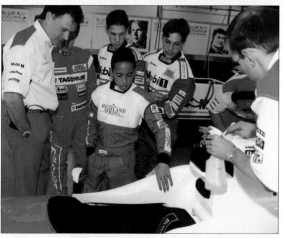

Top: DC and Damon Hill with the already Oakley-clad Luke.

Above right: 1995 was a stellar year for Zip Kart, with three junior championships: Lewis Hamilton (Cadet), Luke Hines (Yamaha) and Gary Paffett (Junior International A).

Centre: Lewis and Gary get a sneak preview from David Ryan of a McLaren F1, a few years before they would both be employed to drive for the company.

Left: What a Royal line-up: Prince Harry and Prince William accompanied by Gary Paffett, Luke Hines, Anthony Davidson, Gareth Howell, Edward Redfern and Nikki Richardson.

This picture of Lewis was taken when BHP productions were filming the TV introduction at around 3am as it was the only time we could use the McLaren factory for filming.

Chapter 21

Hammer Blow after Hammer Blow

Soon after Tina and I got together, she moved into the house I had built on my father-in-law's nursery. I bought another place for Lindy and Kelly and gave Allan the choice of moving in with them or staying in his flat with us. He said he'd like to stay where he was and, while at first it must have felt a bit strange for him to see another woman where his daughter used to be, it worked out surprisingly well. He was a lovely man with a sharp brain and he and Tina soon hit it off. Through Allan, Tina and Lindy became good friends and still are today.

I used to see Kelly every Tuesday and Thursday, and Mum and Dad would still bring her to the track most of the weekends we were racing in England. They just loved having her around them and I think looking after Kelly provided Mum with some of her happiest moments. But, looking back, it is fair to say that I missed out on a lot of Kelly's growing up. Since the age of sixteen, my life has always been at full throttle and centred on kart racing. I don't go down to the pub or take days off to play golf: I concentrate on the job. Like my dad, I've never really learned the art of delegating, so I tend not only to work long days, but often well into the night as well. And weekends have always been for racing, either my own or with my Young Guns team. I can't claim I'm unhappy with the situation – Zip Karts isn't just a job to me: it is a way of life and has been for nearly half a century.

Even today, if I'm not off with Luke or my race teams, I'll still find a meeting somewhere to watch the cadets race. I helped to introduce the 8–12 cadet category and that's where the superstars of motorsport come from. The kids who really stand out in the cadets, such as Lewis Hamilton, Jenson Button, Daniel Weldon, Mike Conway, Luke Hines, Gary Paffett and Anthony Davidson, have all gone on to do well in the sport.

But there's a price for dedication and in my case it meant I saw less of Kelly than probably she would have liked. It therefore seemed a good idea for her to join us on a family holiday in Portugal, even though she could come only for the first week because of school commitments. It proved to be a turning point in all our lives.

On the first day on the beach I noticed she had a lump on her wrist and asked her what it was.

She shrugged. 'Oh, it's where I was hit by a tennis racquet a few months ago.'

I thought it was odd that the lump was still prominent after all that time and, when I questioned her further, she admitted it had grown a bit bigger recently and she was feeling some numbness around it.

I didn't let her see I was concerned but that evening I phoned Lindy and she confirmed their GP thought it was a muscle injury from the tennis accident.

'I don't like it,' I said. 'I think she needs to see a specialist as soon as she gets home.'

Lindy fixed the appointment and shortly after we returned

from Portugal we received the devastating news – Kelly had a cancer that had grown around the nerves and muscles in her wrist. She was taken into the Royal Marsden Hospital and was told an operation was not an option. The cancer had spread too far. Worse, minute spots were found in her lungs. She needed drastic treatment.

For the next eighteen months, Kelly was in and out of the Marsden undergoing a series of gruelling tests and treatments – intensive chemotherapy and a bone marrow transplant. It would have been tough for an adult to take and she was only twelve. She lost all her hair and shed almost 4 stone in weight. On top of that, she had to confront the reality of death for the first time when some of the kids she had befriended on the wards died. Each death was a double blow, sadness at the loss of a friend and fear that it might also happen to her. But she was incredibly gutsy and an inspiration to all of us, never complaining or feeling sorry for herself even when the hospital called her back and she knew she was in for another bout of harrowing treatment. And, whatever differences there have been between Lindy and me, I have to say she was an absolute rock to Kelly, living in the hospital and giving her massive support 24/7 throughout this entire ordeal.

It's hard to describe the feelings you have as a parent watching your child suffering not just a life-threatening illness but also the horrific treatment to try to cure it. The main emotion is frustration and helplessness. You would give anything to be able to take the pain on yourself, but there is nothing you can do but to be supportive and positive and make sure they don't see the fear in your eyes.

In those quiet, three-o'clock-in-the-morning moments I sometimes froze in fear of what the news would be. At other times I persuaded myself that she was young and strong and a Hines, so she would be able to fight it. Sure enough, one day she came to see us, her eyes shining, and said, 'The doctors say I'm OK. They did some tests and said I'm clear.' I didn't know whether to laugh or cry. Instead, I just hugged her. Having learned a lot about the disease, we knew it might be only a short remission, but she believed it was over and done with and started to look forward.

While this was going on, Dad's health was also failing. He and Mum had a dread of doctors and could never be persuaded to go to see them, but as they grew older there was no avoiding it. I'd thought Dad was indestructible until a few years before, when I bumped into him coming out of the toilet at the factory. He put his arms round me and burst into tears. I'd never seen him cry before and I knew something terrible had happened.

He said, 'I've been passing blood for weeks. I think I'm ill. Don't tell your mum, but you've got to help me.'

I phoned my doctor. We didn't have health insurance then but I told him I didn't care, I wanted Dad to see the best specialist, and soon. This was my father's life; money was the last thing on my mind. I told the consultant that, whatever it would cost, just do it. Dad was examined the next day and they diagnosed a prostate problem. They took him immediately into surgery and cut out the infected parts with a laser. Over the last few years Dad had put on a bit of weight and if he'd gone the NHS route they would have operated traditionally and it would have taken him ages to heal fully. It was the best money I ever spent and the experience persuaded me that, all the time I could afford it, I would pay out for BUPA membership.

As it was, with the laser op Dad recovered more quickly than even the doctors expected. The following morning the nurse went to check on him and found his bed empty. They searched everywhere but couldn't find him. As you can imagine, there was a panic until the ward received a call from reception: 'It's all right. Mr Hines has just come in the front door. He's been down the road to buy a paper.'

When I asked him what the hell he thought he'd been doing, he replied, 'I go for a paper every morning. I felt OK, so why not?'

I think the illness gave Dad a sudden sense of his own mortality and he quit smoking and cut back on fried breakfasts and smothering his food in salt, but it was too late to undo the damage his lifestyle had inflicted in the previous sixty years. Now he was struggling with hardening of the arteries and his ankles would swell up painfully but he still insisted on driving to the factory every day from Finchley. It was crap journey – on a good day it took half an hour but mostly it was an hour of exasperation. Eventually I persuaded him to let me buy him and Mum a place nearer work so at least they didn't have to face that trip every day.

I bought a bungalow that seemed perfect. It was less than a mile from the factory and half a mile from my house. Even though they liked the look of it, Mum still wasn't sure she would be happy away from the old neighbourhood, so in the end we had to leave her Finchley house exactly as it was so she could move back if she didn't settle. Dad and I saw this as a small price to pay if we could persuade her to move. Once they were in the bungalow, they both loved it and it wasn't long before Dad suggested we should turn the big loft space into a room for Kelly when she came to stay. It seemed like a great idea so I got some builders in and they started to rip out bits of the roof.

It was a disaster, and before long it became obvious these guys didn't have a clue what they were doing. Mum and Dad were terrified because the walls would creak as they watched TV and cracks started to appear. I sacked the cowboys and called in an emergency firm, who said it was too dangerous for anyone to live there until it was fixed. It took about six months to sort out but Mum and Dad stuck with it and in the end were very happy living there.

Having resolved that, it was time for a bit more diplomacy to win Mum over. It was clear she was finding it harder to cope with the office work but she could be stubborn and had such a pride in the family business that it would be difficult to persuade her to hand over any of her jobs to someone else. I needed to find a way of lifting the burden without making her feel she was being eased out. It wasn't a job I fancied or really felt equipped for but somehow it had to be done.

Dad agreed with me, so I advertised for someone to help with the accounts and office duties. I handled the interviews and produced a shortlist for Mum and Dad to choose from. There were some excellent applicants but one woman stood out for me. Linda Day not only had the qualifications we needed, but she had been working in a small family firm and seemed sympathetic to the dynamic. I don't care what all these gurus say, companies like ours are different. It's not so much the family running the business as the business running the family, and the two are so closely intertwined that decisions that can be taken easily in other companies become more complicated in a family firm.

Linda was terrific when she met Mum and Dad and, to my surprise, Mum was all for taking her on. After a month I heard the words I never thought I would hear Dad say: 'I like her and so does your mother.' Linda has now been with us more than twenty years and been a fantastic support. She is one of that small group of people – like Grant Munro and Jim Paffett – who have been with the firm so long they are now part of the family.

But before I start to sound like Solomon, always making

wise decisions that work out wonderfully well, I should confess I made two other decisions, apparently as sensible and for equally good motives, that combined in a quirk of fate that was to come back to haunt me. At the time, neither of them seemed nearly as significant as moving Mum and Dad or hiring Linda, but they had a much more dramatic outcome.

The first was to get rid of the swimming pool at the house. It was a spur-of-the-moment decision taken after Tina fished out one of our puppies just before it drowned. It hit us that the pup might have been one of the kids and, much as we enjoyed having the pool, we would never forgive ourselves if anything happened to them, so we had it filled in and a lawn laid over it.

The second was at a European Championship meeting at Hockenheim, where the karting was taking place alongside the Group C World Sports Car Championship. We spent some time hanging out with Derek Bell, who was racing his Porsche. Derek and I were the same age and had known each other for years. By coincidence he had married his third wife, Misty, the year I married Tina and there was the same age gap. Strangely, for a little boy who was to go on to become a leading sports car driver, when we tried to persuade Luke to sit in Derek's Porsche for a photo he stubbornly refused. The best we managed was a snap of him on the bonnet. Nowadays, you wouldn't be able to keep him out and he would be a match for Derek or any other driver.

The kart racing finished on the Saturday and we planned to stay on and watch Derek race, but it was blisteringly hot, so we decided on a relaxing weekend at home instead. I drove through the night, eventually arriving back in the early hours, and, because the kids were comfortable, we spent the rest of the night in the motor home in our driveway.

We woke up to one of those perfect, English, shorts-and-T-shirts, early-September days – a cloudless sky, a bone-warming sun with a hint of breeze to stop you roasting. We all agreed we were glad we weren't still in the oppressive heat at Hockenheim and for once, even I was quite happy to miss out on the noise and smell of the racetrack.

I find it hard just to sit still and do nothing. That's not relaxing to me. It makes me uptight and twitchy. So I planned to do some work on my car and then cut the grass. I had one of those sit-on tractor mowers with rotary blades and, even though he was only six, Luke had driven it several times, so I didn't give it a second thought when he asked if he could mow the lawn. I got the mower out of the stables and, reminding him not to get off without switching off the engine, went round the front to start work. Tina had gone indoors and Tuesday was playing in the garden. It had been a great decision to come home.

About fifteen minutes later I heard a scream that turned my blood cold. I raced round the back and could hardly take in what I saw. Tuesday was screaming seemingly without taking a breath. But she wasn't hurt. It was Luke. He had been mowing the patch where the swimming pool had been. He climbed off to move aside the swing but left the engine running and, as Tuesday was sitting behind him, the blades had not automatically cut out. He slipped and as he fell he saw the mower coming towards him. He stuck his left leg out to push it away but the mower kept coming. He put his hand out to stop it and the blades sliced down the length of his fingers from nail to palm.

The first thing I noticed was his hand pumping blood. Then I saw his leg. It bore no resemblance to any human limb. It was just a bloody mess. There were bits of flesh and bone everywhere. I screamed for Tina to bring me some towels.

We wrapped him up, put him in the back of the car with

Tina and I drove flat out to the hospital, which was less than ten minutes away. As I drove I heard this little voice plead, 'Don't let me die.' It was the single most chilling thing I have ever heard.

We must have looked like something out of a horror movie to the staff in casualty: a gore-covered man racing in clutching a bundle so drenched in blood it was dripping on the floor, followed by a distraught Tina in bare feet. The A&E staff reacted superbly, especially the sister Sue Haynes, a friend of ours who should have been going off duty but promised to stay with Luke until he went down to the operating theatre. They threw iodine over Luke, and got a transfusion line into him within seconds. Later they told me he had lost half his blood and if we had been a few minutes later he would have died.

After what seemed like an eternity they stabilised him and took him down to the operating theatre. The doctor came to see Tina and me. He said they would probably have to amputate his leg above the knee. 'He's going to be in the theatre for some time. There's nothing you can do here. Why don't you go home, clean up and come back later?'

When we returned to the hospital they gave us the incredible news that, for the time being at least, they had saved Luke's leg. The doctor explained that, when they got him down to the operating theatre and cleaned him up, they discovered that the nerve running down the back of the leg had miraculously not been severed. It was stretched to twice its normal length but not cut through. When the house surgeon noticed this he phoned Lance Therkildsen, the specialist, for advice. It was only by luck that he got him. Mr Therkildsen was supposed to be setting off on holiday that night but, instead, he dropped everything and drove straight to the hospital. He looked at the shattered bones and mangled muscle and all his instincts told him he should amputate, but he told us later, the fact that nerve was still intact made him decide to try to rebuild the leg.

'We had to give the child a chance, no matter how long the odds,' he said. 'But don't raise your hopes too high. He's not out of the woods yet. We've pinned what's left of the bones together and rebuilt the leg as best we can but the growth plates have been destroyed. His left leg will never grow like the other one and we'll probably have to keep building it as he gets older. His ankle is so mangled we may still have to amputate his foot at some stage. You have to accept that he's never going to be able to run and play football, but at least for the moment he still has a leg.'

The next twelve hours went by in a daze. We took Tuesday to stay with Tina's sister, then packed an overnight bag so Tina could stay at the hospital. I can't remember whether I went to bed or not. It's all a blur. I'm sure I must have cursed myself for letting him on the mower – I certainly have a thousand times since – but that whole night seems to have been wiped off the slate of my memory. I've thought about that day so many times since and of course I blame myself and realise many people will see my decision to let Luke drive the mower as crazy. But it never occurred to me that it was dangerous and I'm sure that, when I was a kid, my dad would have let me drive the mower. And I know I'm not alone: I've watched other fathers at the kart track and they encourage their sons to do risky things. It's the nature, I guess, of motorsport and it doesn't mean we don't feel the consequences as sharply as anyone else.

The next morning I got to the hospital about eight and Tina asked me to go over the road to the supermarket to pick up some things she needed. As I reached the entrance to the shop, a coach pulled up and a load of schoolkids got off and raced up the stairs. That's when it hit me. My Luke would never be able to do something as ordinary as running upstairs with his mates. I sat on the kerb and sobbed. I don't know how long I sat there. I was oblivious of everything and everyone around me. I just couldn't stop crying. Eventually a woman asked me if I was OK and I managed to gather myself enough to reassure her. I went into the shop and found everything on Tina's list. But I don't have a clue how.

We clung on to the fact that they had not amputated Luke's leg but our other problems seemed to pile up. After years with neither Mum nor Dad seeing a doctor, their GP was suddenly working overtime. Mum had been putting on a lot of weight even though she hardly ate enough to keep a sparrow alive. We thought she must be secretly stuffing herself with chocolate but she swore she wasn't and said she was feeling a lot of discomfort. Eventually, it was diagnosed as an ovarian cyst. Her GP told Dad she would not survive another six months without the operation but he still had to use all his persuasive charm to get her to agree and, when the surgeon finally cut it out, it weighed eight and a half stone, at that time the biggest ever removed from a woman.

That year I was asked to make a speech at the annual dinner and dance of the Kimbolton kart club. It's a club our family has enjoyed a long association with – the main straight is named the Hines Straight after Dad – so they all knew her and what she'd been through, and the loudest cheer of the night came when I introduced her as 'Slimmer of the Year'.

With Kelly still having to spend time in hospital for tests, Mum's operation and Luke's accident, there was a spell when I seemed to spend the whole day driving between hospitals. I would go to Harlow to see Luke first thing in the morning so Tina could go home, have a shower and spend a bit of time with Tuesday. The poor kid's world had been turned upside down – she was even taken for her first day at school by her aunt rather than her mum. When Tina got back to the hospital, I'd go on to Barnet to see Mum and then to the Royal Marsden to visit Kelly.

Tina and I saw each other only in passing. I doubt that we spent more than an hour at a time in each other's company for several months. I even abandoned work, just popping in occasionally to make sure it was ticking over. As I drove that endless circuit of pain, I felt like a flyweight who was being battered remorselessly by a heavyweight. Friends looked on sympathetically and we appreciated all their support, but there was not much they could do to help. The rest of the world just kept on going as though everything were still as it should be. But in my world it couldn't have been less normal. Blow after concussive blow was raining in on me. I couldn't go down and there was no referee to step in and stop the punishment.

And it was about to get worse.

Chapter 22
Why?

There was a brief spell during these crises when things seemed to be turning in the right direction. Mum was recovering well from her operation and Dad was holding his own. Incredibly, having endured thirteen operations in eight weeks, Luke came out of hospital well ahead of schedule, and Kelly's hair started to grow back, though she was taken aback that what had once been straight and blonde with highlights was now dark brown and curly.

We'd had a scare when Tuesday was admitted to Princess Alexandra hospital in Harlow with severe asthma at just six weeks old but she had come through that well and Luke was making better progress than we could ever dare hope. We could tell Mr Therkildsen was pleased but he always couched his optimism with caution. 'It's coming along very well,' he said. 'But we have to be prepared for a setback at any time because what appears to be happening can't be happening. His left leg appears to be growing at the same rate as his right.'

We clung on to that hope as hard as we could. The kid deserved some luck – he'd had a really tough few years. He'd been prone to tantrums as a baby and was very slow to talk.

Neither Tina nor I really knew how quickly he should be picking up words but he had passed all the routine development tests for a two-year-old at the health clinic. His health vistor assured us there was nothing wrong and told us his screaming tantrums would pass and his speech improve. We were told, 'He's just a slow starter,' but there was a nagging doubt that something was wrong with him. Luckily, we had a new health vistor assigned to him, someone who saw him through fresh eyes. She realized things weren't right and arranged for him to see a senior paediatric doctor, who referred him to Mr Amen, the ENT consultant at our local hospital. He confirmed Luke had a serious problem with glue ear, a condition where the middle ear fills with a liquid instead of air. However, there was a long waiting list for operations and this was potentially devastating to his health. I wasn't prepared to wait, and thank goodness we now had BUPA membership. Within two days he was operated on at Holly House hospital in Chingford. They took more than half a litre of fluid from his head and told us later that any more delay would have resulted in his being totally deaf and, if the membrane between his ear and brain had ruptured, he would have been brain-damaged. As it was, they saved around 80 per cent of his hearing.

But Luke's suffering wasn't over. Before the end of the year he had his tonsils and adenoids removed and his sinuses drained. He had grommets in his ears and most of the time was in a lot of pain, all of which meant he developed very slowly. He was behaving like a deaf child, refusing to make eye contact and not speaking at all, so he was given intensive speech therapy with exercises to do at home. This needed lots of time and patience but it paid off and he gradually started to talk. He wasn't really ready when the time came for him to start school and struggled to keep up with the other kids. He already had the Hines attitude to life and worked hard, but, just as he started to get on top of things, he had his accident. That kid went through more in his first six years than most people do in a lifetime, so when Mr Therkildsen told us his leg miraculously appeared to be growing I felt it was no more than he deserved.

After our brief respite, the health of those around us seemed once more to go into free fall. I knew there would be consequences as soon as I heard Uncle John was seriously ill with cancer. He and Dad were very close and I don't think Dad would have trusted anyone else with running the snooker hall. John died within a few weeks of being diagnosed and I could see Dad was deeply affected. I'm sure he had been shielding all of us from exactly how ill he was, especially Kelly, who he adored. But now she was apparently on the mend, and after John's death it was as though Dad felt it was now OK to let go and his own declining health became all too apparent.

His doctor decided he needed to go into Barnet General Hospital. I still couldn't allow myself to believe my old man was mortal. Knowing how he had bounced back before, I convinced myself he would beat this one. We sorted out yet another routine for visits: I would go and see him from three to seven, then Mum's sister Barbara would bring her in and they would sit with him until ten.

On the fifth day after he was admitted, I was booked to attend a sportsmen's dinner at Hoddesdon Civic Hall where I was one of the guest speakers along with former Arsenal and Tottenham goalkeeper Pat Jennings. When I went to see Dad he complained that he had cramp in his arm, so I gave him a massage. He didn't look too good and I decided to skip the dinner but he wouldn't hear of it. He said, 'Don't be daft. It's important that you go. Get off early. I'll be OK until your mum arrives.'

'Are you sure? I'm quite happy to stay.'

'Don't muck about – I want you to go. I'll see you tomorrow.'

As I was leaving I bumped into one of our former drivers, Kenny Owen, who I hadn't seen for some time. He asked after Dad and I told him he was upstairs but he was going to be OK. Even as I said it, something triggered in my brain and made me go back up and see the ward sister. I gave her my home and mobile phone numbers and said, 'If anything ever happens to Dad, please ring me and not my mother. She couldn't take a call from you in the middle of the night, but if you phone me I'll go and get her.'

The call came at five o'clock the next morning. Dad had died.

I just stood there with the phone in my hand. The world stopped for a moment while I registered the awful truth of what the nurse had told me. In some ways it wasn't a surprise but it was a hell of a shock. I'd not only lost my father, but also my best friend, my mentor, the man who had made me what I am. The most influential relationship of my life halted in a moment. From my early childhood we'd argued fiercely, we'd laughed a lot, and we'd shared every high and low. Wherever I was in the world, he would be the first person I would phone after a race.

In many ways I was his mirror image, both the good and the bad, and while some fathers and sons who are that similar fall out, with Dad and me it created a bond of love so deep that nothing could ever shake it. Immediately on hearing the news, I was aware of a massive hole in my life that could never be filled. I still miss him every day, and I still wish I could phone him and tell him what's happened at the track. I tried to sum it up on a card on his wreath: 'To my hero, my best friend, my mate.'

When I got the call, I just wanted to crawl into a hole and be alone with my grief but I knew I couldn't. I had to tell Mum and the family and I had to be strong for them. As so often in my life, I lost myself in doing what had to be done. I arranged the funeral and we had a fantastic turnout of people. There were friends from way back, from the bingo hall and the snooker club, from all areas of motorsport, including the governing body. The old man would have been proud to see how much affection there was for him. Of course, he had to have a say in events, turning up late for his own funeral because the hearse broke down. He never was in a rush to get into the hereafter.

Just over a month after Dad's funeral, Kelly was round at our house and I noticed she was limping. I felt sick in my stomach. I asked her what was wrong and she told me she had a problem with a lump in her hip.

'You know we have to sort this out straightaway, don't you?' I said, desperately trying to swallow my fear.

Lindy and I took her back to the Marsden and after several tests they confirmed the cancer had returned. The doctors were brilliant. They sat us down and told us the truth. They gave Kelly so much respect, talking to her as an adult, able to make decisions for herself. They explained they couldn't repeat the bone marrow transplant and chemotherapy but said there was a new experimental treatment that had produced some promising results in America, which they were willing to give to her if she wanted. Otherwise there was nothing they could do.

My gutsy thirteen-year-old daughter asked the question on all our minds: 'How long have I got?'

'Six to eight weeks, Kelly.'

I immediately said we would try the American treatment. If necessary we would go to the States for it. But Lindy was against it and, more importantly, so was Kelly. She decided she could not go through any more painful treatment, especially as the odds were so heavily stacked against it being successful.

Every part of me wanted to scream, 'No, you must fight to the last breath. You must take every chance, no matter how slim. You must never give up.' But I was so impressed with Kelly's courage that finally I could do nothing but bow to her wishes and try to find a way to cope with the fact that my first child would die within a few brief weeks.

I asked if there was anything she wanted to do – go round the world, go on holiday, anything. She said she'd prefer to stay at home where everything was familiar.

It is impossible for a parent to come to terms with the death of a child but, even in that bleak darkness of the soul, things can still happen that raise your spirit. Derek Redfern, the director of Haymarket Publishing and a very good friend, who did a hell of a lot for the Make a Wish Foundation, had contacted me a few months before to ask if I would see a young man who had cerebral palsy and was desperate to go kart racing with me in Manchester. When I agreed, Derek said, 'Let me have your mobile number because Tim is so ill, it might all change at the last minute.'

Tim made it to Manchester and we had such a great time, I said to him, 'I'm involved in an exhibition on twin-engine karts at the London Arena for BBC TV in a few weeks time. David Coulthard, Johnny Herbert, Derek Bell and a lot of famous drivers will be there. I want you to come as my guest. Will you do that for me?'

His eyes lit up. 'Yes, I'll be there.' And he was. After that, we arranged something else for three months down the line, and Tim made it again, clinging on to life to achieve yet another ambition. He not only had a few months more life, they were months that he thoroughly enjoyed.

Kelly had often expressed a wish to meet Philip Schofield, who she had liked since his days in the BBC 'broom cupboard' with Gordon the Gopher. I wasn't sure he'd want to come because he'd recently been the subject of tabloid headlines for an alleged affair and I thought he was probably keeping his head down.

I phoned Make a Wish: 'This time I need you to help me. Is there any way you could arrange for Philip Schofield to visit my daughter Kelly?'

'No problem, I'll get back to you.'

A few days later we received a call. Although he'd never done anything like this before, Philip would come and see Kelly. She was bedridden by this time and I can only guess how harrowing it was for Philip, who was still a very young man, to confront a child he knew was close to death. Kelly eased any nerves he might have been feeling, teasing him about the headlines and asking him if they were true. He responded brilliantly, spending hours with her and making her very happy. I will always be grateful to him, to Derek and to the Make a Wish Foundation, which does such fantastic work.

It was no surprise to us that Kelly had been able to put Philip at ease with her cheeky chat. She was that kind of bubbly, impish girl. Only a few weeks before, I'd been taking her home when we stopped off in a Spar shop to pick up some sweets. We were at the counter and she dropped a right smelly one and, quick as shot, said, 'Dad! You shouldn't have done that,' turned on her heel and walked out of the shop, leaving me to face the music.

I will never forget 15 February 1998. It was a lovely warm day with just a few snowdrops and crocuses starting to push through as though they sensed spring was just around the corner. I went over to take Kelly out in her wheelchair. She had been through a bad spell but that day the sun seemed to give her new life. She was breathing more easily than she had for weeks and she chattered all the time we were out. Apart from the chair, it was like having the old Kelly back, teasing and funny, interested in what was going on round her. We walked for ages and, when I finally got her back home, I picked her up and carried her upstairs to her room. At the top of the stairs she hugged me, kissed me on the cheek and said, 'I love you, Dad.'

I replied, 'I love you too, darling.'

That night I got a call from Lindy. 'You have to come quickly.'

It was only up the road and I drove flat out, but I wasn't quick enough. My little girl, who just twelve hours before had been so full of life, was lying with her mouth open where she had been gasping for a final breath. It was almost exactly six weeks to the day since we had been told there was nothing the doctors could do.

Nothing prepares you for the loss of a child. Even when you know it is coming, it is still so much out of step with the way life should be, that the horror of it is too much bear. Anger, guilt and grief tumble in on one another. Every emotion is so raw that, even when you think you have yourself in check, the slightest thing can churn you up all over again and you are helpless in the face of your agony. There is absolutely no peace. I kept thinking about what might have been. With her personality, Kelly would have become a very special woman, and I would have been in a position to provide her with loads of opportunities.

The constant question was why? Why Kelly? Why an innocent young girl, who had never harmed a soul and had brought so much happiness to so many? There was never an answer. There still isn't.

Perhaps the most amazing thing she ever did during her last few weeks was to plan her own funeral. I don't know how a thirteen-year-old could face doing that, but she did. She chose the music, and the sound of the Bangles singing 'Eternal Flame' in that church will haunt me for the rest of my life.

Throughout this period, Tina was a rock. I'm not an easy

person to live with at the best of times and the double blow of losing Dad and Kelly made me turn in on myself. I even got a call to tell me that Tim had finally succumbed to his cerebral palsy the day before Kelly died. I survived by filling my head with the things I had to do: in arranging the funerals, sorting out the endless paperwork, trying to keep everything together. Tina was left to try to provide Luke and Tuesday with some kind of normality. They coped brilliantly but I'm sure they were affected more than we realised.

For my mum, losing Kelly so quickly after burying Dad was a blow too much. Unknown to me, she had also been diagnosed with cancer but she swore Auntie Barbara to secrecy and, while I knew she wasn't her old vibrant self, I'd put it down to the cyst operation. She had hardly ever been apart from Dad from the day they had married and I don't think she really wanted to go on without him. If it hadn't been for the day-and-night care Barbara provided, I don't think she would have lasted as long as she did. There was a ten-year gap between the sisters, but Mum had always been a young old lady, so they seemed much closer, and Barbara had experienced her own sorrow, losing her husband Fred early on and having to bring up two girls on her own without much money, so she knew what Mum was going through.

Kelly's death was the last straw for Mum and she went downhill very quickly. I had a phone call from Barbara early one morning, telling me I had to go round straightaway. When I arrived, Mum was in her armchair and was clearly very ill. Still she insisted I should go and open up the factory. 'You must look after the business. I want you to go to work. You can come back and see me when you've opened up.'

It took me five minutes to reach the factory and unlock but by the time I reached my office the phone was already ringing. It was Barbara telling me to come back. I raced back but, just before I arrived, Mum died. Just like Dad, she had sent me away. They didn't want me to see them die but I'm glad they didn't die alone. Mum had her much-loved sister with her and I was told that Dad had called for a nurse at the end, so that he had someone with him.

My life appeared to be stumbling from tragedy to tragedy. Even the family red setter, Bonnie, succumbed to severe heart failure and had to be put down. The adrenaline-filled days of winning championships seemed to have happened to someone else in another lifetime. I wasn't even sure I had ever been that carefree, hard-living guy who travelled round the world taking great bites out of life. I certainly had no vision of that lifestyle ever returning. I was numb, merely going through the motions. And my body was paying a price.

Chapter 23

I Meant to Tell You Not to do Stomach Crunches

Mum died on 18 June and I seemed to spend the next few months in a daze, not really caring much about anything or anyone. Towards the end of the year, I knew I had to snap out of it. I had a responsibility to Tina and especially to Luke and Tuesday to try to return our lives to something close to normal. They had been forced to confront enough sorrow at such a young age that they didn't need a father on automatic pilot. Luke's leg was much stronger and he was able to walk about and ride his bike, so I decided we needed to go right away and have a break. I rang our friends Dave and Barbara Hepworth in Australia and asked if they could put up with four lodgers for six weeks. As I expected, Dave said, 'Get on the plane, mate. It'll be great to see you.'

Dave and Barb have been friends for years. I first met them in 1985, when I raced in Adelaide. I immediately took to them and the lovely laid-back city where they live. Adelaide is a fantastic place. Whichever part you are in, you are only ten minutes from the beach, city, hills, river and wineries, so just by stepping off the plane I felt at home and started to relax. It was a terrific holiday and made us all feel better. We did the whole tourist bit, showing the kids as much as we could, including close-up views of kangaroos and koala bears in the wildlife park. We also went to the Gold Coast, where my old mate Barry Sheene and Stephanie made us very welcome. They arranged a barbecue for all the family and Barry took us out on his boat to do a bit of water skiing. I could finally allow myself moments of fun again.

I've always been a sun worshipper and tan easily, so I spent a lot of time outdoors. It was as if the rays of the sun were recharging a battery inside me and gradually warming me back to life. I thought I knew how bulbs feel when the earth warms up and they start to grow again until one day, towards the end of the holiday, I woke up shivering and feeling dreadful. One minute I was freezing, the next boiling hot. I couldn't eat or drink. It was as though I'd suddenly gone down with a bad bout of flu, but it couldn't be flu because the next day I was fine again. That happened two or three more times, including the day we flew home and I have to report that a twenty-four-hour flight spent shivering and aching is not the ideal way to travel. It seemed to drag on for ever.

As soon as we arrived home I went straight upstairs. Tina called the doctor, who said, 'It must be serious if Martin's gone to bed. I'll come round.' He was there within the hour and gave me a thorough going-over, asking whether there had been rats in the river when I was water-skiing. I managed a grin: 'Only one. Me.'

He said, 'Martin, it's not flu or a chest infection. It might be something you picked up in Australia. I'll arrange for you to go and have some tests.'

They took me into Hertford Hospital and for the next six days tested me for everything they could think of until I felt like a pin cushion. They pumped strong antibiotics into me intravenously. The good news was that the Australian Rivers

Authority confirmed there was no evidence of the deadly Weil's disease in the river where I had skied and the doctors were also able to assure me it wasn't hepatitis or any of the tropical diseases they had seen before. The bad news was that they still didn't know what it was. And it wasn't getting any better. Food and drink tasted horrible, even water, and I had lost about two stone in ten days. I had yellow skin, eyes and fingernails, and I was a bag of bones, hardly having the strength to stand up.

They decided to try an ultrasound test and the following day the doctor came into my room and said, 'Martin, we believe we've found the answer. We think you have a tumour. It is probably in the liver but we won't know until Monday.'

I was stunned. Not me too.

It was a scary weekend. I'd just lost three members of my family to cancer. I dreaded the Monday coming round, yet I wanted to know what I was battling against.

The doctor came and sat by my bed. 'You may be a very lucky man,' he said. 'We've found a tumour in the bile duct. It's very unusual. It looks as though it's grown in there and is blocking the bile from draining away. You're being poisoned from inside.'

'And how is that lucky?' I asked, unconvinced.

'Because it's confined and can possibly be removed. It's a very tough operation but if it works you have every chance of being clear. I need to send you to see Chris Russell at the Royal Middlesex in London. He's the top man in this field and I want him to take a look.'

Mr Russell was away and in the days waiting for my appointment there were times when I almost gave up hope. One simple gesture snapped me out of it. Tina was out and I was sitting in a chair covered in blankets. I was so consumed by the illness that I had no sense of a life ahead. That wasn't like me. No matter what happens, I'm usually an optimist. But most of that day I wasn't anything, just terribly ill. I was going over all that had happened in the last couple of years and, if I'm honest, feeling sorry for myself. Tuesday saw me there with my teeth chattering, went upstairs and came back down dragging the duvet off her bed. She spread it over me and lay on top. 'I'll make you warm, Daddy,' she said.

I looked away so she didn't see my tears. At the same time I felt anger surge through me. I was angry with the illness that had sucked the life out of me and angry with myself for giving in.

I thought, I never had the chance to see Kelly become a woman. I'm fucked if the same thing is going to happen again. I *will* see Tuesday grow up. I'm going to beat this, whatever it is.

That was the thought that kept me going over the next tough months. There were many people I loved and wanted to live for, but when the going got really tough, and it often did, I kept the thought of watching Tuesday blossom into a woman at the front of my mind.

I wasn't able to walk from the car to the hospital so my friend Ty Gardner carried me into reception, where a porter met us with a wheelchair. They took me up to the ward and I met Chris Russell for the first time. He was friendly but pulled no punches when I asked him what my chances were.

He said, 'We need to cut out the whole tumour but, if that's not possible, we will have to leave it alone or we'll risk spreading the cancer round your body and killing you.'

'So what if you can't get it out? Chemotherapy?' I asked.

'No, if I can't cut it out there's nothing else will work. I'll do whatever I can to prolong your life as much as I can. It's not a fast-growing tumour so that could be anything from six to eighteen months. But I'm hopeful. If I can get it all out and re-plumb you, you will have a chance. I promise you I'll always be straight with you. And right now that means telling you there's no way you're fit enough to survive the operation. We need to build you up first.'

He said they were going to try to ease the symptoms in the short term. They gave me a local anaesthetic and fed this long flexible tube with a camera on the end, a bit like a toy you would find in a sex shop, down my throat. They obviously liked what they saw because they sent the tube back down with a different instrument on the end, eased a plastic tube next to the tumour and this acted as a drain for the bile. I was semi-conscious all the time and, while there was no pain, it's a strangely eerie experience and you are suddenly aware of your internal organs in a way you have never been before.

But it did the trick. By the time I was wheeled back on the ward, I was ready for a drink. The poisonous bile was slowly retreating from my body. Hey, this was great. Perhaps they had cured me already.

Mr Russell soon put me right. 'It's only temporary. We still have to do the surgery. I'm going to the Middle East to see another patient and then we've got Christmas, so you have three or four weeks to get yourself strong enough to survive the operation. Do you think you can do that?'

'Chris, this is the fight for my life. Nothing's gonna stop me.'

I walked out of the hospital feeling I'd been given a second chance. As I left, the porter who had brought me the wheelchair on my arrival gave me a thumbs-up. We'd never spoken a word to each other but that simple gesture touched me. I was optimistic again. I still looked a sight, yellow eyes and fingernails and a sallow skin where my tan used to be. Not the Hines image at all. I thought a bit of retail therapy would do me good so I went into a shop and bought myself a rather expensive three-quarter-length, navy-blue Boss coat with a quilted lining against the December chill. This'll last me a good few years, I thought, and it is still my favourite coat to this day.

The next day I went down and saw Steve Clarke, a physio who used to run the gym at my squash club. I'd always had a lot of time for him and said, 'This could literally be life or death. I want you to sort me out a diet and fitness programme that will put me in top condition for this operation.' I told him what equipment I had at home and he drew up a plan.

I have never worked harder. I was meticulous with my diet, eating all the right food, drinking the right stuff, even going without my favourite glass of red wine. Three times every day without fail I went through the forty-minute routine Steve had mapped out. It was gruelling at times but I kept repeating the old saying under my breath, 'Fail to prepare, prepare to fail,' and pushed on. When I thought my body could take no more, I thought of Tuesday and drove myself a bit harder. I could feel the difference within a week and by the time I was due to see Chris Russell again I was in the best condition I'd ever been in. I even managed a game of squash the week before I was due to have my operation.

I walked into Chris's office and he didn't recognise me. Instead of the yellow bag of bones he'd last seen, he was faced with a superfit athlete.

'I'm ready,' I said.

He told me to take off my shirt and I saw him look at what I can only describe as a pretty impressive six-pack, testimony to many thousands of stomach crunches. He didn't say a word. It was only later he confessed, 'I'd meant to tell you not to exercise your stomach muscles. What you had was the Whipple's operation, one of the biggest single operations humans can undergo. We had to cut you from side to side, go in through your stomach muscles, put your stomach on a table, remove the tumour, your gall bladder and everything else in the vicinity, re-plumb you and sew you back up. If your stomach muscles are fairly soft it isn't a problem to stitch them together again but when they are taut and strong like yours were, it's a hell of a job and is very uncomfortable for the patient every time he breaths, laughs or farts.' He knew what he was talking about. It was bloody agony.

I was physically and mentally prepared for the surgery. I was helped enormously by everyone around me, who focused on a good outcome. Whatever they were thinking inside, when they were with me there were no long faces, no sympathetic glances, no doubts, nothing but encouragement. Dave and Barbara in Australia offered to drop everything and come over to keep things ticking over so I didn't have to worry about work, a fantastic gesture. I concentrated on positive thoughts, making plans for the company over the next few years and things I would do with the family when it was all over. A few moments still stopped me short in my tracks, especially signing over power of attorney to my solicitor in case I died on the operating table. That really concentrates the mind.

The operation happened at the time of the first Gulf War and, the night before, I was sitting in my room watching some footage of the fighting on television when this Middle Eastern-looking guy stormed in with so many scars and cuts on him he looked like Frankenstein's monster. He was waving his arms and demanded, 'What have you done with my friend? This is my friend's room. Where is he?' It turned out he had been injured in the war for a second time and was looking for the guy he had befriended on his first stay in the hospital. He looked a bit wild-eyed and dangerous. I was in two minds what to do. Should I protect myself if he attacks or run like hell? I settled for pressing the buzzer and a nurse took him away.

Chris Russell came to see me on the morning of the operation. He was a reassuring figure. I trusted him completely and knew that my whole future was literally in his hands over the next few hours. As I started to go under the anaesthetic, I kept telling myself, When you wake up remember to ask them if it's been a success. I was on the operating table for five and a half hours and the nurse said, 'As you were coming round, you must have asked us a hundred times how it had gone.'

They were able to reassure me. Chris had removed the tumour and thrown it away. There was light at the end of the tunnel and thankfully for once it wasn't a bloody express train coming the other way.

The hospital staff were superb, especially Chris, who over the next months and years was someone I came to admire greatly. His attention to detail and his work rate were unbelievable – he'd be there to see me first thing in the morning and back again to check on me before I went to sleep. Anything I needed, I only had to call his secretary and it was there.

The day after the operation, I was lying in bed with a tube coming out of every orifice, feeling so sore I hesitated to shift my position in case I did some damage. I was therefore a bit taken aback when a nurse said, 'OK, Mr Hines, time to go for a walk.'

'I don't think so,' I said. 'I was cut in half yesterday and sewn back together. You've got the wrong man.'

'No, you're the man. Now, out of bed.'

They made me walk – that's a rather posh term for what I actually managed – across the ward. Each shuffle was agony and my stomach felt ready to burst apart along its new seam. But she made me go all the way. It felt as bad as that flight back from Australia and took almost as long.

The next day, the nurse took me for a walk down the corridor, a trolley either side of me with bottles and pipes leading into my body. I bumped into my Middle Eastern mate, also doing his circuit training after an op. I learned he had been blown to bits and had been stitched back together again. We just nodded, each knowing how the other was feeling.

'What's the plan for tomorrow?' I asked the nurse. 'The London Marathon?'

But I was secretly quite proud of the progress I was making and the old competitive instincts started to kick in again. When I saw Chris, I asked, 'What's the quickest anyone has gone home after this operation?'

'Well, I had a lorry driver who went out after fourteen days.'

'Best we beat that, then,' I said.

He laughed. 'Why not?'

When he saw me on the tenth day he said that, if everything went well, I could go home the following day. *Yessss!* I always knew kart drivers had it over lorry drivers. Or they would have if I hadn't developed an infection in the wound overnight. The next few days were disgusting. I will spare you the gory details. Suffice to say the syringes they used to take the infection out were bloody big.

In the end Mr Russell allowed me to go home after fifteen days, provided there was someone to act as a nurse. Tina gallantly volunteered to change the dressings but what she hadn't bargained for was the day I was in the shower and my scar burst open. It was not a pretty sight but after a phone call to Chris and a reassuring visit from my GP it was decided I could stay at home. It meant Tina faced a new challenge: because the infection had not cleared properly, they had to leave a hole open and she had to dress it, and, to give her her due, she did a great job.

Overall, I made good progress. I went back to see Chris for regular checkups, scans and tests. He told me that, while he couldn't prove it medically, he was convinced my problem had been brought on by the incredible sorrow I had been through over the previous twelve months.

He said, 'Martin, no one can stand that level of intense grief without their body reacting in some way. Take this as a warning. You've been lucky this time, but you might not be so fortunate again. Don't work seven days a week. Accept that you've been cut in half and your body might not be able to take the strain of driving a kart. You may never race again. You're not a kid any more, you know.'

The trouble was that I still felt like a kid but I did exactly what he told me – for about three weeks. Even then I went into work for only four or five hours a day and agreed to take a holiday in Barbados so that I could relax and heal. Of course it didn't work out quite like that. On the first day Tuesday was doing her imitation of Tiger Woods on the miniature golf course but her swing wasn't quite as grooved as Tiger's and the club hit Luke. The first few hours of my restful holiday were spent racing around to find a clinic to stitch up the gash in his head. Life was returning to normal in the Hines household

The next time I saw Chris, I said, 'You've never done the scans you said you were going to do.'

'Do you want one?'

'It's not a question of that. I just wondered why you hadn't. Every time I have a dodgy curry and get the runs, I start to worry it might be something else. I've seen so much cancer in recent years, it's gonna take a while to feel safe in my own life again.'

'Martin, I promise you have nothing to worry about. I take your blood and I can tell from that if there's anything abnormal. If anything ever shows up, I'll give you a scan. But in the meanwhile be assured you are doing well.'

With that endorsement, I decided the only way I would know how the body would react to driving was to climb in a kart and try it. My stomach was still very tight and I can't say it was the most comfortable drive of my life, but I did twenty-

Above: Anthony Davidson (Ant) doing what he did best: leading the field in the MSA Comer Cadet Championship category.

Middle: MH helps clean the grass out of the radiator after his trip into the undergrowth in Danielson, 1995.

Right: The Jim Bamba cartoon that told the story of that fateful day in 1996 at IDI-ADA.

Left: 'Some guys get all the luck'. I enjoyed my day modelling with page 3 girl and friend Tracy Kirby when we were first promoting the Zapelli brand of designer kart wear.

Below: Ron Dennis and DC with the winners of the 1996 McLaren Mercedes Champions of the Future.

Top: Luke takes second in the 1996 CIK/FIA Junior European Championships. Both Gary Paffett and Lewis Hamilton took the runner-up spot in 1995 and 1998.

Below: DC tests my super kart for *Autosport* magazine at Silverstone.

Inset: The McLaren BRDC *Autosport* awards 1996. The night I suggested to Ron Dennis he should sign up Gary and Lewis.

Top: The Zip Formula arrives for the new millennium.

Middle left: Max Mosley enjoys a day testing in the Zip Formula and declares it is a perfect entry level formula.

Middle right:The Warren Street boys have grown up.

Right: The Zip bug takes to the fairway in La Manga golf club in Spain, seen here with England football stars Matthew Upson, Gareth Southgate and Gareth Barry.

Inset: Dave and Barbara Hepworth. Without them the 2002 great comeback would never have happened.

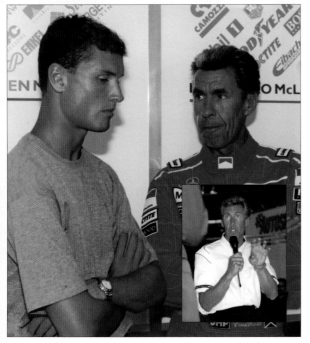

Top: The Zip Eagle landed for the comeback in 2002 at Croix-en-Ternois, French Championship. Grant was always in attendance.

Middle left: The comeback race was a memorable moment in my career.

Middle right: Sir Jackie Stewart and Murray Walker present Gary with his BRDC cheque for £125,000 for winning the national F3 Championship.

Left: A test day with McLaren: I was just keeping DC's race suit warm.

Inset: The Autosport International show was always a great opportunity to promote karting and The Zip Young Guns.

Luke's first win for the all-conquering Vauxhall touring car team at Brands Hatch 2004, with James Thompson second and Ivan Muller third, making it a clean sweep for VX racing.

Top left: This was a once-in-a-life-time moment, when I was awarded the *Autocar* award for contributions to motorsport. I beat Michael Schumacher and Kimi in the process.

Top right: Now that's what I call a GT1: Luke and Philipp Peter with the Corvette C6. They took a fantastic second in the FIA GT Championships in Zuhai 2007. It was Luke's first GT1 race.

Centre: Oliver Rowland wins the 2007 MSA Junior Intercontinental 'A' Championships in 2007.

Left: Oliver and me the week after he signed for McLaren in May 2007.

Above: Dad and lad: the only way to go racing.

Below: The two most important ladies in my life today: Tina and my daughter Tuesday.

Inset: Well, that's the lot for now. Time for a glass of wine.

five laps on a test day at Snetterton and, at the end of it, I was the fastest out there. 'Wait till I'm really fit, fellas.'

There was an amusing coda to the story of my operation. About twelve years later, I started to pass blood and instantly thought I'd got the same prostate problem Dad had suffered from. I saw a specialist, who said, 'I don't think there's anything wrong with you. I think you've just strained yourself.' I remembered that I'd recently taken the Harley out of the garage for the first time in years. I'd ridden only about five miles but I'd bashed my nuts on the tank and that had obviously caused the problem.

The specialist read my notes and said, 'I want to shake your hand.'

I thought it was a bit strange but shook his hand and said, 'What was that about?'

'Well you had the Whipple's operation. Do you know that very few people live longer than five years after that? I've never met one before.'

Not only had Chris forgotten to advise me not to work on my stomach muscles, he'd overlooked scaring me to death by telling me that only a quarter of 1 per cent survive the surgery. Still, he had saved my life, so I forgave him.

And he'd done such a fantastic job that I could now start to think about fulfilling a promise I'd made to Dad before he died.

Chapter 24

This One's for You, Dad

The day before my dad died, he and I were chatting and as usual the conversation got back to karts. He was still upset that I'd recently lost the world championship when my gearbox went on the thirteenth of fifteen laps. I said, 'Don't worry, Dad, I'll win it again.'

After everything that had happened since then, that race at Silverstone – where my old man stood by the side of the track leaning on a walking stick watching me for what turned out to be the last time – seemed like a lifetime ago. But, now that I was in a kart again, the promise I'd given him made it even more urgent that I get back to being quick. After a few races, it no longer hurt to drive – it was bloody uncomfortable but not so bad that I didn't want to keep pushing.

I entered the 1991 World Championship because that was what we did – we raced for the biggest prizes – but, if I'm honest, I must say didn't think I was in with a chance of winning. However, the first two rounds went well and, when we reached Le Mans, the kart was running fast and suddenly there was a chance we might just overhaul leader Perry Grondstra. My qualifying times were good and I started the pre-final on the front of the grid. I knew this was to be probably the most important race of my life. A win would be 95 per cent of the job done and this one was for Dad. I got a great start and quickly settled into an electrifying pace. Everything felt fantastic. I knew I was clear, as I couldn't hear the pack on my heels, but so often in sport, just as you think you have it cracked, disaster strikes. My king bolt sheered, I lost control at 100 m.p.h. and crashed heavily. I was out of the race, my kart was badly damaged and I would be right at the back of the grid for the final. It was another of those hero-to-zero moments and I was feeling pretty low when I arrived back at the pits on the back of the breakdown truck, but Grant Munro pointed out that, provided we could rebuild the kart in time to have it back on the eighth row of the grid, we had only to win the final to take the title.

We worked frantically to get the kart as near perfect as possible. With just five minutes to go, it started to rain, but we'd achieved a near miracle and not even the rain could dampen our renewed optimism. This was going to be the race of my life.

My teammate Ian Shaw was on the third row and we hoped he could keep among the front men and stop anyone opening up too much of a lead. The light went on, the engines roared and sixty karts sped off in a fog of spray. It was a question of closing your eyes and going for it. Most of us made it round the slight right-hander and up the hill into the chicane. But then it was chaos. I still don't know how I got through there safely – there were karts on the bank and more sideways on the track. I was driving blind, surviving on pure instinct fuelled by adrenaline. The carnage at the chicane moved me up several places – including ahead of Ian – and I had three storming laps. I was absolutely in the zone. Naked women could have hung from the Dunlop Bridge and I wouldn't have noticed as I picked drivers off one at a time, leaving them in a shower of spray.

By halfway I was fourth, but it was getting harder, because there were very quick drivers ahead of me now, including Grondstra. For a couple of laps I didn't seem to be making up any ground on him. Having worked so hard to pass all the drivers immediately in front of me, I'd mentally switched off.

I yelled at myself above the sound of the engine, 'What the fuck are you doing, Martin? If you don't pull your finger out, you ain't gonna win a thing.'

You get nothing out of a kart by being kind to it. They are tough little machines, meant to be driven hard. It's rough on your body – the vibration can loosen your fillings and the G-forces make you fight for breath – but, if you want a comfortable ride, go for a Sunday spin in your Mondeo. I forced every ounce of power I could out of my machine. I delayed braking by fractions of a second, I concentrated on being as smooth as I could manage, and I took risks I might normally never have considered. It was a delicate balancing act, because at the same time I was trying to look after my wet tyres on the now drying track and, as the race reached its climax, I believe it was that which gave me the edge.

I went past Perry with three laps to go. Now only Eric Gassin and Torgjer Kleppe, the man I had narrowly beaten for my first world title, stood between me and victory. If I couldn't overtake them, all this effort would have been in vain.

I picked off Eric and went after Torgjer. As I came on to the straight I was still 300 yards behind. The board was out. 'Two laps to go.' *Whaaat!?* That *couldn't* be. I'd been counting the laps. I was sure there was only one left. But the board said two. If it was right, I had time. I didn't need to take too many chances. If it was wrong, I needed to keep pushing like hell. I never trusted the French and decided they had cocked up again.

I drove the best single lap of my career in conditions I hate – that time when the track is neither wet nor dry and every corner brings something new to contend with, a different challenge to anticipate and negotiate. I had a good run up the hill and down to the hairpin, which I took faster than I'd ever done before. We came to the final complex and I was in Torgjer's slipstream. I took a lunge. He twitched slightly and left the door open a fraction.

I went through.

I forced him out wide. He immediately fought back, crossed up and lost time. I didn't realise I was clear and expected him to come straight back at me, so, as the final series of bends came at me in quick succession, I risked wrecking the kart by throwing it aggressively over the kerb. I knew that, if I got it wrong in those conditions, I'd be history. I held my breath, expecting an axle to bend or a chain to come off. The kart bucked like an untamed stallion but I hung on and stamped my foot to the floor, taking the chequered flag. I was absolutely elated. After the year in hell, Hines was back. Once more I had finished the World Championship tied on points with another driver.

FIA official Robert Langford spent some time going through the rule books trying to separate Perry Grondstra and me. We both had two firsts and two seconds and Perry claimed that his next best was better than mine, so he must be champion. Robert, however, said that I should be given the title because I had won the final race. The French officials agreed and I was handed the trophy and declared World Champion. There was a certain amount of argy-bargy and confusion and I learned Ernest Buser suggested to Grondstra that he was champion. It was decided the FIA–CIK committee would make the final judgement. As far as I was concerned, the rules were absolutely clear, but the committee created history by declaring that the title would be shared, a decision I still believe was done only to save Ernest Buser's face. Nevertheless, it still felt like a hell of a triumph to me after everything that had gone before. I was confident Dad would have counted it as one of my best and Mum would surely have said, 'See what happens when you don't say can't?'

The day after the final race I made a copy of the results and sent them to Chris Russell with a bottle of champagne and a note saying thanks. Very few of us are lucky enough to meet a man who can have such a profound effect on our lives. He's quite a guy. He kept monitoring me with blood tests and was clearly happy with my progress. About two years after the operation, he said, 'How are things?'

'Well, I'm back to fourteen hours a day and racing every weekend.'

He laughed: 'I guess that means you're cured. Martin, I meant every word I said about learning to take it easy but what can I do with you? I don't need to see you any more.'

That was the last time I saw him. I wrote to him on the tenth anniversary of the operation just to let him know I was still around and I hope to send him another letter in 2011 and 2021 – and who knows after that? However much time I have left on this earth, I owe to him.

Chapter 25
Cheat!

Being back 'on top of the world' was a great feeling and made me hungry for more. It also brought me another of those moments I could never have dreamed of as a kid and which would have made Mum and Dad very proud. I was invited to a special garden party at Buckingham Palace, along with Britain's other world champions, to mark the fortieth anniversary of the Queen's reign. It was a special occasion and I couldn't help but think back to my childhood – if I'd had a garden like that, I could have built one hell of a pigeon loft.

It was a fantastic moment in my life. Everywhere you looked there was a sporting hero. Tina and I spent most of the day with the boxing guys we had met when I took part in *Superstars*. The highlight of the day was when the Queen arrived, elegantly walking down the steps to mingle with a selected number of her champions, although a close second was Chris Eubank's entrance, monocle and all.

Back on the track, it looked as though I was well on the way to another British title in 1992, when I was leading after four rounds, but then the RAC Motor Sports Council summoned me to a tribunal, accusing me of cheating. They claimed that, when they checked my fuel after the championship race at Knockhill, the octane level was 91.5, which would have been legal in Europe but was above the British limit of 89. I was surprised, because, as usual, I'd just used the fuel BP had sent me. They were my team sponsors and the last thing they would do was put their reputation – or indeed mine – on the line with such an elementary mistake. I contacted them and they issued a statement saying, 'The product was supplied through our distributors Reference Fuels Ltd in good faith on the basis that it complied with the 1992 regulations. We believe that no blame should be apportioned to Mr Hines in these circumstances.'

They even sent one of their top people over from America to speak for me at the tribunal, but, while the sport's ruling body usually take a lot of notice of major companies, they chose to ignore this one. They even took no notice when BP produced evidence that the machine used to test the fuel was intended to be used with virgin petrol. Our two-stroke fuel had oil in it and the equipment manufacturer's own guidelines said that in those circumstances a 5 per cent tolerance should be allowed, which would have put us well within the limit. Despite this, the three-man panel didn't take long to decide I was to be given the maximum £500 fine and my licence was taken away for two and a half years. It was incredibly harsh and made me think there was more going on here than I was aware of.

This was confirmed some years later when a friend of mine who was a top RAC official, and happened to be upstairs in the offices when the verdict was phoned through, told me that one member of the RAC's middle management punched the air when he heard the news and said, 'Yes! We've got the bastard at last.' It seemed that some of the people I'd upset over the years saw this as their golden opportunity to nail Hines.

I was stunned. This wasn't just a ban as far as I was concerned: this reflected on my integrity and would wipe out everything I'd ever achieved in thirty years of motorsport. I had never cheated in my life. As far as I'm concerned motorsport is all about trying to win, but there's absolutely no satisfaction in winning by cheating and I'd be the first to support a long ban on anyone who had deliberately flouted the rules. I paced around outside trying to come to terms with what had just happened. I told my solicitor, Howard Pinkerfield, that I wanted to fight the decision.

'The only thing we could do would be to take them to the High Court and obtain an injunction overturning the tribunal,' he said. 'But that would cost a helluva lot of money. You probably wouldn't be looking at much change out of thirty or forty thousand pounds.'

I made another of my instant decisions: 'Howard, how much is the last thirty years of my life worth? I'll find the money somehow. Just do it, but do it fast, because the British Grand Prix is only a two weeks away and I want my licence back before that.'

Howard recommended I should employ John McDonald, a QC with experience of motorsport. It was great advice. John was fantastic and cleared his diary over the next few days so we could go through every aspect of the case in detail. The hearing was scheduled for a week before the Grand Prix and by that time we were confident we had a powerful argument. I was impressed by the way John did his homework. He found out that Justice Mervyn Davies was to hear the case and planned his presentation accordingly. He stayed very calm and measured throughout while the RAC's lawyer was more aggressive. He wasn't helped much by his evidence, which in one case literally fell apart in the judge's hands.

They were discussing the testing of the petrol and as the judge was looking at a similar container to the one used to transport the sample from my tank, the seal broke. The RAC's barrister tried to make out that it was a one-in-a-thousand chance and handed over another container, only for the same thing to happen. Justice Davies wasn't impressed.

The question then arose how this less-than-secure container had been carried to the test laboratory and the RAC admitted that because their officials had flown back from Scotland, the sample had been handed over to another driver to bring back, and not just any other driver but one of my main competitors.

'And how long was it between the race meeting and the container arriving at the laboratory?' the judge asked.

There was some shuffling of feet and a barely audible reply: 'Three days, m'lud.'

I don't think for a moment one of my fellow drivers would have deliberately tampered with the sample, but there was clearly enough evidence to suggest it couldn't be guaranteed to be uncontaminated and, combined with the report on the testing process itself, I felt we had proved our case. Justice Davies clearly agreed. He called the counsel together and instructed them he wasn't willing to go into a second day. They made their final submissions and he ruled in my favour. My licence and my reputation were returned and I was able to race at Silverstone the following weekend.

I was very fortunate. Although the RAC paid only a fraction of my costs, BP were magnificent in backing me and refunded most of the £41,000 I spent on the case. But what would have happened to a young driver who couldn't have even contemplated taking on the sport's ruling body? His career would have been ended and he would have been disgraced entirely unfairly. It just cannot be right that justice is available only to those who can afford it.

I didn't win the Grand Prix at Silverstone but I made up for it in August and September when I became the first driver to win the World Championship for a third time. The three rounds were all crammed into a few weeks and it was pretty intense racing. I was second behind Simon Cullen at St Wendel in Germany and fought my way back to second at the Osterreichring in Austria despite dropping 50 yards behind the field when I had to go into the gravel to avoid a pile-up. This time Chris Stoney won and, going into the final round at Le Mans, I was two points ahead of Cullen with Stoney just behind him.

We were racing alongside the Truck Racing Championship in front of 75,000 people and the rubber and oil put down by the trucks made the track very difficult by the time of the pre-final. I managed to handle the conditions better than the rest and won from the front, so lined up on pole in the final. It was a humdinger of a race with Cullen mounting an early challenge, then Stoney and I battling it out. We were both pressing hard and I realised if we kept pushing each other like this there might well be a crash. Second place would be good enough to give me the title, so I tucked in behind him and eased my way to the championship.

The following year, I beat Perry Grondstra to the European Championship and I was hoping to be the first driver to take the world crown three years in a row, but Perry at last finished ahead of me by just three points. The final round was at Knockhill and, after the pre-final, he and I were level on points. For once I didn't make a great start and found Gary Tupper between me and my target, and by the time I got past him Perry had opened up a four-second lead, which I was just unable to overhaul. It was disappointing but he was a great driver and we'd had some titanic battles over the years, so I couldn't begrudge him the title.

I felt less magnanimous in 1994, when Perry pipped me again, this time by a 500th of a second. It all came down to the final round in Austria. I set the fastest time in practice but had a disastrous qualifying, failing to post a time because of a broken conrod in the first heat while the second was washed out. Fortunately, the stewards let me race from the back of the grid in the pre-final. I drove like a maniac, breaking the lap record on lap four at an average speed of 119.3 m.p.h., but then I picked up a slow puncture and had to settle for fourth place, with Grondstra a couple of places ahead of me.

I still had a chance to take the title if I could win the final and Perry finished third or lower. The race developed into a three-way tussle between Perry, Ian Shaw and me with some pretty hairy overtaking, although I kept up the psychological pressure on the other two by being just in front each time we crossed the start/finish line. The final lap was touch and go – I was shedding rubber from one of my rear tyres but managed to hang on to win the race, although Grondstra got the tip of his nose cone ahead of Shaw to deny me the world crown.

It was a bittersweet race victory. I was disappointed not to be world champion but proud of the way I had overcome the odds and again achieved the fastest lap. My racing had also been acknowledged with membership of the exclusive British Racing Drivers' Club, but not without my usual battle against bureaucracy.

The BRDC membership is a who's who of British motorsport who enjoy the club's plush headquarters at Silverstone. I'd wanted to join ever since being invited inside after the superkart demonstration at the British GP. I'd trod the plush carpets many times since – I made a point of being friendly to the doormen and they usually let me through with no questions asked – but it wasn't the same as being a member. You can join only if you are nominated by two members and to be a full member you have to meet certain racing criteria. At one time karters were excluded because our races were too short, but they relaxed the rules and one day, when I was talking to a very old friend from the sixties, Sidney Taylor, the former owner of the famous Steering Wheel Club in West Bromwich, he asked why I wasn't a member. I admitted it was one of the few things in the sport that had eluded me.

'We'll soon change that. I'll propose you,' he said.

Another good friend, Ross Hyett, agreed with Sidney and supported my application, and it probably took a couple of months before my nomination reached the board. It was one of those things that you don't talk about a lot but that make you check the post each morning, looking for the distinctive envelope. When mine eventually arrived it offered me associate membership. That's what they give sponsors and other non-drivers who do a lot for the sport and I was seriously pissed off. I'd won more titles than any of the cheeky buggers on the board, so I rang Martin Brundle, who was chairman at the time, and asked him what the hell was going on.

He said, 'The board were impressed by your achievements but decided you couldn't have full membership because you race on kart tracks, not motor-race circuits.'

I went nuts. 'Martin, that just goes to show how much the board know. I've raced and won on most of the major circuits in the world – Le Mans, Daytona, Hockenheim, Zolder. We've had a bloody kart GP at Silverstone for years now. I think it's a fucking cheek offering me associate membership and you can tell your board they can stick it up their arse.'

Martin realised they'd made a mistake and agreed to take it back to the board. The next month I got a letter of apology and the offer of full membership.

A couple of years later I was at Silverstone having a cup of tea with one of the BRDC committee members and he said, 'Martin, I have to tell you, one of my favourite meetings was when we finally made you a member. It was all a bit boring and I was starting to drift off when I heard Martin Brundle say, "And Martin Hines says you can stick your associate membership up your arses." That made us all pay attention and certainly put some life into the meeting.'

A few years later Luke was made a full member and it's rather special when father and son can sit together in the company of heroes you've had since you were a kid in the most elite racing drivers' club in the world.

My return to the top had been a thrilling and satisfying time, not least because I'd managed it while still concentrating on the progress of two other drivers, who I believed had a great future.

Chapter 26

A Stunning Drive by Hines – Luke Hines

If I had proved I'd overcome my cancer, the other patient in the family was also making pretty spectacular progress. Over the months Luke kept going in for X-rays and each time Mr Therkildsen shook his head and said, 'I don't really believe it, but the leg's still growing.'

He was so impressed he asked Tina to take Luke to a seminar of surgeons from all over the country that he was addressing. He showed them X-rays of Luke's original injuries and invited them to speculate on the possible outcome. Most plumped for amputation. They then met Luke and each of them examined his leg and weren't particularly impressed until Mr Therkildsen pointed out that Luke's left ankle had been smashed to a pulp and half the pieces of bone were missing. On top of that the green, growing platelets had been severed from his tibia, yet miraculously had started growing. There was no medical explanation for what they were seeing.

Mr Therkildsen said, 'What I want you to take on board is that things happen in nature we cannot understand. Clearly, children can have incredible powers of recovery and regeneration, so, no matter how bad the situation might appear, don't ever give up on a child.'

There was a bit of tension between me and Luke at this time. He wanted to drive karts like his Dad and do the other things boys do, but I was still feeling guilty about what had happened to him and was determined I would never put him in harm's way again. He was not happy about being wrapped in cotton wool, so eventually I asked Mr Therkildsen's opinion. I was hoping he would tell Luke it was too dangerous and that would be an end to his pestering. Instead he said, 'Why not let him do whatever he wants to do? His left leg's still growing and is as strong as his right, so there's no physical reason why he can't drive, and he's been through so much that he deserves a bit of fun.'

He had that right and, even allowing for a father's bias, I have to say that I doubt if many kids could have handled what he did with such guts. Soon after the accident I said to him, 'Luke, it is dreadful what's happened to you but, no matter how it turns out, I don't want you to use this as an excuse. You have to tackle life as it is, not how you wish it had been. And always remember: it could have been worse.'

From that day on, I never heard him complain that he was unlucky or that it was unfair that he had suffered so much. Indeed, he seemed determined to live life as though nothing had happened. That's not quite true. I understand that when he became a teenager he would occasionally show off his scars to girls and claim they had been caused by a shark attack in order to impress them! Ah well, the apple never falls far from the tree.

By modern standards, Luke started driving karts late, making his competitive debut at Buckmore Park at the age of nine, and in his first year he was no great shakes. There were the inevitable whispers that 'He'll never be as good as his dad' or, if he did well, they'd say, 'It's only because his dad makes sure he has the best kart.' At that stage it was too early to know whether the first was right, but the second was definitely crap. When it comes right down to it, the difference between winning and being second or third is the fella in the seat. Of course you need a machine that is competitive but it's the driver who is the most important part. For instance, Lewis Hamilton wouldn't have won as many Grand Prix if he'd been driving a Minardi rather than a McLaren, but I promise you he wouldn't have been finishing down in sixteenth or seventeenth place.

Luke either didn't hear the negative comments or chose to ignore them. He certainly soon showed the doubters they were wrong. He started to make rapid progress and was a worthy member of the Young Guns team.

With every special driver I've been involved with there have always been one or two Eureka moments when I've said to myself, 'This kid is special.' It happened with Luke at the final round of the British championship at Shennington.

Going into the race, Luke knew he wasn't going to be champion, whatever happened. He and his teammate, Nicky Richardson, had been head and shoulders better than the rest all season and deservedly Nicky had already sewn up the title. Even if Luke won every race he would still be two points behind, but he had figured out a new goal for himself. Only a handful of drivers in eight years, including Jenson Button, had ever won all three heats – one from the front, one from the middle and one from the back of the grid – and then won the final. 'I'd like to do that, Dad,' he said.

Conditions made it unlikely. It was lashing down with rain all day, the track, which is always tough, was treacherous and visibility was down to a few feet. But he won his first race from the front and managed to work his way through the field from the back to take the second. He was driving well and looked to have the measure of the other drivers and the conditions. I tried not to let him see I was getting keyed up, thinking he just might be able to pull it off.

He got himself into a reasonable spot to attack early in the third heat, but, as he came round the pit complex and up to the hairpin, another driver skidded, collected him and knocked him off. He spun out on to the banking with one wheel off the ground. He couldn't find any purchase to get going again and, by the time the marshals lifted him off, he was about 100 yards behind the back marker.

The other fathers knew what we were hoping to do and came over to commiserate. I was gutted but said, 'That's how it goes. I just hope he can still get a good grid position and win the final.'

The next ten laps were among the most incredible I have ever seen. Forget the fact it was my son in the kart, a kid we once thought would never walk, let alone race, for this was some of the most brilliant driving I've witnessed by anyone – and I've watched all the best. Luke simply tore through the field – his fastest lap was two seconds quicker than anyone else – and on the last lap he overhauled Colin Brown and clinched the win. As he drove back to the pits all the parents and engineers clapped him in.

I was choking back tears. I said, 'Luke, that was amazing. That had nothing to do with your chassis, your tyres or your engine – that was purely down to your talent and your determination not to be beaten. I couldn't be more proud of you.'

He started the final from the front of the grid and won by three seconds. He'd done it. He may not have been champion, but no one had driven better that year.

It's moments like that which make running the Young Guns every bit as exciting as racing myself. People often ask me if I miss competing and I guess there's a bit of me that still thinks that, if I put my mind to it, I could be competitive, but I also know that watching exciting kids grow into superstars and knowing I played a part in their success is just as rewarding. And the body doesn't ache as much afterwards.

Chapter 27
Young Guns

One youngster clearly wasn't destined for a career in karts. Tuesday had survived all the traumas of the past few years brilliantly. It would have been very easy for her to use what was going on as an excuse for not doing well at school or to play up for attention, but she never did. She was as bright as a button, brilliant in the classroom, very popular and mentally was a teenager from about the age of six.

But karts were not her thing. We were at Knockhill for a TV event and had set up a small circuit for the youngsters to race round, and I asked her if she would like to have a go. She was a bit tentative but decided to try it out. About three-quarters of the way round the first lap she pulled off the circuit. I raced over to her wondering what had happened and found her crying.

'There's a fly in my visor!' she said.

That was the end of her karting but she was certainly no wimp and, after her ice skating came to an end when the local rink closed, she went on to become a useful showjumper, having ridden since she was six. This was the only time the family separated: Tina drove the horse box to the various shows with Tuesday and I was at race meetings with Luke.

Thank goodness for mobile phones! I spent a fortune on giving and receiving running commentaries on each of the kids. Tuesday's show jumping came to an end when a couple of falls damaged her back. She also became distracted by every father's dread: boys. Interestingly, although not crazy about karts, she has developed a passion for fast cars, so I wonder if some of the motorsport genes crept through.

We were a lively family, always on the go and there was plenty of chat and laughter but there was one thing we all felt but didn't share with each other – a belief that our house was haunted. When Lindy and I gained permission to build the house on part of her dad Allan's land, we found a wonderful builder to handle the job. Jeff went the job about enthusiastically as though it was his own house but sadly he passed away before completing the upstairs and we had to get someone else to finish off. It was now 18 years later and Tina and I had been living there for 14 years. We had some structural problems caused by an extension and we decided it would be better to knock the old house down and rebuild a new place in a classic style.

We moved into the bungalow I'd bought for Mum and Dad while the work was being done but one evening while Tina was waiting for the electricity to be cut off before demolition, she was reminiscing with Allan and they both admitted that they had heard things go bump in the night. She broached the subject with me, confessing that she had often been frightened to be there when I wasn't around because things seemed to get noisier when I was away. I admitted that I'd always thought the place was haunted by Jeff and that I'd often heard what I thought was hammering on brick work and thought it was him finishing off the house. I hadn't said anything to her because I didn't want to scare her. As we thought back, we recalled that the kids had claimed to see ghosts upstairs and we wondered if they had actually seen something, especially when we remembered the number of times we would hear banging and thumping upstairs but could never find any source. One of our friends belonged to a spiritualist church and told Tina how to exorcise the old house before rebuilding started. She must have done a great job because the new house has warmth and a friendly, welcoming feeling and is much, much quieter.

Even if Tuesday didn't fancy karting, there were always queues of kids who did. We had factory drivers from the very early days of Mart's Karts and they soon became part of the family. Two of the first were Buzz Ware and John J Ermelli, a couple of real characters. Buzz's daughter Louise used to spend a lot of time at our house with my Mum while he was at the shop working on his kart.

We've had a lot of good drivers down the years. It's a simple idea: you have people winning races then make sure everyone knows they are part of the Zip team. Kids want to emulate them, so you sell more karts. It follows that an important part of my life is looking out for the best young drivers. It's not a hardship because my favourite sport is cadet racing – eight- to twelve-year-olds with 60cc engines on their karts racing at up to 60 m.p.h. As far as I'm concerned it's the best form of motorsport in the world today. It's the nearest you are likely to find to a level playing field: the smaller drivers have an advantage because they are aerodynamically better off while the bigger kids have a bit more strength. And the advantage of lighter drivers is reduced by adding lead to their kart to bring them up to the limit. They all drive the same type of engine and use the same type of tyre and, since by far the majority are on Zip chassis, it's about as fair as you can make it.

When I'm building a team, I start by looking for a leader or two, then add the other guys I know will bust a gut to beat them. It's a policy that has worked for me since my early days. When I was the Zip team leader we also had drivers such as Reg

Gange and Dave Buttigieg in the team and they loved nothing more than 'beating the boss'. We were intensely competitive between ourselves, which made us almost unbeatable as a team.

Once I've identified a potential Young Gun, I have to work out what I need to do to persuade them to drive in my team. It helps that we've got the best karts and that I've discovered a lot of top drivers. Kids know that being chosen as a Zip factory driver brings a lot of status and the promise of being noticed by the right people in motorsport. But I also have to be careful not to tip off the opposition, who might go in with a fancy deal to try to nick them. If that happens, I tend to say to the dad, 'I'm not changing my offer. It's up to you – do you want your kid in a winning kart or not?'

Fathers are probably the biggest downside to running a team. Not all of them, but far too many. Over the years I've had some right up-and-downers with dads who believed they knew better than I did, especially when they thought I wasn't pushing their lad enough. I've always believed it is less important for a young driver to win every race he enters than for him to be improving all the time. In fact it's vital he doesn't win every race because one of the things you have to learn as a driver is to cope with disappointment when you are shunted off or suffer a mechanical failure. At that age they are adding experience, know-how and a will to win to whatever talent they were born with. Sometimes it's a good idea to put a youngster out in a slightly slower kart so he has to work harder to compete. That soon shows up the kid with the desire to produce the maximum from his machine

The two most important qualities a driver needs is a competitive streak – he must hate being beaten – and what I call 'feel'. Feel is hands, feet and bum – everything that touches the kart – working together so that the driver is aware exactly what is happening around him. A driver with feel adjusts that vital fraction of a second faster than one who hasn't got it and squeezes the last bit of power out of his kart. I've also noticed that the kids who have feel find it much easier to adapt when they switch from one formula to another. Whereas it will take a reasonably good driver ten or twenty test days to be at home in a new formula, these guys slot in almost immediately. It happened with Luke – I took him from a kart and put him in Formula Ford and he was right on it in a couple of laps. Gary Paffett was the same and I'm working with a new young kid, James Colado, who astonished everyone when he first sat in a single-seater. In a strange car on a track he didn't know, he was the fastest out of fifty drivers, all more experienced than he was. He's got feel.

As well as interfering dads, the other thing I won't put up with on my teams is tantrums or grizzles. There was one lad – I won't embarrass him by naming him – who was a terrific little driver but whenever things went wrong he'd bawl his eyes out. I got pissed off with him but I didn't want to throw him off the team, so I called all of them together for a meeting. I'd bought some 'Baby on Board' stickers from Mothercare with a picture of a stork carrying a baby and said, 'You see these? There are two sizes. Anyone who acts like a baby will be looking at the smaller one in the middle of his steering wheel while everyone else will see the bigger one on the back of his seat. And he'll have to race with them on.'

A horrified voice said, 'You wouldn't!'

'Oh yes I would. And you know I would. This is serious motorsport and you have to think and behave like young drivers, not spoilt brats in nappies.

I had to use the sticker only once.

We've had some great drivers down the years. Some drifted out of the sport when the karting days were over because we didn't initially think in terms of a progression to the bigger formulas. In the seventies I remember thinking Jackie Brown and Johnny May were exceptional drivers, but they slipped through the net. The first time I can remember thinking, This kid will become a Formula One star, was when I watched David Coulthard at Rye House. I first encountered DC when he was about thirteen. He was driving in a team in Scotland run by David Boyce, who used to sell Zip karts and equipment. David has nurtured a lot of top-class Scottish drivers, including Allan McNish, but DC was a special driver for me.

DC was already winning everything in Scotland – he was Scottish champion for a number of years in a row – and needed more competition, so David would bring him, his dad and mum and sister Lindsay down to race at Rye House. They knew if he could win there, he had a real chance. The family were incredibly dedicated and must have made a lot of sacrifices to drive up and down between the track and their home in Twynholme, often motoring through the night.

I was very impressed with DC's ability and attitude to driving and offered to take him to some meetings abroad, racing in a team with Paul Rees. The pair of them were chalk and cheese. DC was a great chaser. If for some reason he was on the back of the grid, he was always able to work his way through to the front. He seldom made a mistake. Paul Rees was more fiery. If the two of them came to the last corner together, do or die for victory, you would be thinking perhaps Paul would take it. But half the time he'd crash in the process, whereas DC was always calm and in control. He would always finish. Paul Rees was an exceptional driver and might possibly have made it, but unfortunately he didn't have the financial backing. DC's father Duncan could provide the funding required but he gave his son so much more as well and much of the success Team Coulthard has achieved over the years stems from Duncan's advice.

Of course, that worked only because DC was a good

listener. When they first came to Rye House he was very quiet and you could hardly coax a word out of him, but by the time he was seventeen he was already relaxed in front of a microphone, happy to mix with the sponsors and, if required, to go up on the stage and say a few words. I'm sure that was Duncan working in the background and making sure he learned about PR as well as driving.

When it was right for DC to move out of karts to Formula Ford, I phoned my pal Ron Carnell at the Duckhams Quest Team.

'Ron, when you're sorting out your team for next year, Coulthard is your man.'

I gave him a full rundown on DC's career, his strengths and where he needed to improve. I kept pestering him and couldn't believe it when I read he had signed someone else.

I rang him: 'Ron, you've just made the biggest mistake of your life.' And so it turned out.

David was sensational, sweeping everything before him, taking the title, becoming the Dunlop 'Star of Tomorrow' and going on to become the first winner of the McLaren/*Autosport* Young Driver of the Year Award.

That year I was invited to the Duckhams award dinner and, when it came to the speeches, the chairman said, 'Before we move on to the prizes, I have a message for Ron Carnell. Ron, when a good friend of ours like Martin Hines tells you to sign a driver, will you please do so in future?' Everyone knew I'd been pushing DC's case and laughed. Ron managed a smile through gritted teeth but he took it in good part and we have remained friends.

I've always enjoyed following DC's career. He's remained the same level-headed guy despite all the fame and attention he receives. I went to all his debut races in every formula and recall that, when he was practising for his first Formula Three drive, he was down in the dumps thinking he'd never master it. But he's one of those drivers who have feel and by the time of the race, a couple of days later, he had slipped into it and was competing up at the front. His record speaks for itself – thirteen Grand Prix wins, the fourth-highest points scorer in the history of the sport and the top British points scorer ever. I was thrilled when he stepped back on the podium at the 2008 Canadian Grand Prix. It couldn't happen to a nicer man.

Another great father-and-son team were Jason Plato and his dad Tim. Jason was a very different driver from DC. No one could ever describe him as shy and retiring – controversy seemed to follow him around and he didn't give a damn. Yet, because of the charm that made him a natural on TV in programmes such as *Fifth Gear*, few took exception to him. He was exceedingly quick and didn't like being behind anyone, so he would often try to squeeze his kart through gaps that were a little too small. Drivers in front of him couldn't give him an inch of space or he'd dive in, forcing his way through.

In his early days he was run by Neil Hann, who now owns S1, to my mind the best of the championships for junior and senior international drivers around at the moment. He came over to Zip and had several successful years, but, as he came to the end of his karting days, we had something of a mixed season, money was tight and we almost decided not to go the next year. Tim and I talked it over and agreed to give it one more go and I am so glad we did. Jason was brilliant and as a result the next season he secured a drive in the Alpha Spider championship and took it by the scruff of the neck, winning every race.

He also plagued the life out of Frank Williams, camping outside his office until the great man agreed to give him five minutes of his time. Jason managed to persuade Frank to allow him a test and finally was given the job driving the Williams

Renault Touring Car. That's the sort of determination I'm looking for in drivers. It's a style he's carried into a phenomenal touring-car career, starting with three poles in his first three races and a thoroughly deserved British Touring Car Championship in 2001.

Although I've been involved with hundreds of excellent drivers, the outstanding kid who has the F1 stamp comes round only about every four years or so. Anthony Davidson was clearly one of those. We called him Ant, not just because of his name, but because he was so small. Like his older brother Andrew – Randy Andy from *Big Brother* – Ant wasn't short of confidence. He was the master of the one-off quick lap that knocked the other drivers out of their stride. At times he wasn't the fastest driver in a race but he was incredibly difficult to beat. He just wanted to win more than anyone else. One of my earliest memories of him was in the British Championship at Kimbolton. I saw him come down the long back straight, holding off the other drivers into the tight left-hander before the right-hand hairpin. They were quicker than him on the straight but there was no way they were going to out-brake him. I stood and watched the whole race from that spot. He had karts swarming all over him but he wouldn't be beaten.

Like all successful drivers, Ant had great support from his family, especially his dad Denis. It was Denis who bought him his first kart and, as soon as he realised his son was no ordinary driver, he encouraged him to go all the way. He has kept a log of every single meeting in great detail, lap by lap through testing and right through the race. If you were in a hurry and spotted Denis coming with his book in his hand, you ducked out of the way because you knew it wouldn't be a brief chat.

After his karting career, Anthony followed the well-trodden path of Formula Ford and Formula Three before breaking into

F1. Along the way he, like DC, became McLaren/*Autosport* Young Driver of the Year. I believe he has the talent and determination to go on and become a big name in the sport over the next few years.

In 1992 we were running under the name of Vauxhall Zip Kart team and one of the Vauxhall PR people wrote an article in which she described the drivers as 'young guns'. When I read it I thought, What a great name! And from that moment we were officially called the Zip Young Guns. We painted up the trucks and karts and it was amazing how quickly the name caught on. About the same time, Murray Walker started to talk about all up-and-coming F1 drivers as young guns, which didn't do us any harm.

The first team remains one of the best ever to carry the name. It was led by Anthony Davidson, even though he was only twelve years old, and included Luke, Gary Paffett and Wesley Barber. All of them have gone on to be outstanding in their chosen branch of motorsport – Gary and Anthony in F1, Luke in GT1, while Wesley has won in single-seaters in Britain and the USA.

The Young Guns teams have been enormously successful and brought through a lot of drivers who have starred in other formulas and are going to become leading drivers in their field. Oliver Turvey is currently in Formula Three with Carling motorsport. Mike Conway is a year or so younger than Luke and won the 2007 British F3 championship. He is now in GP2 and a test driver on Honda's F1 team. Our 2001-2 USA British Cadet champion James Calado is driving Formula Renault with Fortec.

In the early 1990s we were joined by two other drivers who are often in the headlines. Neither of them went on to drive F1 – although I think one of them could if he'd wanted to. But I gather his family might have objected.

Chapter 28
By Appointment

'**M**artin, how would you like to make a couple of karts for the future king and his brother?' It was Martin Howell phoning out of the blue.

I hesitated for a nanosecond and said, 'Why not?'

It turned out that Martin and Bob Pope, the guys I had helped launch indoor karting, had arranged some secret sessions for Princes William and Harry. The boys had loved it and now they wanted to try outdoors. The track at Buckmore Park was booked and only Martin, track boss Bill Sisley and I knew when and where it was happening. We were sworn to utmost secrecy. I had a couple of Young Guns suits made so William and Harry would look the part and built two karts. I'd imagined they would want numbers one and two but in fact the security guys insisted on 10 for William and 11 for Harry, the numbers used instead of names by the secret service in the case of an emergency.

They wanted to take part in real races, so I had to provide half a dozen drivers from my team but I couldn't let them know what they were going to do. I rang the night before and told them where to meet, and it was only when we were in the motor home on the way to Buckmore Park that I revealed who they would be racing against. Even so, the secret leaked out somehow. The track is in a dip overlooked by the M2 and on the other side of the motorway there are some high trees where the security guards found a number of photographers with massive lenses on their cameras perched like vultures. They dragged them out and sent them on their way. We were allowed to take our cameras in but, in those pre-digital days, the films were taken by palace officials to be developed and the prints sent on to us.

Yet, for all the security, pictures still reached the press. The next day I had to drive to Donington and, when I stopped at a service station, I was amazed to see every front page had a picture of William and Harry driving Zip karts. That was followed up by a series of features in several magazines, including *Hello!*. Vauxhall were our sponsors at the time and I reckon they got their money's worth that one day alone. But I swear it wasn't me who put the pictures out.

Despite all the security, it was a very relaxed and informal day. We were briefed on the etiquette: Princess Diana was to be addressed as ma'am, the boys by their names. We were introduced and within a few minutes the two princes were off playing with the other lads while their mother joined us in the motor home for a chat about what we had planned. It must have been successful, because we were asked to stage several other days and each time William and Harry became more confident behind the wheel and a bit quicker. And each event seemed to attract even more press coverage, especially when Princess Diana chose to bring the boys karting rather than attend the Queen Mother's birthday celebrations.

Over the years since her death, there have been acres of rain forest used to print stories about Princess Diana. I can speak only as I find, and she was always fantastic with us. She was very relaxed, clearly adored her boys and was happy because they were enjoying themselves. I have certainly dealt with many parents who weren't nearly as easy to get along with. In fact, I had only one problem with her. On one occasion I wore my Harley-Davison jacket that I'd kept from the days when I rode a Harley. She was wearing her Hard Rock Café windcheater and said, 'Martin, that is a very nice jacket. I think I'm going to have that one day.'

'No you ain't, ma'am,' I replied. And she never did.

All this was going on about the time of the rumours about the 'Squidgy' tapes and, as soon as the newspapers realised I had met Princess Diana, they plagued me with calls wanting me to tell them what had been said. But I liked the woman and, anyway, didn't fancy spending the rest of my life in the Tower, so I didn't say a word.

We used to have a handicap system to give the princes a chance against the Young Guns who had been driving regularly for years. William and Harry would have a start, followed in order by our slower boys, then the fastest lads setting off about ten seconds behind. It made for some good racing, but Harry wasn't too chuffed when he was beaten by William and decided to do something about it.

I became aware there was a problem only when William, who was playing computer games with Luke and Gary Paffett at the back of the motor home, looked out of the window and said, 'Martin, go and see what Harry's up to – I think he's cheating.'

When I got outside, Harry was standing next to his kart with Johnny Herbert, who was acting as host for the day.

'What's going on here?' I asked.

Harry said, 'There's lead on my kart and it's slowing me down. I want it taken off.'

'Sorry, you can't do that. The lead's on there because

William weighs more than you do, so it evens things up and makes it fair.'

'I don't want things to be even. I want to win.'

He looked at Johnny Herbert for support, but Johnny shrugged and said, 'There's nothing I can do. Martin's in charge and, if he says the lead must stay, that's it.'

Harry wasn't happy. He took a spanner and tried to prise the lead off. I was impressed by his enterprise, determination and, above all, his desire to win.

I said, 'Harry, you can't take the lead off. For one thing, William's spotted what you're doing and won't let you get away with it. But one day you might be in a position to do me a favour, so I'm going to help you out. We won't fill your petrol tank to the top.'

He looked at me suspiciously. 'But that will mean I can't finish the race.'

'Don't worry. There'll be enough for you to finish the race but you won't weigh as much as the other karts. You'll have achieved what you wanted without anyone knowing.'

He liked the sound of that and grinned. I've not been at all surprised that he got into several scrapes while he was growing up, or that he insisted on fighting in Afghanistan. Even back then he was a character in his own right, someone who quickly made up his mind what he wanted to do and went about it wholeheartedly. William was a good driver, picking up the basics very quickly, but Harry had that extra something. Driving came more easily to him and I think that, if he had wanted to, or been allowed to, he might have become a reasonable racing driver. He'd impressed me by his attitude and the way he'd improved each time he'd driven.

And remember: he was racing against Luke and Gary Paffett, two youngsters I was convinced were going to be superstars.

Chapter 29
And This is Gary

One of the things I emphasise to all my young drivers is that motorsport is a team game. You may be the guy in the driving seat, the one who bathes in the glory and has his name in the paper, but without the team behind you, especially your engineer, you ain't diddly squat. Driver and engineer must be best mates. They must constantly talk to each other, party together and share everything, except perhaps girlfriends. The relationship must be so tight that the guys in the pit don't think twice about crawling out of bed at six in the morning and working through to the early hours of the following morning because they feel the victory is theirs as much as the driver's.

I've always had a great relationship with my teams and once flew round the world to spring a surprise on Steve Eaton, who was in the pits alongside Russell Anderson when I won the 1983 World Championship. Steve was a very funny guy and a great mate. He was not only a terrific mechanic, but was one of those people who can even make the boring process of travelling fun. On one of our trips to Australia, Steve met Cheryl, the sister of one of my friends and moved in with her.

For a period after his visa ran out, they came back to the UK and stayed with us. He was just the latest in a long line of 'lodgers'. We always had open house with members of the team staying over or sharing our holidays and Christmas - Colombian driver Gonzalo Tunjo was with us for 18 months. When Steve sorted out his visa problems they moved back to Australia and we heard they were planning to marry in Adelaide and wanted Tina and me to be there.

Our friends Dave and Barbara Hepworth phoned to see if we were going and I said we were but wanted it to be a surprise. They were immediately up for it and agreed to help, along with another couple we knew well, Bob and Deb Loveday. We telephoned Steve and told him as much as we would have loved to have been at the wedding, we couldn't get away. We had a couple of returned phone calls, pleading with us to change our minds, but we kept saying it was impossible.

There were a lot of racing people going over from England, so we had to be a bit careful not to be spotted in case someone let slip they had seen us. We decided to fly into Sydney and spend some time there before travelling down on the morning of the wedding. We were greeted at the airport by a huge crowd of young people and I thought, Blimey, someone's let it out that I'm coming! But then I found out they were waiting for Michael Jackson. They took no notice of me at all; not good for the ego. Sydney was a washout. It never stopped raining, Bondai beach looked more like Dunkirk and Tina and I ended up staring through the raindrops running down the window of the tour bus we'd taken just to stay dry. I phoned Dave, who told us it was sunny in Adelaide, so we decided we'd head there and hope we could keep out of sight.

The wedding was going to be held at Hardy's winery at Reynella, about 20 miles outside Adelaide, and when we did a recce we realised that if we took Bob's car – he's a private eye so it had heavily tinted windows – we could approach very near on the day without being seen. We found the glade where they were going to have the photos taken and it was perfect for our plan.

Tina and I went back to sunbathing in Dave and Barbara's garden but had to make a dash for it when the dogs started to bark and we heard someone coming round the back. Tina dived into the loo and shut the door and I rushed behind a shed. It was rough, overgrown ground and, as I stood there in just a pair of shorts, I couldn't help but remember the stories I'd heard of Australia's snakes and deadly spiders. Woodcote at 140 m.p.h. is fine, but poisonous spiders are something else and I shuddered at the slightest movement in the grass.

I hadn't moved quickly enough, anyway, and Ballsy, another mate from Oz, had spotted me. We made him promise not to let on he'd seen us, threatening that he would need a new nickname if he breathed a word.

Our plan worked perfectly. There was a slight hitch when we found the gate to the winery locked and I had to lift Tina over in a very tight-fitting number. It wasn't elegant but we just about managed and took our position hidden behind the shrubs.

The wedding party came out and, after the family photos were taken, Dave took his cue and said, 'It's a pity your mate ain't here.'

Steve said, 'Yeah, that's the only disappointment that Martin couldn't be here'

At that I came in from one side, Tina from the other, and the whole place erupted in cheers. There were lots of hugs, a few tears and then a fantastic party. The old team was back together and we always knew how to party.

After winning sixteen major titles I felt a bit like an old gunslinger with nothing left to prove except that he could still outdraw the kids who fancied going up against him. There were some good young drivers out there but I still fancied my chances of showing them a clean pair of wheels. However, some things had changed. Luke was starting to reveal signs of real talent and I discovered I got as much of a buzz out of helping him develop alongside my other Young Guns as I did out of driving. And Gary Paffett had excited the hell out of me from the first day I saw him drive.

I'd taken Luke to race at Clay Pigeon, a track between Dorchester and Yeovil, and noticed this youngster in a Zip kart. He was very sharp, unflustered in a crowd and had the measure of drivers who were clearly older than he was. I went over and said hello to his dad, who introduced himself as Jim Paffett.

'And this is Gary,' he said.

Jim told me they drove club events only in their own neck of the woods because they couldn't afford to travel the country. He was clearly chuffed that I'd picked out Gary from the rest of the other drivers and even more pleased when I offered him a deal that meant he could buy his kit at trade prices. I said to Gary, 'Just make sure you have your Zip stickers displayed prominently.' He nodded enthusiastically, his eyes shining as if to say he would have Zip tattooed on his chest if necessary.

I kept an eye on his progress and was impressed with his results. Jim was not having such a good time. His MOT garage wasn't working out and he told me they might have to quit karting and were thinking of moving back to Kent, where they had originally lived. I had a feeling about this kid and made a snap decision.

'Jim, you've been around karts for years and I can always use a good mechanic. Why don't you come and work for me? We'll enrol Gary into the same school as Luke and I'll see what I can do about some accommodation.' I also gave his wife Jan a job in the office when they first moved up to Hoddesdon. It was one of those impulsive acts you do because they feel right. From that day, the Paffetts became part of the team.

Luke and Gary went everywhere together and on one trip in 1993 I was able to introduce them to their first superstar. It happened in the week leading up to the Superkart GP at Silverstone. With F1 cars testing on the circuit ahead of the British GP, kart drivers were not allowed in until after 7 p.m. on Thursday, but, because of my long association with the event, we were let in at midday and given the prime parking spot for our motor home behind garages one and two, where McLaren were set up. The kids were already excited because they were going to race on a small circuit we set up for cadets near Woodcote, and as we started to walk around they were wide-eyed, realising they were in the middle of the McLaren camp. Just at that moment Ayrton Senna came out of their huge Marlboro motor home.

'Martin, what are you doing here?' he asked.

It was probably the first time the lads realised I really did know Brazil's triple World Champion as well as I'd said. I told him we were preparing for the kart GP, then added, 'Ayrton you must meet these young men, who are looking to take over from you one day.'

The kids were completely awestruck but he was so friendly they soon relaxed and they started to feel like film stars when a TV company that was making a documentary about Ayrton asked him to greet them all over again, this time with the cameras running.

In many ways I treated Gary better than my own son. Gary was a year older and, while Luke was still a novice, Gary was already on it and winning. He would always be just that bit ahead, so, inevitably, when we had to find the budget to move him up to single-seaters, there was less for Luke following behind.

On top of this Luke was still having problems with his health. He came second in the 1994 Cadet Championship but soon afterwards we noticed a change in him. He no longer wanted to play his computer games and he even talked differently. It was as though he were getting younger, not older. We continued racing but, while you couldn't say he was driving badly, he'd lost his sparkle. He also became lethargic, especially in the mornings, not wanting to get up and, once up, falling asleep all the time. He was not eating properly and complained of stomach ache. The normal thoughts of bullying ran through our minds but were soon dismissed by the school and, when his skin started to look pale and his eyes sunken, Tina and I decided we needed medical help.

Once again we were lucky in our choice of doctor. She immediately recognised that Luke might have ME post-viral syndrome, which was still a controversial illness at that stage, with many doctors not certain it even existed as a separate complaint and some papers labelling it 'yuppie flu'. But our GP not only picked up on the symptoms, but took them seriously, although she told us treatment was still in its early days. We started to research ME and turned for advice to a friend, who we had watched go from being the vibrant life and soul of every party to needing to be pushed around in a wheelchair since being diagnosed with ME. We were determined this was not going to happen to Luke. We were recommended to consult a London specialist, Dr Paul Sherwood, a retired surgeon who believes in the power of massage. As well as running a successful clinic, he's written a number of books on the subject. He soon confirmed Luke's diagnosis and came up with an explanation of the probable causes.

He said, 'Luke's lymph glands are blocked, probably due to a tiny piece of tonsil left after the operation he had when he was two, and which has started to grow and become infected ever since. If you add that to the fact that he was pumped full of antibiotics for months after his accident, his immune system's shot to pieces.'

Once again, Luke had to endure an operation. They removed the last vestige of tonsil and then, back at the clinic, the work began on clearing his lymph glands. Travelling to London almost daily became too much, so Dr Sherwood allowed our physio, Steve, to carry on the programme. For what seemed an age there was little sign of progress, then one morning Luke came into the bedroom to see Tina and me and it was immediately obvious he had changed. He was sharper and was talking like his old self again. He will never be completely cured – cold weather affects him and, if he has a particularly gruelling race weekend, he needs to rest for half a day to recover – but he never complains and once again we were fortunate in having people who knew what they were doing and a sympathetic and supportive school.

Meanwhile, Gary was living up to all the promise he had shown when I first spotted him. In 1994 he was runner-up in the British TKM championship and went one better the following year as well as earning second place in the Europeans. The day he clinched the British title – 24 September – Luke also won a major championship and David Coulthard won his first F1 GP in Portugal. I slept very contentedly that night.

There was also another new kid on the block and he was a bit special too.

Chapter 30

Ron, I'd Like You to Meet Lewis Hamilton

Princes William and Harry weren't the only people Martin Howell and Bob Pope introduced me to. It was they who first put me together with Ron Dennis, the McLaren supremo, a meeting that was to have a profound effect on many people's lives and create a new stepladder between karting and F1.

Again, it started with a phone call from Martin. He had organised a special kart meeting with all the F1 manufacturers putting a team in. Ron was driving along with Ray Bellm and Nick Mason for McLaren, but they needed a fourth and Martin wanted to know if I fancied it.

We had a great day and Ron and I hit it off straightaway. Shortly afterwards he asked me to supply him with a couple of karts and a trailer for his children. I already knew enough about him to realise I was taking on a daunting task – Ron was a stickler for detail and would want everything 100 per cent with all the bells and whistles that would make his outfit the best. Screw up on this and a promising new friendship might not only be off on the gravel but smashed against the Armco barriers. The karts were no problem, but we had to bring some people in to help make the trailer. In the end it was spot on, right down to the push-button gas doors, and it was the perfect match for Ron's Merc 4x4.

Over the years our friendship grew and by chance Tina and I were having dinner with Ron and his wife Lisa the night he signed Nigel Mansell to drive for McLaren in the 1995 season. There had been plenty of speculation in the press that Ron had persuaded Nigel to give it one more go and they had made the announcement that afternoon. Over dinner, Ron said how difficult it was to find and keep the right drivers and I took the opportunity to get something off my chest I'd wanted to say for a long time to someone in his position.

'Ron, you guys spend millions on finding and developing your drivers, but I reckon you're starting too late. For just a fraction of the money you pay out, you could be sponsoring the best young kart drivers, teaching them your ways and moulding them into perfect McLaren team members. Along the way you would enjoy great PR because you would be helping kids who might not have the chance otherwise. And at the end of it you wouldn't have to pay them as much because those that made it would have to repay what you'd already invested in them.' He seemed interested, but as the wine flowed, the conversation changed and no more was said.

But I was sure I was on to something and sketched out a package of TV events that would include the top kids in the country. I needed a six-figure sponsorship and decided to go back to Ron. He had lots of contacts and an introduction from him would be a great help.

I spelt it out: 'This would be the cream of British kart drivers with regular exposure on terrestrial TV. The racing will be terrific – we'll only allow the top twenty-eight drivers in each class to compete – and I'm sure we can build up good viewing figures. And, incidentally, it'll give people like you the opportunity to spot drivers at a very early stage.'

He asked me a few questions then said, 'Shake my hand. I've bought it.'

I was taken aback. Before accepting, I made sure he wasn't just doing this out of friendship. I saw this as a long-term project and wanted a sponsor who was committed to it as much as I was. He assured me he was interested only because he believed in it, and we shook hands. The McLaren Mercedes Champions of the Future was born.

The most important thing now was to secure terrestrial television coverage, so I contacted Marie Nicholson of BHP, the leading motorsport programme makers, and outlined my vision of the project. This would be a serious TV spectacular, setting a benchmark for karting on TV. She was as impressed with my enthusiasm as Ron had been. All we had to do now was persuade ITV. We met Kevin Piper, who was head of sport at Anglia, and, while he was grabbed by the idea, he was concerned the board at Anglia may not be as enthusiastic. But, between them, Marie and Kevin did a fantastic job and somehow they pulled it off. I contracted Keith Huewen as our studio commentator and DJ David 'Kid' Jensen at trackside. The stage was set for the biggest innovation to hit karting for decades and it is no coincidence that new stars such as Lewis Hamilton and Gary Paffett emerged from that opening series.

This was a super professional roadshow with everything done as though we were staging an F1 GP. All the major figures from motorsport came to the events and the viewing figures soon started to climb. Above all, it did what it said on the tin – over the years, the people who were the stars of *Champions of the Future* went on to be top-class drivers in whichever formula they chose. The first final, at Buckmore Park in October 1996, saw Gary crowned at one end of the age range and Lewis at the other. Exactly ten years later those two were contracted to McLaren and battling it out on the track again to see who would partner Fernando Alonso in 2007.

Lewis won and went on to catch the imagination of the public in a way no British driver had for years. Journalists were desperate for every detail of this young phenomenon's life and my phone almost went into meltdown with a constant stream of callers wanting to know about this incredible new talent. I was happy to confirm that the talent was incredible but it was certainly not new.

I had first seen him at Rye House when I was there with Luke and Gary. As always, I took in the cadet practice and races and could hardly believe what I was watching. To make racing safer, there is a system by which new drivers have a black number plate for their first eight races – a kind of 'L' plate that warns other drivers, 'Be careful, I'm new and might do something completely stupid.' This particular day there was an eight-year-old kid with black plates near the front of the field when he should have been at the back, and he certainly wasn't doing anything stupid. I think he finished fourth overall that day, which was incredible. On top of that he was black, which was quite unusual in karting at that time. I knew I had to find out more.

I sought out his dad, Anthony, introduced myself and asked him how many races Lewis had been in, expecting to hear it was his eighth.

'This is the first one,' he said.

'Bloody hell! That kid is seriously talented. What are you planning to do?'

Anthony explained that it was a struggle to fund the racing, even though he was holding down two jobs. But he recognised that Lewis was a rare talent and was determined to do all he could to help him fulfil his dream. I invited them to the factory the next day and we sorted out some technical backup and discount on parts, and that was the start of a relationship that lasted seven years in karts, and remains on a personal level today.

As I've already said (though in different words), my life would be much easier if all kart drivers were orphans. Fathers can be the bane of my life. The majority seem to find it impossible to stand back and coldly assess if their son has the talent, the determination and drive to win. Only a few drivers have that magic combination but, instead of recognising the fact and settling for some fun racing, most dads make excuses and fool themselves. They think that, if they throw money at the problem, it will sort itself out, but even the best machine is no use without the right driver. In the end, their unreal expectations make their own and their son's disappointment even greater.

Anthony Hamilton wasn't one of those fathers. I don't think it's an exaggeration to say that, without Anthony's guidance, Lewis wouldn't be where he is today. He not only nurtured the kid's natural will to win, but instilled in him how to be focused and how to act. It was Anthony who steered him through the minefield of motorsport so that he came out the other end unspoilt and untarnished. They both got great support from Lewis's stepmum Linda and his brother Nick, who is very much part of the team.

It took no time at all for Lewis to climb through the ranks. At around 5 foot tall, wiry and strong, he was the perfect build for a kart driver. He had a fierce will to be first, combined with great feel and an ice-cool brain He was simply too good for most other kids. I can still see in my mind's eye the day at Clay Pigeon when he produced an almost impossible break from third on the grid to take the lead. Clay is a very fast start – you come off into a left-hander, down into a tight right hand corner and immediately into a chicane. With the quality of field he was racing against and the way the circuit is, there was no way he should have taken the lead. He made it only because he was so determined that he would not be denied. The three karts locked together with Lewis in the middle of the sandwich. Displaying nerves of absolute steel he got his wheels in front going into the chicane and from there on made the race his. It was one of those defining moments when I knew he was something special.

He had an instinctive ability to spot even the smallest opportunity and take advantage of it. I still occasionally watch the clip on YouTube where, on the last lap in a Champions of the Future race, he is lying fourth approaching the final chicane. There looks to be no way through but he has the savvy to let the three in front of him fight against each other while he takes a different line, whips past them on the outside and goes on to win. I've seen him do that so often. It's not luck: it's a superb driving brain working at maximum revs.

At the McLaren/*Autosport* awards dinner that year, I took Lewis and Gary Paffett to meet Ron Dennis.

I said, 'Ron, you should sign both these boys up. They are the future.'

Lewis, immaculate in his tiny dinner jacket, shook Ron's hand and said, 'Mr Dennis, one day I'm going to drive for you.' We all laughed but both Ron and I were impressed by the youngster's focus. He already knew where he wanted to be and was willing to do whatever it took to arrive there. He was different from all the others because he had such a sensible head on his shoulders – he may have been a child in years but his attitude was that of a seasoned, professional driver.

Karting is a rare sport in that it brings fathers and sons together in a relationship in which they are equal. There can be great tensions and even rows but it is a closer bond than most fathers and sons enjoy, sometimes to such an extent that the dads forget to make allowances for the fact that they are dealing with a child who will sometimes do dumb things.

I seldom remember seeing Lewis act like a child. Even in the early years he had fantastic mixture of focus, aggression and a touch of arrogance, and without those qualities you aren't going anywhere in motorsport. If he had a bad day, he didn't have a paddy or cry. The winner in him had the hump but he channelled that into finding out what went wrong. He wasn't afraid to analyse his own performance, nor scared to criticise the preparation of his kart when he felt it fell short of the required high standards.

From an early age Lewis had a champion's ability to pinpoint a problem while driving and communicate that to the people working on the kart. He could be exacting with his dad, just as Anthony could with him, but they were both aiming at the same thing: making the kart go quicker.

The thing I admired most as I got to know him and watch him drive was that he was an out-and-out racer. If things went wrong, he didn't give up and say to himself, 'It's not going to be my day.' He tried to work out a way to drive round the problem, to tease every available ounce of power out of the kart despite the setback. Few drivers are the total package – Lewis is.

His progress was faultless. He won everything there was in cadets before making the move to Formula Yamaha in 1997. This was a major step up which he made with absolute ease and took the championship in true Lewis style.

Ron Dennis was clearly impressed and signed him to the McLaren driver development programme. He included an option on him for F1, making him the youngest driver to sign an F1 contract. He provided him with a McLaren truck and full support while he continued to drive alongside our Young Guns team. Even before that, he'd helped cover the cost of his racing. You could tell Ron was excited by the youngster. He watched his progress and would phone me to ask how he was doing. I didn't even have to exaggerate when I told him how much promise he had. 'OK, keep me in touch and, if he needs anything, send us the bills.'

Lewis's next step up the ladder was the Junior Intercontinental A, the highest junior category in this formula, where he would receive another huge jump in power and grip from the sticky Bridgestone tyres. Lewis at thirteen would be battling against seasoned campaigners up to three years older than he was, but even this didn't faze him. He battled from round one with the very best the formula could throw at him and managed second place in his first season, losing out on the title by a couple of points to Fraser Sheader after a few mechanical mishaps.

Following that, he went to Europe and raced for Top Kart, an Italian company whose karts we distribute in the UK and who make our cadet formula engines. He was competing against all the leading teams, who were throwing millions of pounds at it and were able to test two or three days a week while he had to learn about new tyres and driving on unknown tracks; but against all the odds he again came second. It was a phenomenal achievement and meant that, after years without a challenger in Europe, we had now achieved three second places in the past few years, because Gary and Luke had also beaten the system. All three of them were unlucky not to finish first.

We all knew Lewis was a potential World Champion. He eventually became European champion in 2000 and the following year, still only sixteen years old, raced karts against Michael Schumacher, who rightly noticed that Lewis's great strength is his racing mentality. It was time for him to step up to single-seaters.

I think there were a few anxious moments at McLaren when

Lewis went into Formula Renault and had a tough first year. They had expected him to become an instant superstar and perhaps a few doubts crept in. My own feeling was that he would have been better taking an intermediate step up into Formula Ford or my own Zip Formula, where he would have learned to work on mechanical advantage rather than aerodynamic trickery before moving on to cars with wings and down force. I believe all drivers should go through a stage where they learn to drive by the seat of their pants. I also feel Lewis suffered comparisons with Kimi Räikkönen, who was believed to have swept the board in his first year in Formula Renault, but in fact that was a myth. Kimi had driven in England the year before and not done well, and so had gone unnoticed, and had also driven single-seaters back home in Finland, so he too took a while to adjust. Sure enough, the following year Lewis showed that he was now completely at home with the car and won the championship. He followed that up with success in Formula Three and GP2 before Ron decided he was ready for F1.

Although I love watching the Grand Prix, I have to admit that I usually record those that are going on across the other side of the world and watch them when I get up, but I set the alarm for Lewis's F1 debut in Australia and it was worth every second of lost sleep – to achieve a podium finish in his first race was outstanding. I sent him a text message with just one word: 'Fantastic'.

But, as we now know, it was to get even better. Some people said it was just because he was in the best car but they overlooked the fact that Ron Dennis could have had the pick of drivers and he chose to put Lewis in the best car because he knew what a great talent he was. It's incredible now to think that no one – not even Lewis, I suspect – dreamed he could finish second in the world championship in his rookie year, yet when he did everyone felt disappointed. And, to my mind, rightly so. He should have won it. In my view McLaren made some appalling errors and ridiculous decisions during the final Grand Prix in Brazil. They were trying to be too clever. He only had to follow Räikkönen round to win the title, but they left him out too long before changing his tyres.

But you have to admire the way Lewis handled the disappointment and bounced back for the 2008 season stronger than ever, even though his car was not the fastest any more. Arguably, it was third fastest after Ferrari and BMW, yet his stunning victory in Monaco just underlined what a complete driver he is. I can't remember before seeing someone hit the wall, pick up a puncture and go on to victory, all in such style in dreadful conditions. While some of the best drivers in the world were making mistakes, he drove faultlessly.

Even more impressive was his victory in the British Grand Prix at Silverstone. I watched the race from 'Hamilton Hill' together with Tina, Tuesday and a cross-fingered Linda Hamilton. It was just like the old karting days again and reminded me of all those occasions we've been together at races at different venues over the last 14 years. Of course, this was no ordinary venue and the whole occasion had extra significance because if you believe what you read in the papers, Lewis only had two more chances to win a Grand Prix at Silverstone before it is moved to Donington in 2010. I'm not so sure. I tend to believe this is just another throw of the dice in the ongoing game between Bernie Ecclestone and the BRDC. I very much doubt that Donington can make all the changes needed to the circuit and the roads in two years even if, as reported, there is an enormous pile of money to throw at it. You never know, Bernie might own Silverstone in two years, so my money is on us all being gathered again at the Abbey chicane and hopefully seeing another masterclass from Lewis.

He will do well to top his first British GP win though. I think it is certainly his greatest drive to date, especially when you consider the pressure that had been heaped on him in the media, the expectations of the home fans and the good old British weather. I have spent 40 years watching some of the most talented drivers in the universe in all possible conditions and Lewis's victory by more than a minute at Silverstone – and remember at the age of 22 – was nothing short of Senna-like and I can't pay him a bigger compliment than that. The pressure he endured driving on intermediate tyres throughout in the most challenging of conditions was quite remarkable. He remained super cool and wasn't tempted once to squeeze the throttle pedal too hard,

We had several glasses of wine in the Hamilton family motor home afterwards and I asked Lewis, 'What did the team say when you came up to lap Alonso and Raikkonen?'

He gave me a cheeky grin and said: 'You are OK to back off and sit where you are.'

I could tell how much he loved it as he lapped them both but, to be fair to them, they showed great sportsmanship in slowing and getting out of his way. It was a wonderful afternoon and certainly answered those critics who were quick to jump on his back and it showed the rest of the world what some of us have known for years – this guy is not only a great driver, he has incredible guts and character.

People often ask me what difference being black has made to Lewis's career. In the early days we were all certainly conscious of the fact that he was almost the only black kid in karting but as the years went on I think it has become irrelevant. I believe the comparison with Tiger Woods is very powerful. Both were black in a white sport and therefore had the eyes of both communities on them, either critically or in admiration. It was an added pressure that white sportsmen didn't have, yet Tiger and Lewis rose above it because of their talent and also the way they went about their business. They used the pressure to help them focus. If they had a bad day at the office they knew it would attract extra attention. They accepted it and would go out next time and perform better than ever. Both have gone beyond being great black sportsmen and are now just world-class sportsmen.

It's given me enormous satisfaction to see Lewis come through, take his place as one of F1's superstars and to know I had a little part to play in his success both with the support I was able to provide in the early days and by creating the Champions of the Future series, which meant he and Ron Dennis met probably six or seven years earlier than they might otherwise. Several people ask me if seeing the fame – and cash – of drivers such as Lewis and David Coulthard makes me regret never having a go at F1 myself. I can honestly say no. When I was at the peak of my karting career, the opportunities weren't as clearly available as they are today and the thought never crossed my mind. I also believe that, while I was a top kart driver, I didn't necessarily have the feel to adapt to the single-seater. Of course, like every other motorsport fan in the world, I wondered what it would be like to drive an F1 car. And, thanks to Ron Dennis, I got the chance to find out.

Chapter 31

Now That's What I Call a Party

Motorsport is full of amazing characters with big egos and often a reputation for being something of a bastard. You hear loads of stories of how ruthless this guy has been or how that bloke shafted someone. But there have been stories like that about me, so I tend not to take them at face value. I don't think of myself as a tough person to do business with but I've been bitten enough times to try to stay one jump ahead of the game and most of those who tend to criticise me for driving a hard bargain are the people who have tried to put one over on me and failed.

Because of this, I always find it interesting to compare the public image with the person I meet. To read some reports, you would think that Bernie Ecclestone is the devil incarnate, a James Bond villain intent on world domination and stashing every penny he can lay his hands on in a private vault hidden somewhere deep within a mountain.

I've met Bernie only a few times but I have to say I didn't have that impression at all. I think he's one of the shrewdest people in any walk of life and he has done more for motorsport than any other single individual. Just think where

F1 was twenty years ago. We enthusiasts used to follow it avidly but 90 per cent of the people in the street were hardly aware it was going on. Now, largely thanks to Bernie and the way he has packaged the sport for TV, it is attracting nearly 600 million viewers and each Grand Prix generates more than $200 million.

Sure, Bernie takes his share of that, but I don't think that's what motivates him. He hasn't enough time to *burn* all his money, let alone spend it. I'm sure Bernie sees it all as a contest and the money is how he measures whether he is winning or losing – though I doubt he often thinks of himself as losing.

He transformed a product that at times is not the most interesting of spectacles – most people, including those who know a lot about the sport, can't really see much from the grandstand. You just catch a glimpse of a helmeted head flashing by in a car and it's difficult to know whether success or failure is down to the individual gripping the wheel or the guys in the pit lane controlling the computer. Yet millions of people are enthralled by every minute, even watching practice sessions. Onboard cameras and other technical advances for coverage have helped. The ever-present possibility of a massive shunt keeps some people watching.

But the real reason more than a hundred thousand people turn up at tracks across the world and the BBC coughed up an enormous sum of licence payers' money to snatch back the rights from ITV is that F1 is a soap opera. It is *Dallas* with turbocharged storylines packed with thrills, spills and testosterone, larger-than-life characters, beautiful women and enough money to have even the innocent looking over their shoulder for muggers.

The 2007 season was a classic soap story. If you had sat down at the start of the year and written a script, you couldn't have improved on reality. Indeed, I reckon a Hollywood writer would have had his work thrown back at him if he'd packed into one script the Hamilton–Alonso battles, the McLaren spy scandal and the amazing finale fought out in the Brazilian sun, where the rookie just misses out. But that was exactly what kept the media and the public enthralled throughout the season and the man who was switched on enough all those years ago to know which way the sport had to go to survive was, I believe, Bernie Ecclestone.

Then there's Ron Dennis. I have spent a lot more time with Ron and done a lot more business with him than with Bernie, but I wouldn't claim I know him all that well. I'm not sure many people do. He is something of an enigma. I have enormous admiration for the fact that he left school at sixteen to become an apprentice mechanic and from there rose to be the driving force behind one of the most successful racing teams in the world, a feature in the *Sunday Times* Rich List. Yet, on the couple of times I've mentioned how much I respect what he's achieved, he's just brushed it aside as though he doesn't want to think about the past.

Ron is the kind of guy you can be sitting with having an amiable social drink and a few minutes later he will walk past you, eyes narrowed, and totally blank you. It's not rudeness or arrogance: it's just that he is completely involved in what is on his mind in that moment and the rest of the world is irrelevant.

This may all be explained by the fact that he's a Gemini. I hadn't realised he was born on 1 June until Tina and I were invited to his fiftieth-birthday celebration in 1997 – and what a party that turned out to be! Whatever anyone says about Ron, no one can claim he doesn't like a good time or that he lacks imagination.

Our invitation said we had to meet at an airfield on a Friday night and would be home again late on Sunday. It also contained a bizarre list of things we had to take with us, everything from formal evening dress to the strangest swimming cap we could find. Most of the things were so unusual Tina had to spend two days shopping for them, yet when we arrived at the airfield we were told to put our cases to one side because we wouldn't need them!

Instead, a button was pushed and the front doors of a hangar eased open, revealing a row of benches and changing screens. Within a few minutes many of the biggest names in motorsport were kitted out in army uniforms. We were then split up into six teams of eight. There was plenty of laughter, some of it quite nervous, when each team had an SAS man attached to it. Tina and I were in the Orange team along with Keke Rosberg, Martin Whitmarsh and John Watson and their partners.

The military theme continued when we heard the distinctive sound of helicopters approaching and a few minutes later they appeared low over the brow of the nearby hill like something out of *Apocalypse Now*. We all clambered in and were whisked off to a field in the Cotswolds, where we were transferred into old-fashioned army trucks with canvas sides and driven at high speed along country lanes to a campsite in the middle of nowhere. Two-man tents were dotted around the field, which was surrounded by woodland. What the hell was going on? This is certainly not what Tina expected when she bought an expensive new evening dress.

We may have felt like army rookies but no raw recruits had ever been to a camp like this. There was a luxury shower and toilet block, a barn that turned out to be an open bar stocked better than most five-star hotels, and the mess 'chow' was a whole pig, roasted in a covered pit, Polynesian style. The party was in full swing as dusk fell but the merriment was interrupted by a siren and a voice over the Tannoy warning there was an air raid. Within seconds we were in the middle of one of the most spectacular and certainly the loudest fireworks display I have ever experienced. The explosions were deafening and shook the ground and I reckon were as close a simulation of an air raid as you can get without actually dropping bombs.

Ron's sense of humour came to the fore with the next item. Having survived the 'bombing' we were treated to a big-screen showing of the Korean War medics movie *M*A*S*H*, after which the celebrations went on well into the night.

Some of us perhaps partied more than we would if we'd known what was to follow the next day: a series of events, ranging from paint balling to stripping a cannon and transporting it across a river. We crawled under nets and climbed over barriers, all to gain points for our team. Even with hangovers, motorsport people are highly competitive and, with our SAS men barking advice, the Orange team did OK. The action was interrupted only for one of the most splendid lunches I've ever enjoyed, served in a picturesque farmyard while we sat on straw bales.

That evening, tired but elated, we were taken to Sudley Castle, once the home of Catherine Parr, the only queen to survive Henry VIII, and now owned by Henry Brocklehurst, close friend of Liz Hurley. We were shown to a group of pretty stone cottages, where we found that our suitcases had been unpacked and our clothes beautifully pressed and laid out ready for the evening. We dined magnificently in the medieval banqueting hall and were entertained right royally with music and dancing. After a leisurely Sunday morning and lunch in the castle, we were picked up by helicopter once more and taken back to our cars.

None of us who were invited will ever forget that weekend, which, typically of Ron Dennis, was carried off with great style and immaculate planning. He and I have had several disagreements over the years but I am always proud to say he is a friend. Most of our bust-ups have been because I tend to say what I think without worrying too much about the effect it will have, as Ron has pointed out to me on more than one occasion. One day, after I sounded off far too quickly, he said, 'Martin, you should wait twenty-four hours before opening your mouth because it may seem different then.' It's advice I have never forgotten and have followed on more than one occasion, but it's not always easy. I can't bear it when people hum and haw around a subject and then go away and slag you off behind your back. Say what you think and let's get on with it.

Just because I've told Ron when I've disagreed with him, it doesn't mean that I don't like the guy and I reckon he must quietly feel the same way, because he did let me loose on one of his stunning F1 cars.

Chapter 32

Upside Down and Nowhere to Go

It all started at one of those charity dinners where they raise shedloads of money by auctioning off things you normally can't lay your hands on. I like to support these occasions and have bought a number of items over the years, including some magnificent photographs that line my walls at home. This day I was one of the people who bid to go round Silverstone for a few laps in a McLaren road car driven by Martin Brundle. I'd arranged that, halfway round, Martin would let me take over the driving but it never came off – the gear lever went on the car just before I was due to go out. 'Don't worry,' Ron said, 'I'll make it up to you.' He did, and how.

A few weeks later I got a call from Dave Ryan, the New Zealander who joined McLaren in 1974 and became their team manager.

'Martin, can you come down for a seat fitting? Ron's going to let you have a go in the McLaren.'

'Sure, but why do I need a seat fitting for a road car?'

'It's not the road car: he's going to let you drive Mika's new car.'

'I'm on my way.'

It turned out that I fitted Mika Häkkinen's seat perfectly and was also given a set of his overalls with MH on. I've still got them and, even if Ron wants them back when he reads this, he's got no chance. Dave told me they wanted me to do some aerodynamic testing at Danielson, a big airfield circuit just south of Magny Cours, where the French GP is held. Now, if you ask most F1 drivers how they would feel at the prospect of several days' straight-line testing, they would claim they had to wash their hair and couldn't make it, but I was quite pleased – quite pleased in the way I would be if I won the lottery and been given a ticket for everlasting life on the same day. There truly was a god, his name was Ron Dennis and he had just handed me one of the greatest gifts I'd had in my life. Of course, being Ron he had to take the gloss off just a bit.

Dave said, 'The racers tend to mess about after a while but Ron thinks since you are, as he put it, very mature, you would take it seriously.'

When I arrived at Danielson I found the crew were treating me with some suspicion. I think word had got round that I was the boss's pal and was probably there to spy on them. I was certainly too old to be a racing driver in their eyes, so they were looking for a hidden agenda.

The first lunchtime, one of them asked me what I wanted to eat.

'Whatever's on offer, I'm not bothered,' I replied.

'No, you're the driver. We'll provide you with anything you want.'

'Really, I'm not bothered, whatever the chef thinks is good will suit me. By the way, if you're going into town, could you pick me up some film?' And I handed over some cash.

There was a laugh from behind me and one of the mechanics said, 'I told you he wasn't a racing driver. He's offered to pay for something. No driver has ever done that!' We'd broken the ice and from then on everyone relaxed.

That afternoon I sat in an F1 car for the first time. It was so tight in the cockpit I had to wear two different boots – one of Mika's and one of my own that had a slightly different-shaped toe and didn't drag on the cockpit above the throttle pedal. The crew talked me through how everything worked. I was excited but not nervous. I recalled that, a few years earlier, David Coulthard had tested one of my Superkarts at Silverstone for *Autosport* and afterwards he'd said, 'It's fantastic. If you shut your eyes you could imagine you are in an F1 car. The acceleration and grip are very similar and the braking is better.' I trusted DC completely,

'OK, Martin, we want you to just drive down to the end of the straight and back to get the feel of it. Nothing too quick, just get your bearings. Go out of the pit lane slowly, then, when you're on the straight, hit the accelerator. You'll see a green light come on and that will help you change up at the right revs. Signal when you're ready and we'll start the engine.'

I took a breath, raised my hand and the engine burst into life. It sounded as though I were sitting in the middle of a jet engine during takeoff. I sat there revving it to bring it up to the right temperature, then eased the car away. Then I hit the throttle. I will never forget that moment as long as I live. The whole machine shot forward, pinning me back in my seat.

'David Coulthard, you fucking lied to me,' I yelled.

This was nothing like a superkart. The bloody thing was enormous. I couldn't see the ground in front of me and when I turned the wheel, I couldn't see the corner. The wheels looked as if they belonged on a tractor compared with kart wheels. And the noise! Jeez! You could drown out a rock band with one of those babies. Most of all, I couldn't get over the sensation of speed. To be fair to DC, after five days, when I'd become used to the car, I could see what he meant, but that first run is burned into my memory even more vividly than the first time I drove a kart. I can still run it in my mind's eye like a movie and it still sends a tingle down my spine.

When I got back to the pits one of the guys said, 'If you've never driven one of these before, how come you got away without stalling? It's such a difficult clutch that everyone stalls the first time.'

I laughed. 'Yeah, but probably they haven't driven a 250cc superkart with a Rotax dry-plate clutch. If you can get one of those off the line without stalling, you can drive anything.'

I couldn't wait for my next drive. They put a new set of boots on and out I went. I hit the power, changed up to second, up to third – and found myself in a field. The car had just turned right on me. I thought, Oh no, Ron'll kill me and never let me drive again. I clambered out. I started to pick up the bits. The crew arrived and said they would clear up but I insisted on helping.

'See, we knew you weren't a real driver. They never tidy up after their shunts.'

The crew put my mind at rest about the crash. 'It wasn't your fault,' they said. 'You hit a bump and went up in the air. As you came down on one wheel, the other turned and with cold tyres you had no grip. It was just one of those things.'

That night I could hardly sleep. I was frightened I would find out I was dreaming and it wasn't really happening. I couldn't wait for the next day, to climb back into that magnificent machine. The next few days flew by. Whenever they called me in, they said it was OK for me to stretch my legs but I wasn't going to risk it. They might not let me back in. I just sat there and relished every minute. I knew I was too old ever to race one of these monsters but at least I now knew what it felt like to have all that power at your fingertips.

The guys must have been happy with the way I drove – or the way I paid my whack – because a few weeks later I was invited to go to Spain. McLaren were having some problems and wanted to find out if the front wings were moving under the down force. They had a very sophisticated system to test it with infrared lights shining on to the side of the cockpit to a gauge with a camera that would record any deflection from the norm.

My job was to go up the straight into a right-hander, up to the top into a big 180-degree swoop, then come back down the straight to another loop and back to the start. They told me to do one lap reaching 120 m.p.h. on the straight to warm up the tyres, then, on the next lap, take it up to 160 m.p.h. I would have to push really hard to maintain that speed for the time they needed for the test.

The first day went really well. That night they said they had learned a lot, so wanted to try something new. 'When you reach around the 160 m.p.h. mark we want you to pull the clutch in.' It sounded easy enough. I came off the loop, hit the throttle, watched the speed climb to 160 m.p.h. and then pulled the clutch in. It was as though I'd slammed on the brakes full force. I couldn't believe how quickly the car stopped. For a moment I thought I must have braked, but my foot was still right down on the throttle. It was just incredible that the air pressure against the car could have that effect just by shutting the power off. They sent me out again. By this time I was feeling really confident, not realising my flaw as an F1 driver was about to be dramatically exposed.

I was coming off the loop back towards the straight. There was a white line at the edge of the track with an expanse of grass to the left of it, or so I thought. In fact there was a 6-foot-deep drainage ditch right up to edge of the track so full of grass that it looked like part of the field.

I was on the power a bit early as I came round the corner. The back just stepped out a little bit, which brought the front wheel over the white line. No problem, just a quick correction and away we go. Or it wouldn't have been a problem but for the chink in my driving technique. I was used to driving a superkart with absolutely direct steering and where lock to lock is a quarter-turn of the wheel. On an F1 car with its rack system and power steering you need half a turn to obtain the same amount of movement.

I reacted with a quarter-turn. Not enough.

By the time I realised I wasn't getting the movement I needed, my wheel was in the ditch. The car somersaulted and I ended upside down and unable to release myself. The engine was still going and fuel was running over the back wings. I realised that at any minute I might be barbecued like Ron's party pig and hoped the crew had seen what had happened. Strangely, I also found time to worry about what Ron would say.

Right round the outside of the circuit was an oval track where they test buses to the limits of their endurance, and fortunately one of the drivers spotted me and radioed in that there was a car upside down in the ditch. Within minutes a whole armada of vehicles was on the spot. One of the team cut the engine and then they dragged me out. They checked me over in the ambulance but I was unhurt and went to help the crew sort things out. I was impressed how thoroughly they searched for every last bit of the wreck, sealed it up and sent it back to the factory. They missed only one small bit – I'd slipped it into my pocket and I've still got it at home.

I felt dreadful. Not for what had happened to me but because I had written off Mika Häkkinen's new car and, even though the mechanics tried to reassure me and tell me that the ditch should have been filled in years before, I knew there was plenty of room and I hadn't needed to cut that close to the white line. It was definitely my fault.

We were sitting around later when one of the senior members of the crew came in looking a bit embarrassed. They had forgotten to ask me to sign the disclaimer saying I wouldn't hold them responsible if anything happened to me. They needed me to sign it now or their jobs were on the line.

'You are joking,' I said. 'I ain't signing nothing. I'm gonna sue you.'

Their faces were a picture. I let them suffer for a few seconds then said, 'Don't be silly, fellas. I'm only joking. Give it here.'

All the way home I was thinking about what I was going to say to Ron. I had wrecked a week's testing and written off a huge chunk of money, so I guessed he wouldn't be too pleased.

Early the next morning I phoned the factory and spoke to Dave Ryan. I told him how it had happened and asked him how Ron was.

'I think it's fair to say he was a bit tetchy last night. He's at home; I'd call him if I were you.'

When I got through Ron was clearly not in the mood for small talk or even concerned about my health.

'What the fuck happened?' he demanded.

I went through my story in detail.

'Are you making excuses?' he snapped.

'No. It was me in the car. It was my fault.'

'OK. I can live with that. As long as you aren't trying to put the blame on someone else.'

That was the last we spoke about it.

McLaren covered the story up very well but of course there were soon stories on the motorsport rumour mill and a couple of months later I received a letter from Sweden from SAAB, who make jet fighters as well as cars. It read,

Dear Mr Hines,

We have heard you are extremely good at low level aerodynamics in high speed vehicles. Unfortunately we had an accident last week and lost our top test pilot so we have a vacancy to test our new jet fighter. With your recent experience in Spain we would like to offer you the job. There are lots of perks and the salary is enormous.

Yours sincerely,
Jan Kumbersen.

The only person I could think of who might try such a wind-up was Mike Nicholson, who was in charge of Vauxhall Motorsport, the sponsors of the Young Guns team. I sat down and composed a letter to him:

Dear Mike,

As much as I appreciate the help you have given me and the team over the years, I have now been offered a very lucrative job in Sweden that will take my career in an entirely different direction. Therefore I would just like to say that Vauxhall can stick their team and their money where the sun doesn't shine.

Yours sincerely,
Martin Hines.

I faxed it over and within a minute the phone rang. 'Martin, what the hell's this about?'

It quickly became apparent it hadn't been Mike who sent the hoax letter. Luckily, he saw the funny side of it. I faxed him a copy of the SAAB letter and he phoned me back.

'It's a great job. Who could it be?'

I suddenly fell in. 'Mike, look at the signature. Jan Kumbersen is your bleedin' boss. It's Ian Coomber and son.' I'd known Ian for some time and his son Mike was a former Young Gun; they'd obviously got wind of what had happened and decided to pull my leg.

That wasn't the end of the wind-ups. Ian Coomber had also told Derek Redfern at Haymarket, the publishers of *Autosport*, and he sent me a very authentic-looking letter on McLaren notepaper, signed by Ron Dennis, advising me in scathing terms that any thoughts I had of becoming an F1 driver should be forgotten. It was accompanied by a bill for £5,877,960, which included, among other items:

Monocoque MP 4/11 (new) £1,800,000.00
Mormo steering wheel (unused) £1,450.00
Diarrhoea tablets (large box) £4.50
Team laundry (underwear) £6.60
Books – 'He taught me all I know' by D Coulthard, special offer £2.95
RAC post accident scrutineering £48.00
RAC bar bill £620.00

The giveaway was 'Fee to D Redfern not to print the story £5,000.00' And he even included 25p for the stamp to post the bill!

Ron would have enjoyed that. He would not only have felt it was justified to wind me up, but would also have seen it as revenge for some of the stunts I'd pulled on him. My favourite was when one of his drivers was leading a race and had to withdraw because of problems with the throttle cable. On an F1 it is an electronic fly-by wire, but in a kart it is a straight cable with a solderless nipple. I sent Ron a letter saying how sorry I was that he'd had a problem and concluded, 'Please find enclosed packet of solderless nipples. They might help. We usually put two on to be sure.'

The next week Eddie Jordan had a similar problem, so I dropped Ron another note suggesting that, if he'd finished with the solderless nipples, he might like to pass them on to him.

I like little jokes like that. They lighten things up and give a bit of balance to what can be a highly pressured lifestyle. I'm not sure Ron always agrees, but in this instance he found a way to get his own back. When Alan Henry wrote *McLaren: the Epic Years*, he included a chapter about my 'mother of all testing shunts'. He even included a picture of the somewhat disembowelled car. Alan expected Ron would knock that section out before it went to print but – lo and behold! – it was left in and I'm sure it was Ron's way of having the last laugh. And why not?

But I still think the moments Ron likes best are when I find him great drivers such as Lewis Hamilton, Gary Paffett and perhaps Oliver Rowland in the future.

Chapter 33

What if I Told You We're Buying a Racing Car?

In 1996 Gary Paffett won the Junior Intercontinental A Champions of the Future series with Lewis Hamilton picking up the Cadet title. Gary was fifteen years old and it was time for him to start thinking about moving to single-seaters, which meant I had some decisions to make. This was where I would normally hand him on to another team, but, having virtually quit driving, I had a bit of extra time for other things – well, at least another couple of minutes a day – and I was reluctant to let him go. We had formed a good team, so why not keep it going? Why not see how far we could go together? No one had ever taken a driver all the way from karting to F1 but that only increased my desire to have a crack. It would be expensive but, as the man said, 'Money is like manure: it's no use unless it's spread around to help things grow.'

At the time, I was running a competition for Vauxhall to find a future motorsport star. The final consisted of six drivers going head to head at Donington with the winner gaining a place in Jim Russell's racing school. The school provided three days' tuition in a single-seater and at the end of it there was a race. There were ten schools over the season and the winners

251

of all the races went forward to a winter series. Whoever came out on top of that was given a scholarship and a free entry into the following year's Formula Vauxhall championship. John Kirkpatrick, who runs the school, reckoned Gary was one of the best prospects he'd seen for years, and he wasn't wrong. Gary dominated his course and blew them away in the final. We'd got our free entry. All we needed now was a car.

At this stage you normally go to an established team and pay them to let you run in their car, so I approached Van Diemen. They were a top team, running Antonio Pizzonia, who went on to race F1 for Jaguar, but they appeared to be under the same illusion as many other people that, when it comes to readies, I am about a fiver behind Bernie Ecclestone. The reality is that I'm probably a quid behind his dustman and whatever spare cash I have tends to be put into racing. I don't regret that or begrudge it, but it doesn't mean I'm willing to pay the asking price, so when they quoted me a particular sum I managed to convince them that the only thing green about me was my lawn.

'*You* guys should really be paying *me*,' I insisted, 'because, believe me, this kid is going to win the championship.'

After some haggling it became clear that they wouldn't drop below a hundred grand for the season and they emphasised they were being *that* generous only because they agreed he was a great prospect.

It was a lot of money. I chewed it over in my mind and talked to some friends whose opinions I respected but who wouldn't be insulted if I ignored their advice. The logical path was to try to find a sponsor and take the Van Diemen offer, but a little voice nagged away that we ought to be able to do it more cheaply than that. What if we bought our own car? After all, we had built up a team of good engineers at Zip who were willing to work hard, never said, 'That's impossible,' were happy only when winning and, importantly, could put up with me. Anyone at Zip who didn't have those qualities quickly found themselves down the road.

My friends were united in the view that it would make more sense to put my cash through a shredder and then set fire to it than to buy my own racing car. They pointed out that the teams have the best facilities and the best equipment and are provided with the best engines. 'That's what makes them special,' one friend said.

'Yeah, but I don't have special money,' I replied.

I decided to try out my ideas on Grant Munro. Grant had been team manager and chief engineer of my superkart team for a number of years and would be an important member of the crew I was planning for Gary. I trusted his judgement and common sense.

'What would you think', I asked, 'if I told you I was going to buy a racing car and a truck to go into Formula Vauxhall with Gary Paffett?'

He didn't blink. 'Be a bit different, wouldn't it? But it's got four wheels and an engine and we've got a good driver, I don't see why not.'

I think I'd already made up my mind anyway, but it was nice to find one person who didn't think I needed a straitjacket, so I got out the magazines and started combing the small ads for second-hand racing cars.

I found an S/H Formula Vauxhall Junior. We took delivery and as we checked it over we realised we had one particularly steep learning curve to overcome. Having worked on karts for years, we realised that the black art of suspension was a complete mystery to us. There was also the small matter that Gary was still a novice in single-seaters and, much as we were keen for him to test our new car, I did have to keep reminding him not to bend it, because we couldn't afford the repair bills. To his eternal credit, he never moaned once, retained his enthusiasm at fever pitch, and didn't bust the car. He won the novice section of the winter series and finished fourth overall, which was phenomenal. He was ready to step up.

Formula Vauxhall had two classes. There were twenty-four drivers in Class A and six novices in Class B, who were at the back of the grid and had a number of restrictions on them such as fewer new tyres, but the class gave them the chance to gain experience driving against some good drivers. With Gary's talent and my ego, most people in the sport expected me to put him straight into Class A. Some even told me they thought he could win it. But if I do have a good opinion of myself it's not just because I'm tall, slim and good-looking. Over the years I've learned lots of lessons and even those decisions that look like instinctive punts are based on what I've gleaned while getting oil under my fingernails, negotiating in boardrooms and learning to drive faster than my rivals. Apart from perhaps his dad, no one had a higher opinion of Gary's talent than I, and I was confident he would indeed do well in Class A.

But I was sure he couldn't win it. He had too much to learn about his car and how to convey that to his team so they could tweak the setup until it was exactly right. He would be racing on strange tracks against drivers who had already been out there two years and had the backing of wealthy, experienced teams. His crew were good but they too were learning as they went along. We would go into Class B.

If Gary was disappointed at the decision he didn't show it. He won every single race in his class and even managed a podium finish alongside Pizzonia, the overall series winner. That was unheard of. It was a stunning first year and achieved on a shoestring. We were racing against teams who tested two or three times a week but we couldn't afford to go out there other than on the official test day. Not only would it cost around two grand a time for track hire, tyres, petrol and mechanics and engineers, but it was all too easy to have a shunt and do a few thousand pounds' worth of damage to the car. On top of that, we were funding our racing through what we earned from Zip, so we had to make sure we looked after the business. Incredibly, we made it through the season with a total repair bill of a miserly £664 – about the size of a top team's mechanics' bar bill.

Gary had earned us a free entry for the following year but yet again there were siren voices urging me to throw him straight into Formula Three. There was no way I was going to do that. He still had plenty to learn – I tell all my kids that the moment they think they know it all is the time to quit motorsport – and, more important, I wanted him to have the word 'winner' against every year on his CV. He already had it next to Class B. Now was the time to whip their arse in Class A. Then we'd go and do the same thing in Formula Three. Much better be number one for three years in a row than to cut corners and be second or worse. No one remembers the runner-up.

We had to go out and buy a new car to meet the new Class A upgrades on brakes and other bits and pieces. I thought about selling the old car to pay for the new one but, being a sentimental kind of chap, I decided to put the very first Zip single-seater racer in store under a cover. I was soon very glad I had.

The first few races went well, but when we got to Croft Gary had a major shunt. He was a bit impetuous trying to overtake and flipped the car about five times. A wheel shot off, hit a spectator's car, then bounced into Dave Richards' helicopter, doing about £50,000 worth of damage. Instead of flying off, leaving us peasants on the ground in a shower of dust, Dave had to rent a low loader and tow his chopper home. Fortunately, his son was in our Young Guns team at the time so he forgave us.

Gary's car was totalled. We were down twenty-five grand and, having got through the first year without insurance, I'd gone the same route this time, so no relief there. There was nothing for it but to salvage whatever upgrades we could from the wreckage, buy some others, and fix up last year's car.

We had missed out on the points at Croft and Gary was much more subdued in the next couple of events. We picked up a few points but we didn't win. I wondered whether the crash was playing on his mind but it didn't seem to be bothering him. Much more, I think, was the fact that he was driving the Class B car and didn't think it was as competitive. It was a mental block he needed to overcome before the final race at Silverstone because we needed to win with Ryan Dalziel finishing outside the top three, to clinch the championship. And all the big teams were throwing massive amounts of money at this last race. Qualifying was OK but not brilliant. We would start about eighth on the grid in the final, when Gary produced one of the best drives I have never seen.

It was one of those occasions when you need to be in two places at once. This being impossible, I went to the World Karting Championships in Italy with Luke and spent enough on my mobile keeping in touch with the pit back in England to keep Vodafone in business for years. Between those calls and the number of times I read the *Autosport* report, it sometimes feels as though I'd been there. As Gary went down to the *parc fermé*, it started to piss down with rain. They were given ten minutes to change to wet tyres but there was no time to make any setup adjustments. That suited us, because it made it more of an even contest and we had the trump card: Gary Paffett could drive by the seat of this pants better than all the other drivers.

His first lap was just out of this world. Ignoring spray and the horrendous conditions, he powered his way through the field and fought his way up to second. A number of people who know good driving compared it to the famous first lap in the 1993 European GP at Donington, where Ayrton Senna defied the conditions to overhaul the much quicker cars of Damon Hill and Alain Prost just on nerve and his matchless ability to drive when traction control was not helping.

Gary took the lead in the second lap and then disappeared from the field. He was lapping at a stunning two seconds a lap faster than everyone and clinched the championship with ease. He was deservedly named as the McLaren Young Driver of the Year.

The following year Gary was even sharper in the British National F3 Championship. We did a deal to run with another good friend, Fred Goddard Racing, and went out and bought an F3 Dallara, powered by Renault, and employed another old mate, Peter Berry, to engineer the car. It was not long before the commentators referred to the championship as Formula Paffett, such was Gary's absolute domination. By the end of the season we had not only taken virtually every pole position but won every UK race and picked up the £125,000 BRDC prize fund, which was absolutely crucial in our masterplan to obtain the funding we would need for the next season in Europe.

Gary's progress through the ranks remains one of my proudest achievements, because we didn't have the tricky engines they say you must have to be competitive; we didn't have the massive budget and all the gear of the big teams. We just had a second-hand car, a second-hand engine, a great crew, a fantastic driver and a combined determination to win that made us unstoppable. We were a great advertisement for the sport but we were a one-off and would always be unless the system was changed.

Chapter 34
Putting Zip into Single-Seaters

No one will ever convince me there is a shortcut from karting to F1. A lot of drivers have tried to jump from a kart to F3 without the stages in between but that is like leaving primary school and going straight to university. It might seem like an attractive idea but it doesn't work in the long term.

You have only to think of Jarno Trulli, a karting world champion, and Giancarlo Fisichella, runner-up in the European Championship. They were two of the most talented drivers of their generation but they missed out on part of their education by going straight to F3. They then moved on to F1 and with all their ability have won only four Grands Prix between them, including Fisichella's victory in Brazil, which was pretty well by default.

To my mind, it is vital to have a well-structured series of steps that help drivers learn their trade and adapt to new conditions so, when they finally reach F1, they can do themselves justice. Under the current system, which takes very deep pockets or a bank manager who makes sub-prime lenders look like misers, motorsport has always been expensive. It was once a pastime for toffs who wanted something more exciting than grouse shooting, and, while it has moved on a bit, many talented drivers have missed out because they didn't have enough spare cash.

I remember a fantastic guy called Steve South, who was one of the few people I knew who was quicker than I was in a kart. I thought he must be one of the 'silver spoon' brigade when I heard he went to Harrow school, but it turned out to be Harrow County, not the posh gaff up the road. In what is a familiar story, Steve got incredible support from his dad, Reg, who was involved in the early days of electronics and spent every penny on their dream of an F1 berth, and it looked to be working out when Steve won the British F3 championship in 1977. About that time I watched him test for Lotus at Snetterton alongside a young Elio de Angelis. You couldn't split them, but when I asked team boss Peter Collins which one he was going to sign, he admitted, 'They're both stunningly competitive – you can hardly separate them on times – but we'll probably sign Elio because of the finance. His family own about an eighth of the universe while Steven's got about tuppence.'

Steve did get one F1 entry, deputising for Alain Prost in the United States GP, but didn't qualify, and his career was cut short later that year when he was involved in a horrendous accident in Canada and had part of his leg amputated. I still see him once a year at the British GP and he looks just the same but I often wonder how far he would have gone if he'd had financial clout.

If anything, the situation has grown worse since Steve's day. The top-entry-level teams are booked up months ahead by people with a load of wedge. The kids whose dads have to hold down three or four jobs to earn a stake are able to find a place only in the lower teams, reducing their chances of winning to almost zero. And not only do the rich kids have the best cars, but they can also afford to test a lot more. You don't have to be a fan of Karl Marx to know this ain't necessarily going to produce the best drivers.

My experience with Gary Paffett convinced me that motorsport needed an entry-level formula that was affordable and fair for all drivers, somewhere every kart driver with potential would have the chance to show what he could do in a single-seater. I also wanted to create a formula that would make drivers better. We would do away with aerodynamic aids and sticky tyres and make drivers learn their trade by the seat of their pants. They would develop feel in the same way Ayrton Senna and Michael Schumacher had, by the driver, rather than the designer and engineer, controlling the machine. It was time to take a blank sheet of paper and create the ideal formula from scratch.

I wanted a car that was well balanced, with good front to back ratios, and a reliable, aluminium engine that would allow a lot of track time. The petrol heads love having the car in the garage, fine-tuning their fine tuning, but the driver needs to be out on the track. I also wanted a car that wouldn't cost the earth to run. That meant analysing the three most expensive components – tyres, the crew and damage from accidents – and finding a way to make them much less expensive.

I reckoned I could slash about 80 per cent off the average tyre bill while at the same time providing a setup that would produce better drivers. We wouldn't need slicks and wets because we would race on treaded tyres that would be OK in both wet and dry conditions. They would have enough grip but not too much, making it more difficult to drive, so skilful drivers would have an advantage; and, because the tyres would be made from a harder compound, each set would last longer.

Running a team takes a big lump of dough. You have to pay the guys, rent somewhere for them to work and on top of that buy and maintain the trucks to transport the cars to and from meetings. For much of the time, all that money is sitting around, doing nothing. I figured we could reduce a driver's costs by a hell of a lot by running all the cars centrally. We would put all the cars on the grid and get them to and from meetings, so, instead of twenty-four trucks, there would be just three. One engineer would look after four cars and there would be one mechanic, employed by us, to every two drivers.

Now I had to tackle the horrendously expensive problem of shunts. Many years before this, karting had been a dangerous sport with some kids being seriously hurt, mainly because of interlocking wheels. I introduced glass-fibre bodywork that protected the front wheels and we filled in the gaps between front and back wheels to stop karts interlocking. Within a year, accidents in which the driver was taken to hospital dropped by around 75 per cent. Gary Paffett's Formula Vauxhall crash reminded me of those bad old karting days. He went up the inside of another driver, tangled with his front wheel and boom: £25,000 worth of damage to Gary's car. The other kid was down ten grand and we almost lost the championship. I reasoned that if we applied the same principles to a single-seater as we had to karts, it would not only make racing far safer, but would greatly reduce the amount of money you had to pay out on bent and busted bodywork.

The figures were looking good. Normally, you would reckon on around £150,000 to £160,000 to join a top Formula Ford team. Then you had to put aside another ten grand or so for accident damage plus paying the VAT. I worked out I could provide a better product for £35,000. Suddenly, what had started out as 'I wonder if' had moved on to 'why not?' and was now 'bloody hell, this could work'. The more I thought about it the more the new Zip Formula – I'd given it a name already – made sense.

It would be racing where the drivers with the big bucks didn't have all the advantages. We would know the best setup and deliver 24 identical cars to a meeting ready for testing with their engines and gearboxes sealed and the same level of wear on the tyres for everyone. There would be one test day before a race when the driver could change his setup as he wanted within the rules, but, even if you offered me a million quid, you couldn't have a car at any other time for testing. And to prove to everyone there was no hanky-panky or favouritism, a team of scrutineers paid for by the championship but working for the governing body would publicly take the first three cars in each race and check random components, including the gearbox, to demonstrate they were the same as all the others. This was going to be as level as a playing field could be.

I talked over my plans with Martin Whitaker, who was Ford's head of motorsport. I'd known him since his early days on *Motoring News*, and kept in touch when he was at the RAC and later worked as chief press officer for Bernie Ecclestone. In recent years he had arranged for Ford to sponsor the Zip Young Guns. My timing was perfect. He had felt for a while that Formula Ford needed rebranding and agreed to provide some of the development cash. As with all the best sponsorship deals, there would be benefits for everyone. I even suggested we should make the cars diesel-powered because that would give Ford diesels street cred and boost sales, which weren't so good at the time, but they decided against that.

I took a deep breath and built the first Zip Formula car. I knew we would need some expert help and brought on board Alec Bottoms, the guy who all those years before had sold us Zipper karts. He'd later moved on to single-seaters and his expertise alongside the always dependable Grant Munro meant we could produce a prototype. It was a cracker. We didn't take bits and pieces from other cars: we had every component built just for us. There were no compromises. We learned from others' mistakes and built a car that was nigh on perfect. It was the first junior steel-chassis single-seater to pass the FIA carbon-chassis impact test, something the others are still trying to catch up on today.

The whole development was done in utmost secrecy. Most people in Ford didn't know we were working on the formula for the new millennium and the head of their motorsport – a top official from the parent company in the States – first set eyes on it when we rolled the prototype out of the back of a van behind a block of flats in Hoddesdon. They liked it. Now all we had to do was to sell the idea to the sport.

Chapter 35

OK, We'll Do it Ourselves

Zip had taken a massive step, moving from kart manufacturers to a fully fledged race car, learning as we went along. It had been an enormous gamble on something I believed in passionately, but now I had to prove there was a market for the new formula. I approached Peter Gaydon and Denys Rohan at the BRDC at Silverstone, where they had control of the racing school. I felt our new car was perfect for them. At the time, they were using Formula Ford cars, which were much more expensive to buy and run, and to my delight they agreed. They also saw the potential of harnessing the Zip Formula with the name of the BRDC driving school and selling the package to countries around the world that were just starting to show an interest in motorsport.

I arranged for Martin Whitaker to meet them and over the next few weeks we put together a deal. The BRDC said they wanted twenty-six cars – thirteen white and thirteen red – and were so enthusiastic about the project they agreed we could have free use of their small test circuit at Silverstone whenever we wanted it. As with Ford, this was a mutually beneficial partnership. They asked for certain modifications on the car, including upgrading from a 1,400cc to a 1,600cc engine and going from a 38-cm wheel down to 33 cm, because it was more forgiving. We thought both those suggestions improved the car and readily agreed, even though it meant more expense because we had to redesign the geometry of the suspension to accommodate the new wheels.

I wasn't alone in thinking we had come up with an important breakthrough in entry-formula cars. Influential columnist Marcus Pye wrote in *Autosport*, 'The decision of Silverstone to invest in the exciting Formula Zip single-seater for its Northampton and Croft schools could prove to be the catalyst for its adoption worldwide.' Denys Rohan said, 'This is a strong and safe chassis, powered by proven Ford Zetec 1600 engines; it will enable licensed instructors to develop young drivers' ability on track with the opportunity for graduates to race the same cars in the 2001 BRDC single-seater Championship.'

Everything was going well and I was as excited as hell.

Over the years of doing business with companies all over the world, I've found out that a lot of people are reluctant to put agreements in writing, especially those who are pushing at the door of the executive toilet – they don't want any mistakes to be directly traceable to them. But I like to have a record of what's been agreed, so, whenever I make an oral agreement with someone, I follow it up with a letter or an email confirming what's been said. It gives them the chance to come back if they remember it differently and if they don't reply I take that as the deal. That's what I did with the order for twenty-six cars and I heard nothing to contradict me. As far as I was concerned we had an agreement and we set about turning a kart factory into a fully functional production line for single-seaters.

We now had a bunch of cars in various stages of construction, with a value of £25,000 each but, when I approached the BRDC for a part payment, nothing came back. I began to feel nervous when I heard that the American company Octagon had taken over Silverstone and the BRDC, and, sure enough, as soon as I started to push for some cash, I got the excuse that it wasn't down to them, and we had to tackle Octagon. The next I heard, one of their directors wanted to come down and inspect our factory.

We started to hear criticisms of the car, niggly points that were clearly unsound and have been shown to be so over the last eight years when the reliability of the cars has been proven time and time again. But they wanted to challenge the arrangement, which would have left me with a tab for three-quarters of a million pounds. I took the 404 pieces of paper I had kept while negotiating the deal, including the email from them saying what colours they wanted, to my solicitor and he said I had a cast-iron case but he also warned me that, if I took the BRDC to court, the case might drag on and the publicity would kill the formula. I believed passionately that this was the future of entry-level racing and decided to say 'Fuck 'em!' and prove them wrong – not in court but on the track.

That was going to be difficult enough, but it became a gargantuan task when Ford also pulled the plug. It was at a time when the company was bleeding money and one of the areas to take a hit was motorsport. Martin Whitaker was out and the new broom decided he wanted nothing to do with us. That was OK, except there was still some money due under the deal we had. I guess they thought I'd go away but this time I decided I had nothing to lose, so Martin Hines with his little factory in Hoddesdon threatened to take the mighty Ford empire to the High Court. In the end we settled for arbitration, where we agreed a settlement. By the time I paid the solicitors, I was no better off, but it's important not to let people push you around, no matter how big they are.

None of my friends actually said 'I told you so' but I'm sure a few thought it. Once again, I was faced with a choice that could see me fulfil a dream but also ran the risk of breaking the company. I had two cars complete in my factory and several others on the way. I could shove them in a corner with a sheet over them and spend the rest of my life wondering how good Zip Formula would have been, or I could push on, using my own cash to fund it. I can't remember giving the quit option much consideration. It was a no-brainer. We would run the Zip Formula without help.

One of the proudest days of my life was that damp, cold but occasionally sunny November day at Brands Hatch when we staged the first Zip Formula event. We had nineteen novices lined up on the grid facing a testing, slippery circuit. We ran two races, which were packed with incident and excitement. Cars were going round Paddock Bend in the wet two or three abreast and sliding through with their backs hanging out. Drivers lost it coming out of Clearways and reversed into the Armco at 100 m.p.h. The stewards made a rush to help them but, to their amazement, they weren't needed. Unlike with Formula Ford, the rear wing on a Zip Formula car is a big bumper, so there was no damage to the rear wheels, the gearbox and the suspension. The drivers were able to stick it in first gear and rejoin the race. It was old-fashioned racing, the like of which hadn't been seen since the 1970s. The fans loved it. It was like the old 1600 Formula Ford at its best. Loads of people came up to me and said it was the best day's racing they'd had in years and they thought I was on to a winner.

The Motor Sports Association, the governing body of all motorsport, was keen to create a series of stepping stones for drivers and agreed the Zip Formula should be the entry-level category, followed by Formula Renault and F3. On top of my other risks I had to give them a £100,000 bank guarantee that

I would keep the formula going for at least three years. I realised they thought this was necessary to protect the drivers, but in my case drivers were only renting the cars from me, so it didn't really apply, but I signed the form anyway. If I was going to end up sweeping the streets, what was another hundred grand?

In our first year we ran a twelve-round championship with full coverage on Sky Sports put together by my mate Andrew Marriott. The drivers knew their only cost was £35,000 for the season and accident damage, and the biggest bill we sent out was for £3,000, with the majority of them between two and three hundred quid. We didn't have one car somersault over another, and, to show how reliable the cars were, in the first sixteen races we had only four non-finishers because of mechanical problems – two throttle cables, a fuel pump and a puncture.

I had only one driver complain. He moaned that his car wasn't as fast as the others, especially his mate's. I promised him I would look into it and for the next meeting I put his pal's engine in his car and vice versa. He was still slower and, when he came to bitch to me again, I explained what I had done and pointed out it might have more to do with his ability as a driver than the car. We never saw him again!

We had two and a half years of great racing. Our first winner was Mike Spencer, who went on to Formula Renault with Motaworld and was very successful before running out of sponsorship. Our second winner was Tim Bridgeman, who later won the BMW championship series, then raced in the States and is now in the UK Porsche Cup. He has said that he owed his success to his time in Zip Formula. Oliver Turvey, another Young Gun winner of the McLaren/*Autosport* Young Driver of the Year award, learned his single-seater craft in Zip Formula and is destined for great things.

The cars were fantastic and all the drivers enjoyed racing

them. Even Max Mosley, the president of the FIA, took time off from his other activities to come to North Weald airfield and drive one, the first time he'd been in a single-seater for thirty years. He said, 'The performance is really impressive. It's a proper little racing car and great fun to drive.'

We'd overcome more obstacles than the winner of the Grand National to reach where we were going, but there was one we finally couldn't crack: the fact that the fat cats with money still call all the tunes in motorsport and weren't happy to see a small Hertfordshire company with its hand in their cookie jar. At the end of the second season, I heard a rumour that Formula BMW was coming to England as the official entry-level formula. I ignored it for some time, confident the Motor Sports Association would honour the contract they had with me. Zip Karts may not be quite as big as BMW but a deal is a deal. Then I read an article confirming BMW would be launching the following year. I phoned MSA chief executive Colin Hilton. He was up North and said he couldn't come back down.

'No problem,' I said, 'pick a motorway services station and I'll meet you there.'

We met at six that night on the M1. Colin was clearly embarrassed. He mumbled on about how important BMW were and how much money they had spent developing their formula and how the MSA just couldn't ignore them. What could he do?

'You can tell them to go forth and multiply. I've spent a bloody fortune developing a true entry formula, which is what motorsport needs, and we agreed that there would be no other entry-level championship allowed.'

But I knew I was fighting a losing battle. If I'd carried on, BMW could have used their showroom network to provide sponsorship to drivers, and I couldn't match that, so the best kids would have left. Sometimes you just have to know when you can't win, but I was seething. The injustice of it churned my stomach like an acid. My eyes struggled to focus. I said as calmly as I could, 'Colin, I'm incredibly disappointed. I think what you're doing is wrong. I'm withdrawing my formula immediately. And I'm telling you now, if you come after me for the hundred grand guarantee you'll have to sue me for it and I'll make sure you receive so much bad publicity, you will wish you'd never bothered.'

I didn't hear from them.

A lot of other companies were delighted when they learned Zip Formula had folded. Unlike them, I'd been motivated by a love of the sport and because I get a charge out of watching talented young drivers progress, regardless of their background and bank balance. I made no profit but I proved the doubters wrong and still kept the costs to the bare minimum. Some companies hated the fact that we had forced them to cut their bloated profit margins. Suddenly they had been faced with drivers asking why they should pay £250 for a wishbone when I was selling them for half that. Even the improved safety factors pissed off those people who make money out of rebuilding broken cars or replacing smashed-up components. Suddenly you could buy into a Formula Ford team for £100,000 – much cheaper than it had been but still three times more than Zip Formula, while, at the same time, one major manufacturer cut some of their replacement parts by up to 50 per cent. We may not have won but if nothing else we helped reduce the costs for the competitors.

Losing the chance to continue with Zip Formula hurt. But I am confident it isn't dead, but is just waiting for the right opportunity to come charging back. And that may not be too far away, because the sport is crying out for change. Formula BMW quickly packed up at entry level and is now just a support for F1 with ten races a year. Anyone wanting to drive in it needs approximately £250,000. The situation is dire. When we started out with Gary Paffett there were two classes of Formula Vauxhall and two Formula Ford championships, in all accommodating around seventy-five drivers, of who only around twenty-five would go up to the next stage. Currently, we only have about sixteen drivers in Formula Ford. Someone is going to do the maths soon and realise we are going to price ourselves out of drivers before very much longer.

Karting has a problem too. Even allowing for the 'Lewis Hamilton effect', which followed on from a surge created by Jenson Button, which came after a boom from David Coulthard, there are still only a similar number of licence holders now to what there were in 1967.

It takes thousands of karters to produce a Lewis Hamilton and the supply line is in danger of drying up unless the sport does something radical. It doesn't take a genius to realise that there is a limit to the number of people with enough disposable income for even the £35,000 for Zip Formula, let alone four or five times that amount. If things go on as they are, only millionaires will be able to race cars, very much as it was in the early days of motorsport.

But the Zip Formula is viable and it is proven. Those early cars have more than shown their worth. They are now eight years old and being used very successfully in Bahrain. I am convinced we have created something that could still be huge, and not just in Europe. With the growing passion for motorsport in China and the Middle East, it is only a matter of time before we are manufacturing again, and my main ambition in life is still to create a Junior World Formula that is a level playing field. If anyone else feels the same way, you know where I am!

Chapter 36

Old Men Don't Make Comebacks – or Do They?

I had given way to the inevitable when I withdrew the Zip
Formula, knowing there are times when you can't beat the
odds, but most of the time my instinct is to fight the bastards.
I'd taken on the RAC over the petrol and won, and I'd also
fronted down Ford, so I certainly wasn't going to roll over
when I felt we were badly treated by one of Italy's leading
motorsport clothing companies. The irony was that initially
they approached me, saying that they had two distributors in
England who sold a lot of their gear but didn't do much in
karting. Would I be interested in distributing just their kart
clothing? I said I'd love to and we reached an agreement, but
as soon as the other distributors found out about it they kicked
up a fuss, threatening to withdraw from all the motorsport
distribution, so my deal was cancelled.

There was not much I could do about it if they wouldn't
supply me, so I decided the only way to fight back was to set
up in opposition. I sat down and started to dream up possible
names, finishing up with about a dozen that sounded as though
they might be a genuine Italian clothing manufacturer. I gave a
copy of the list to every member of staff and told them to take

it home and read it through. Four days later I asked each of them to write down whatever they could remember of the list and based on the results, Zapelli clothing was launched.

It wasn't difficult to succeed. I just copied everything the other company was doing and slashed the price by 50 per cent. For some reason they were not happy but I pointed out to them that they had given me the idea of selling clothing and, as they had gone back on their word, I had no option but to launch my own range.

I added, 'And, as for the price, I can produce them, provide a good margin for retailers and still make a reasonable profit, so perhaps it's your figures that are out.'

Within a few months they had to cut their prices by 30 per cent. Their change of heart cost them a lot of money one way or another and after a few years they came back to me and appointed me as their kart clothing distributor. Zapelli still exists, selling gloves and our wetsuits, which are probably the bestsellers in Europe – I even see Italian drivers wearing them.

What with little ventures like that, the day-to-day running of Zip Karts, developing Zip Formula and looking after the careers of Gary and Luke, I began to adopt the Beatles' 'Eight Days a Week' as my theme tune. So it's difficult to explain why I chose 2002 to stage a driving comeback.

If I'm completely honest, I never really wanted to quit driving, but I couldn't see how I could do everything else and maintain a high standard and I wasn't willing to be an also-ran. Gary and Luke were taking up a lot of time and the passing of Mum and Dad meant I was the only Hines in the family business. When people talk about orphans they usually mean children, but to me it applies to everyone who has lost both parents. No matter how old you are, it changes your view of life, or it did mine. When Mum and Dad were alive I could go racing knowing they were looking after the business, but now it all fell on me and, more than ever, I felt a duty not to let them down. I was determined nothing should go wrong with the company they had started all those years ago in the bike shop in Finchley.

My biggest problem was finding a way to cram everything into a day. Even when I eventually climbed into bed, the brain still took a while to shut down and let me snatch some sleep. I often wondered what my cancer surgeon Chris Russell would have said if he could see my lifestyle. It was challenging but it also gave me a lot of satisfaction, especially watching Luke and Gary making such good progress, yet, even though I was feeling good, there was a small ache that was not satisfied. I would watch the superkarts and a devil on my shoulder would whisper, 'You could still beat them.' I thought I'd kept my longing to myself but I guess it must have shown because in the autumn of 2001, when I was chatting on the phone to Dave Hepworth in Australia, he said, 'Why don't Barbara and I come over for three months? We could build a new kart and have a go.' I told him not to be so bloody silly!

We started work on the kart a couple of months later.

A lot of experience went into developing a superkart we thought could challenge the world, but we couldn't be sure until we saw it perform on the track. Sky TV approached me about filming a feature on the Zip Formula and asked if I would take a car up to Knockhill in Scotland. It was a mere eight-hour drive and there was no fee, but, as always, I reckoned the exposure would be worth the trek and agreed. It would also give me the chance to test the new kart – and the old driver – without any prying eyes around. I took Grant and Dave with me and have to admit I started to feel a butterfly or two as we approached the border.

We arrived on a typical Knockhill spring day: a bleak wind fired stinging rain horizontally into our faces and the bone-chilling cold helped us to understand why the Scots invented whisky and drink too much of it. Even under those conditions, seeing the circuit again for the first time in a few years got the juices going. It's demanding and dangerous and I love it. It's a great test of a driver with two or three places where you always feel you could have done better, squeezed a little more speed out of the kart and nailed it. One section in particular, where you climb a steep rise to a chicane with a blind right-hander at the top, after which the track drops away, is a classic test of a driver. Overdo it and you go straight off and crash; get through and you think, Why didn't I go faster through there? The only way to beat Knockhill is to be aggressive, but, if you push a fraction too hard, Knockhill will beat you. I sat in the motor home looking out at the unrelenting weather and said, 'Martin, you are fucking nuts.'

My spirits weren't exactly raised when I realised the only wet tyres we had were nine years old and more like mahogany than rubber, but I had a boost when I got my old overalls out and they still fitted perfectly. My two companions, whose profile had rounded a little over the last decade, were disgusted. My body clearly hadn't gone to seed – but were my reflexes as good as they used to be? Would I be able to cope with an untested kart if things started to go wrong? Would I be able to drive as fast as I needed to in order to put it through its paces?

There was only one way to find out. I agreed to do three laps and see how it felt, but said to the others, 'If I go out there and find I can't do it any more, then we forget this whole stupid business.'

Dave said, 'Fair enough, mate. But if you go well we'll have a go at one race. Agreed?'

I nodded. The engine fired and the noise, the vibration and the smell hit me like the charge that sparked Frankenstein's monster into life. Adrenaline coursed through my body and within a couple of yards it was as though I'd never been away. I did a quick doughnut to celebrate, then went out to give our new baby its first taste of action. Even though I was feeling good, the first lap was a bit tentative. I didn't want to make an idiot of myself. I eased round the first corner, up through the chicane and felt as though I was in full control, though still a bit concerned that it might come back to bite me. As I crossed the start line again I decided to give it a bit more of a go. In the wet it's all about keeping your head, feeling the steering and the grip on the track, and to my surprise it seemed almost too easy. I could push it a bit harder, and did. As I came past Dave and Grant, they were hanging over the pit wall looking very relaxed. By the end of the third lap I was as fast as I had ever been at Knockhill in the wet. When I came into the pit, the pair of them had big silly grins on their face. They knew we were going racing again.

We did another fifteen or so laps that day and the newly designed kart was a good 'un. I didn't want a lot of hoop-la on my comeback, so Grant found a race in Croix en Ternois, a twisty circuit about half an hour's drive from Calais. I wanted the preparations to be spot-on, so I did a deal with the circuit to do a day's testing the week before the race. I had won the European Championship there in 1993 and still had all the data on our times at that meeting, but things had moved on and I was concerned that, while we may be as fast as we used to be, the rest could now be a second or two quicker. If that were true, there would be no point in racing. Don't get me wrong: to my mind, the guys who finish from eighth and below are the heart and soul of karting, the people who keep the sport going. But I had always driven at the sharp end and could see no point in starting all over again if I was not absolutely on the pace.

The test day went perfectly. I drove around two hundred laps and, when we checked it against some recent results, we were competitive. What's more, we kept modifying the setup and felt very confident our kart was as good as it could be.

The meeting itself was held on a scorching hot weekend and proved to be one of the most memorable of my life. We were up against some good drivers, especially Damien Payart, a young Frenchman who had come to the fore since I retired and was on his home track, but we still qualified on pole. I knew that he often took two or three laps before he was confident his tyres were warm enough to go flat out, and I took full advantage, going straight into the lead and holding it. Racing thirty-five laps in 36°C is a bit like going ten rounds with Mike Tyson in a sauna, but at the end, while Damien stayed in his kart and his crew threw buckets of cold water over him, the old man was up on the podium jumping up and down.

Not only was I back winning races, the old fuck-you instincts were still there when the French officials claimed my air box was not the sort used in Europe, so Damien – surprise, surprise, a Frenchman! – would be declared the winner.

'Hang on just a bloody minute,' I said. 'You scrutineered the kart before the event and nothing was said. That filter was on then, so you're either incompetent and didn't see it, or you saw it and let me race. Either way, you aren't going to get away with robbing me.'

There was a lot of shrugging and Gallic arm waving and a few expletives in English and French. I'd put up with French shenanigans for thirty years and now it was starting all over again. To hell with them!

I said, 'Look, you do what you like. I came here to see if I could be competitive again. I know I won, I know I was the fastest and I know I am the champion. So stick your cup where the sun don't shine. I don't need it.'

Old Men Don't Make Comebacks – or Do They?

The organiser said, 'Martin, we have known you many years and we are delighted to see you again. We shake hands and you keep the trophy and we say no more about it.'

It had been a gruelling race and I wondered if I was going to suffer a lot of aches and pains the following day. But I woke up ready to take on the world, in fact feeling much fitter than I used to after races earlier in my career when the vibration created all sorts of trouble with my back, my shoulders and arms, and my fingers would turn white in the cold. At one stage, a doctor had told me I should quit racing because I was damaging the discs in my spine and they were becoming fragile and might shatter, leaving me in a wheelchair. I ignored him but I did start having regular massages and have been every week since to Steve Clarke, one of the best physios I have had. For years I have played squash twice a week, seldom walk anywhere if I can run, always take the stairs and have a fantastic metabolism. I didn't do any special training for my comeback but I was in the best condition of my life. So why not have a go at another big prize?

Chapter 37

Hines versus Kleppe: the Rematch

As fate would have it, the first round of the European Championship at the Nürburgring in Germany was ruled out because of fog and I realised there was still time for me to enter and see how we went, especially as the next round was to be at Donington Park, a place where I had seldom been beaten and where I had won the World Cup and *TV Times* races.

There was a certain amount of disbelief expressed when word got round that I was having a go at the European title. A few people told me it was impossible for me to mix it with the boys at the front of the grid at the age of fifty-six; some warned me I was risking my reputation if I made myself look foolish; others just shook their heads and said, 'I always knew Hinesy was nuts.'

The comeback was creating quite a stir in the karting world and, despite my naturally retiring nature, it was good to be back in the spotlight once more. News had even reached as far as Sweden, as I found out when I bumped into Lennart Bohlin, the guy I had raced against all those years ago in the European Championships. Lennart was always one of the hardest men to beat because he was so consistent. He and I had enjoyed some titanic battles, especially at Donington, where I always managed to pass him at the same part of the track. He knew it was coming but never quite worked out how to stop me.

'What on earth are you doing here?' I asked.

He smiled: 'They told me you were coming out of the old folk's home to drive again. I couldn't believe it, so I had to come and see for myself. I've also brought my overalls in case you can't manage it.'

That really touched me and said a helluva lot about what a great sportsman he is.

I got a great buzz being back at a circuit as a competitor. It was Donington's 'Thunder in the Park' meeting with the F1 Minardi two-seaters and Euro F3000 also running and Damon Hill entertaining the crowd, not as a driver but a rock musician. Maybe if I didn't go so well, I could join his band!

The Friday test day on my first shot at the European Championship for nine years wasn't hugely successful. I'm sure there were more than a few people waiting for me to trip up and, to be honest, we did, because we had nothing but fuel-starvation problems all day. The only consolation was that the laps I managed to complete were bang on the pace.

Things grew worse the following day, which was timetabled for warm-up practice in the morning, then straight into qualifying and one final, with the second final to come on the Sunday. I needed to do some serious laps to make sure the fuel problem was completely sorted but one of the guys in the team had fitted new carbon rotary valves on the grounds that they were a bit lighter and created less friction, so might buy us a tenth of a second. It was a great theory but he hadn't thought to test them beforehand. After half a lap my engine seized and I again missed out on practice.

Anyone who knows me will tell you that I am the mildest-mannered of men, seldom raising my voice or getting cross, but to say that I went ape shit would be a massive understatement. I would imagine people at nearby East Midlands Airport could hear me above the whine of the jets.

We got the kart back together, complete with the old valves, and went out to qualify. One or two of the younger drivers had already put in good times and were clearly confident they could send the old man back into retirement with his tail between his legs. But the kart was going great and I didn't feel so bad myself and enjoyed knowing that my experience was going to be one of the keys at Donington, where you had to respect the track, which was often slick from the kerosene dumped by planes as they came into the airport.

I was just starting to relish the prospect of showing the young pups a thing or two when the fuel surge returned and I had to go in. I'd done only six laps and I think it is fair to say that my language was once again a little strong when I arrived back at the pits. I had a rant about the engine, the kart, the track and the bloody stupid idea of making a comeback in the first place. I made sure I followed Chris Russell's advice not to internalise frustration and barked at anyone who came anywhere within a few yards of me. After a while, I calmed down enough to ask how quick I'd been.

Grant said casually, 'About a second quicker than the rest.'

'You see,' I said. 'I told you it wasn't too bad, didn't I?'

For some reason, a shower of objects descended on me from my crew.

Damien Payart not only wanted to show me that a new order had taken over but also to gain revenge for the defeat on his home turf. For once he got off to a great start, leading from another veteran driver, Bobo Westman. Older than sixty, Bobo thought I was one of the young upstarts.

Payart's race was finished when a water hose came loose,

leaving the two geriatrics out front for the whole race. I managed to nose ahead of Bobo at McLeans on the final lap, and, when he tried to come back at me at the Melbourne Loop, he spun off and, by the time he'd recovered, I'd won the race.

The turning point in the second race came as early as the first lap when Payart and Westman clipped each other and speared off. I managed to miss them by no more than 5 mm (about a quarter of an inch) to take the lead. I was controlling the race from the front but almost threw it away on lap six, when I read the pit board as saying I was eight seconds in front when in fact it was *point eight* of a second. As I eased slightly to protect my tyres, Poul Petersen came flying through and I had to work like hell to get back past him. I managed it in the end and took the chequered flag to make sure of maximum points. Second over the line was Torgjer Kleppe, my old rival. The senior citizens had seen off all the young bucks and I bet Lennart was secretly thinking he could have been among us if only he'd driven.

Before heading off to Le Mans for the final round I decided to fulfil a lifetime ambition by racing at the famous Laguna Seca circuit in Monterey, California, just off the fabulous Highway One, one of the most spectacular roads anywhere in the world. Laguna Seca is famous for a bend called the corkscrew, where you come over the top of a blind bump before dropping away in a spectacular sequence of corners. It's the kind of experience everyone should try before dropping off the perch. I was also looking forward to racing against two former motorcycle superstars, Eddie Lawson and Wayne Rainey, who had both turned to karts, Wayne despite being paralysed in a horrendous bike crash that ended his career at Misano in Italy.

I watched the cars and bikes test and saw how they dropped

away at the corkscrew and thought this was going to be one of the greatest experiences of my life. It turned out to be something of an anticlimax. Don't get me wrong: it was special. But, unlike in a car or on a bike, where you are up reasonably high and so enjoy the full impact of the heart-stopping drop, in a kart you are so low you tend to be looking along it. I'm glad I've done it but it wasn't as spine-tingling as I'd expected.

In fact the whole meeting didn't turn out exactly as I'd hoped. Not knowing the quirks of the course, I wasn't as fast as some of the Americans and would probably have finished around sixth, but never got that far because in practice I had a shunt on one of the slowest parts of the course. I came out of the kart and then landed back in it, damaging my ribs. We strapped them up and filled me with pain killers but it was still too sore to drive. Le Mans was around the corner and I didn't want to risk aggravating my injury. I tried two or three laps but there was no way I could drive and ended up as a spectator. When we got home, I spent a lot of time being massaged by Steve and he got me back in shape in time for the European showdown.

I was fastest in the first qualifying round and got off to a flyer in the second but then my engine seized and I could only watch as others took advantage of improving conditions to go past me. I started the pre-final from third on the grid but hadn't gone far when my second engine seized up on me. François Vinuales won the race but, more important from my point of view, Torgjer had taken fourth place and was now only a point behind me. And I didn't have an engine for the second race. Gary Paffett, Grant and I gutted both dead engines and managed to salvage enough to cobble together a new one in time for the final race. It was just a question of how well it would go.

Damien Payart opened up a good lead with Bobo Westman

chasing him. I eased my kart into third place, knowing I just had to stay ahead of Torgjer. I managed to open up a six-second advantage with two laps to go, which should have been plenty but suddenly I realised I had fuel-feed problems. I daren't take too many risks but, with him eating into the space between us, I couldn't afford to nurse the kart too much. The tension was unbearable. I couldn't believe we'd come so far in such a short time to have the prize snatched from us at the last minute. As we went into the last lap, Torgjer was closing fast. I drove as fast and as smoothly as my sick engine would allow me and, with him breathing down my neck, just managed to scrape over the line a split second ahead of him. I was European Champion by four points and proudly collected the trophy I had first won in 1977.

Winning a major championship once more against such tremendous odds stood alongside my World Championships in 1983 and 1991 as one of my most satisfying victories and provided me with one of the proudest nights of my life.

I was nominated for the *Autocar* award for the greatest contribution to motorsport alongside Michael Schumacher, who had won it the year before, and Kimi Räikkönen. Just to be listed in that company was very special. At the dinner, they announced each name, reading out our achievements, and mine boiled down to the life-long enthusiasm for motorsport and coming back to win the European Championship after a nine-year absence.

They reached the bit where they announcer said 'And the winner is... ' And, as he paused to rip open the envelope, I noticed someone at the nearby Ferrari table leave his seat, crouch down and start to edge forward ready to pick up the award on behalf of Michael Schumacher.

'. . . Martin Hines!'

I was gobsmacked and also amused to see matey try to squirm

his way back to his seat without being noticed. I went up and collected the award, which enjoys pride of place on my desk. It will always be one of most prized possessions because it came not just from karting but from the wider world of motorsport.

There was nothing left to prove as a driver; now it was time to concentrate once more on trying to make Gary and Luke into world champions at F1 and GT1.

Chapter 38

A Kick in the Bollocks can Break your Heart

The Zip Formula experiment cost me hundreds of thousands of pounds and probably shaved a few years off my life. The same could be said about my backing Gary Paffett. But it was never about the money in either case. With Zip Formula, I wanted to give more young drivers the chance to show their potential whatever their background. With Gary, it was the challenge of taking an exceptionally talented driver every step of the way from cadet karting to F1 glory.

We were making good progress.

After his success in the British F3, everyone in the pit lane knew Gary was the driver to have on their team. We tested four times for Jaguar against some of the best young drivers around and each time Gary blew the rest away. Jaguar clearly rated him because they offered us a deal to make him their lead driver, partnered by James Courtney from O_2. Bruce Jenkins, the Jaguar team boss, assured me it was a done deal, and, best of all, instead of costing £350,000 it would be covered by the £125,000 prize money we had just won. There was just the formality of having it signed off by Ford in America. According to movie mogul Sam Goldwyn an oral contract ain't worth the paper it's written on. In January, I received an email saying the Americans wanted Andrew Lotterer instead of Gary. We were scuppered. John Booth, who had also wanted to sign Gary, had kept a berth open until 18 December but then had to fill it, so we couldn't go back to him. I was incensed. They'd even charged me several grand towards the cost of Gary's test days, then signed Lotterer, who hadn't even tested. I don't mind standing my round but this was taking the piss.

I had only one option open to me. My old karting rival Keke Rosberg was running a team in the German F3 championship, so I arranged for Gary to sign for them. The smart arses, who knew bugger all about the situation, said he was running away from British F3. That was crap and an insult to a kid who had never ducked a single challenge. In fact, the German F3 championship turned out to have bigger fields and a higher standard of competition, has since become the European F3 and is now the route followed by most of the top drivers, including Lewis Hamilton and Paul Di Resta.

Gary was an immediate star. He finished out of the top three in his first year only because the team had problems with the engine, but the second year there was no one to match him. He led the championship from the first meeting and took the title with seven wins.

We had a deal signed to drive the F3000 with the new Brand Motorsport. Or we did, until they packed up after the first race in Monza, leaving us staring a lost year in the face. But a driver as good as Gary was never going to be left completely high and dry. I got a call from Mercedes asking if he would like to drive a year-old car in the German Touring Car Championship (DTM) for Team Rosberg. We bit their hand off. We had already tested the car, staying over for a couple of days after clinching the F3 title at Hockenheim, and Mercedes had been astonished how quickly Gary adapted to the new formula. Within twenty laps he had been ready for pole position. At the end of the year he was promoted to the works AMG and came second in the DTM championship to Mattias Ekstrom. He should have won it but was disqualified in one of the races for finishing with not enough fuel in his tank – a mistake by the team and a stupid rule, but they could hardly let a young British driver take the win in Germany on D-Day, could they?

I was now spending a lot of time trying to piece together the right deals that would lead Gary into F1. It was a bit like those old vaudeville acts where the guy keeps half a dozen plates spinning at once, always making sure he keeps them going when they start to wobble. Some of the companies were a bit surprised to hear from me, thinking that my relationship with Ron Dennis meant Gary would automatically team up with McLaren, but they hadn't expressed a firm interest. I was free to go elsewhere. The only doubt I had niggling away at the back of my head was that I wasn't sure that Gary wanted F1 badly enough. I was always telling him to take every opportunity that came up to tell the press 'That was a great win – but what I really want is F1.' But he didn't do it often enough to my mind and I just wondered if he was happy being a big star in DTM.

Nevertheless, I started talks with Peter Sauber who was very keen on Gary, and we went to see him at his factory in Switzerland. Peter is a great bloke, a real motorsport enthusiast, and he was very encouraging, saying they knew what Gary could do and were impressed with the way he had progressed through the ranks. We were so sure that we were on track for an F1 drive that we started negotiating Gary's release from his DTM contract, but then Canadian Jacques Villeneuve came on the scene and upset the applecart. It was a time when F1 was having problems in the USA and I don't know if pressure was put on Sauber to take a North American driver, but at the last minute our deal was off. Peter Sauber acted very correctly, phoning me to tell me before I heard it elsewhere and adding that it was nothing against Gary but just the situation they found themselves in.

I was devastated. I was certain that Gary and Sauber would have made a great team but these things happen in motorsport, where there are always more drivers than berths. We were destined to spend 2006 back in DTM and, despite his disappointment at losing out on the Sauber deal, Gary took on drivers of the calibre of Jean Alesi and Mika Häkkinen, and blew their wheels off to be the champion. Nothing could stop him.

I sat down with Gary and Martin Whitmarsh at the British Grand Prix and we hammered out the basis of a deal to make Gary a McLaren F1 test driver. We shook hands and I said to Martin, 'We've got a championship to win. After that, I'll come back and see you to finalise the details.'

I'm not a great believer in lavishing praise on people but the day Gary clinched the DTM championship in Hockenheim I told him that I thought what he had achieved was brilliant. He had been absolutely superb that weekend. When you are driving a machine that is virtually an F1 car with a Mercedes shell on it, everything has to be spot on, right down to positioning exactly on the mark to ensure your pit stops are achieved in the minimum possible time. He drove with absolute precision that day, never making a single wrong move, which was even more remarkable when you think that he was racing under the pressure of leading the championship knowing he could become the youngest British driver to take the DTM crown, and also that his future in F1 probably depended on how well he went. He showed his true character that day. One of his great strengths is that he doesn't go over the top when things go well – he's always understood that we race to win, so it's not that big a deal when we do – and he doesn't get too down if things go wrong. If we don't win, we don't sink into depression or moan: we analyse what went wrong whether it's the car, the driver or something outside our control, and set about putting it right.

We partied long and hard after Hockenheim and when I got home I phoned him to say, 'You deserve your shot at F1. I'll go and see McLaren next week, then you need to come and see me the following Wednesday and we'll sort everything out.'

He never turned up. I rang him but there was no reply. I asked his dad where he was and, if he heard from him, to say I needed to talk to him urgently.

A call came at 8.30 the next morning at home but it wasn't Gary. It was my factory, asking if I would go straight in because there was a solicitor from London with a package. I said I'd be half an hour but the guy didn't wait. I assumed it couldn't therefore be too important and carried on with my usual jobs before getting round to opening the box. It contained a massive folder. When I first started to read it, I thought it was another Derek Redfern wind-up but then I realised it wasn't. I read it through twice to make sure I'd understood it. Basically, this was a file from Gary saying I was a crap manager, that I didn't know any of the people who counted in the sport, and therefore he did not want me to manage him any more. I had the same sick feeling in the pit of my stomach as you have when you are kicked in the balls.

His dad still worked with my Young Guns team and I called him into the office. I pushed the papers across the desk and said, 'What do you know about this, Jim? Looks as though Gary doesn't think I can take him where he wants to go. He wants out.'

As Jim shuffled through the documents, the colour drained

from his face as though someone had turned on a tap and allowed the blood to run out. All he could say was, 'I don't believe it.'

I was in a state of shock. I wanted to go and find Gary and have it out with him there and then, but this was too serious to go off half-cocked. I remembered Ron Dennis's advice and took my time. Gary had never said a word to me to suggest he was unhappy. The solicitor who had delivered the package was one used by Ty, my mate for twenty years, the guy who had carried me into hospital for my cancer op. He loved his motorsport and travelled all over with us and eventually, when I couldn't travel to an event with Gary, Ty would be there to look after things. He even popped up in the background on TV from time to time, with one cruel commentator saying, 'Now we know who ate all the pies.'

I suppose alarm bells should have rung when one or two German journalists asked me if Ty was Gary's new manager, but I just explained I was still the manager and Ty was more like an assistant. I suspected that it was not just the German press who had begun to have the wrong idea. I rang Ty, who denied any involvement. That was the last time I ever spoke to him.

One blow was bad enough. Two was shattering. I'd given Gary fourteen years of my life and spent a huge chunk of money on his career. What hurt most was that I had treated him better than my own son, who often didn't get the drive he deserved because there wasn't any spare cash. Luke has never rebuked me over that but if he had bumped into Gary soon after hearing about our falling out I think it might have been quite ugly.

Because I couldn't speak to Gary direct, I rang Martin Brundle and asked him to act as a go-between. Gary had already told him what was going on and Martin had agreed to take him into 2MB, the company he ran with Mark Blundell. Ironically, two years before, when we thought we'd got the F1 deal with Sauber, I'd approached Martin about taking on the management of Gary. I knew he would need a full-time bag carrier to sort out all the day-to-day stuff when he was on the F1 circuit and I wouldn't be able to do that. But Martin said he couldn't because he was chairman of the BRDC and didn't have the time. Now it seemed he had the time and the inclination.

I contacted a solicitor and he tore their case to shreds, demonstrating that every claim was pitiful, and I said to Martin Brundle, 'If Gary wants to go down the legal route that's OK with me, but I don't think it would be good for his career, so I suggest you come up with something we can all agree on.'

I'd had a deal with Gary that set out how much I'd invested in him and the percentage of his wages he would pay me back each year until it was clear. It was a very fair deal – he didn't pay a penny until he had made a reasonable living, so it might have taken him five years, ten years or even more before he paid me off. Maybe he would never be able to pay it all back. It depended on how successful he was. We were all happy with that. It had been renewed each time it ran out without any quibbles and had seen us successfully through fourteen years together. But a strange thing happens when ordinary lads start to earn big money. I heard boxing trainer Brendan Ingle say that some of his world champions were happy to pay his 25 per cent management fee when it was £25 out of £100, but they balked at £250,000 out of £1 million. Maybe Gary had been happy with the deal when I was doing the paying out but now he didn't fancy it as much.

Nothing could compensate me for the sense of betrayal or the loss of a dream, but eventually we thrashed out an agreement of long-term, staged payments that would at least repay some of the money I'd spent. We also issued the obligatory press release in which Gary thanked me for the guidance I had given him since he was eleven years old, and added, 'The shared goal of succeeding in Formula One has now become a reality.'

I thought that would be the end of it but six months later, when I was at an airport in Syria with Luke, I received a phone call from Ron Dennis. He felt that Gary wasn't going as well as he'd hoped and thought it was because he had the debt to me hanging over him. Ron wanted to pay me off. What would I accept? We had a bit of a haggle but he was pitching it far too low for my liking. Eventually, he phoned back with a more acceptable figure and he took over my contract.

Jim Paffett is still a valuable member of the Young Guns team and I still rate Gary very highly. I reckon that, if you put him in equal equipment with Lewis Hamilton, there wouldn't be much between them. I still talk to him when I see him but I don't seek him out. I will never forgive him.

My dad always used to say, 'Don't get bitten by the same dog twice.' So he would have given me rollicking when he saw me take Oliver Rowland under my wing. Oliver is a proper talent who stood out from the crowd in the Zip Young Guns. From the start you could tell he had what it took to be an F1 driver. He had feel and was another of those drivers who could go from back to front through a crowded field. He proved it magnificently at Shennington in 2007 after a dictatorial official had first instructed the drivers to slow down on the warm-up lap, then shunted Oliver from pole to the back of the grid for driving too slowly. His answer was fantastic, winning the race with one of the best drives I have seen and underlining to F1 teams just how much potential he has.

I got passes for the British GP and made sure he met the

right people in the pit lane. Pretty soon everyone realised I thought this kid had what it took to be another Lewis Hamilton. McLaren didn't seem interested but several other teams were, and we had talks with one team on the basis of having Oliver race for me for another two years, then, when he was sixteen, I would give him six months in the winter driving Zip Formula getting used to single-seaters and the new tracks, before we would race (and win) Formula Renault and F3, by which time he would be ready for their team.

McLaren obviously got wind of this, because Martin Whitmarsh was soon on the phone enquiring about 'that kid you introduced us to at Silverstone'. I pointed out I'd told them first and kept them updated by email, suggesting they should support Oliver because he'd even less cash to spend on karting than Lewis when he began, but they hadn't come back to me and we were now quite a long way down the road with other teams.

'Come and see me tomorrow,' he said.

I did and it was clear they wanted him signed up. It didn't take long to do the deal and I'm told that, when Ron Dennis first met Oliver, he got that old sparkle back in his eye and was 100 per cent behind the agreement that would see me run him in a Zip kart, then move him into Europe in a Topkart chassis, just as we had Lewis. It all looked to be going so well when he won the British Championship in 2007 and Oliver seemed happy because he said in an interview, 'I'm privileged now to be a member of the Young Guns team. I'm also fortunate to have the support of Martin Hines and his influence has been crucial in getting me a contract with McLaren.' And even McLaren's in-house magazine recognised that I'd found them another gem, saying: 'Martin Hines recruited Rowland to his successful Zip Young Guns Team. Hines is renowned for spotting talent and has mentored a long line of drivers including Lewis Hamilton and Vodafone McLaren Mercedes test driver Gary Paffett.'

But pretty soon problems started to loom on the horizon. I had the impression that Oliver may have thought that, by signing the McLaren contract, success was assured. I tried to tell him that you've never made it in motorsport until someone is paying you huge sums of money to drive their car, and in many ways that is still only the beginning, because there will always be hungry kids looking to unseat you.

There is always a danger that, when they enjoy the first sniff of F1, kids start to believe they are God's gift and become cocky. I have never put up with it and always made sure my Young Guns keep their feet on the ground – with Luke and Gary I used to give them all the crap jobs such as cleaning awnings when we got back from a meeting and they have never acted the prima donna. I wasn't having the same success with Oliver.

I became alarmed when he started to pick up points on his licence for dirty driving. The system is similar to the one road drivers face – twelve points and you face a ban – and in a three-month period after signing for McLaren Oliver picked up ten. One of the incidents particularly angered me when he took off two drivers who were alongside him coming out of a hairpin. After the race, I took him into the transporter and gave him the biggest dressing-down he's likely to receive in his life and threatened to throw him out of the Young Guns team if he ever drove like that again.

He was going to be under pressure when the new season started but, to be honest, I felt it would be good for him. He needed to learn to drive hard but clean and knowing he faced the possibility of a three-month lay-off would have concentrated his mind. In autumn 2007 we invested in developing a new chassis ready for him to go into KF2. We took him to the Monaco Kart GP in October, where he dominated the action and would have won by miles but his engine blew. Still, we had shown he was competitive and could look forward with confidence to the new season.

Then in January I received a call from Martin Whitmarsh – the man who had told me he'd got doubts about Gary Paffett because he hadn't shown me the loyalty I deserved – to tell me they were taking Oliver out of Zip and putting him into the Tonykart team, one of my biggest rivals. I think it was their way of keeping him out of the firing line in England but, ironically, Oliver's 2008 season, which will have cost McLaren heaps, was probably his worst year for results since he had driven a Zip Kart back in 2001. McLaren desperately wanted to win the European championship but he finished a fair way back in fifth place.

Perhaps now McLaren will see that it is not so easy for young drivers to step up. It worked out with Lewis, but his circumstances were different. Oliver was left with a strange foreign team at just 15 years old. This might be OK for mature 19-20 year old racers but not for a talented young man who needs a friendly-but-firm hand leading him though the minefield to F1. I do hope Oliver turns things round in 2009 as when he was with the Zip Young Guns he had talent and enthusiasm comparable to that of Lewis.

Even with these setbacks, I remain a glass-half-full man and, while Gary and Oliver were giving me grief, Luke was making me prouder than a dad has the right to be. After a year of troubles at Seat, where he managed just one win, it was time for him to make the next, colossal step to GT2, where he drove a Panoz, the American muscle car that is an awesome beast and a daunting car to master even for an experienced driver. Luke quickly showed it who was boss. This was real seat-of-the-pants stuff but his mastery, especially in the wet, was something to behold, and I smiled as I thought back to the day when we couldn't entice him even to sit in Derek Bell's Porsche.

Being the son of Martin Hines hasn't always been easy. I've rattled a few cages over the years and also enjoyed a lot of success, so, between my detractors and admirers, Luke was always likely to be labelled as either 'successful only thanks to his old man' or 'good but not as good as his dad'. Believe me, when it comes to driving GT, Luke is in a different class from me, and I couldn't be more delighted that he has established himself as world-class entirely on his own merits.

In his rookie year he had six outright wins and twelve podiums. That was good enough to move him up to the FIA European GT1 championship, the saloon cars' F1. Again he was in a mighty car, the Corvette C6, a beautiful brute that needs a top driver, and in Luke has one. I can't help but mention that, despite the fact that Gary was always a year ahead of Luke and had more resources poured into his career, Luke reached GT1 before Gary made it into F1. Perhaps the motorsport gods do make sure justice is done in the long term.

Chapter 39
Watch This Space

I started work on this book on 13 February. I hadn't planned it that way, it just happened to be the first day I could get away to Spain and spend some time looking back. But when I realised the date I wasn't at all surprised because the number 13 has cropped up so many times in my life. I first noticed it about twenty-five years ago, when I realised that for some reason Dad had arranged for the company's financial year to end on 13 July – he never did explain why. The numbers of all our bank accounts end in 13, the house I bought for Kelly and Lindy was 13 Park Road, and our place in La Manga is 26 – perhaps because it cost me twice as much!

Number 13 is traditionally considered unlucky, so I suppose it's no surprise that Kelly was 13 when she died and Dad passed away on Friday the 13th, and I lost the 1989 World Championship on the 13th lap at Silverstone when my gearbox blew, the last race my mum and dad attended. But there have been plenty of good things happen to me as well: I won a World Championship on the 13th, the snooker club was at 13 Woodhouse Road, while *Kart and Superkart* and my Hermetite sponsorship both lasted 13 years.

I'm not claiming any of this has a particular significance but it has always struck me as odd how often that number keeps cropping up. Perhaps the most bizarre occasion was when I sold one of my Porsches. My advert produced about a hundred responses but I agreed to hold it for the first guy who called, a doctor who lived in the West Country. He said he was leaving home with £1,000 deposit and if he liked the car he would get a bank draft for the rest. It was love at first sight and as we chatted I told him I still had all the original paperwork to go with it.

I dug it out and said, 'What's the date?'

He replied: 'The fourth of April.'

I couldn't believe it. I hadn't touched those papers since the day I bought the car but here I was selling it 13 years to the day after I'd bought it.

Oh yes, in case you hadn't noticed, this, the final chapter, is No. 39 – three 13s.

Putting your life down on paper is a strange experience. Memories pop out of nowhere of events and people you haven't thought of for years. Other things are still so vivid that they have never been far from the surface – some so good, you still smile when you think of them and some so painful you cannot help but choke back the tears.

Setting out my story like this has confirmed what I always suspected: I am my father's son. I am what I am because of the genes he handed down, what he taught me and the business he passed on to me. Without him I'd have had nothing. It's a great legacy but it is also a responsibility. I'm a workaholic because if anything went wrong with the business, it would mean I had let my old man down. In a way I am a prisoner of the company, more often than not still working seven days a week. I'm not complaining – I never wake up thinking that I don't want to go to work. I may think for a minute that it would be nice to spend a week stretched out on a beach but then I remember the pile of jobs, emails and messages that would be waiting for me when I got back, and decide against.

What will happen when I decide I can't carry on? I'm not really sure. Luke is not ready to take on the mantle yet. He is a great driver and superb at working with kids and motivating young drivers, which makes him an integral part of the Zip Young Guns Team. He has inherited a wonderful temperament and warm nature from his mother. Like me, he can spot a good driver and fortunately for him he has inherited his father's looks, but he doesn't have my aggression and the hardness you need to succeed in business, although he has plenty of time to work on that. Anyway, he has the small matter of a GT World Championship to think about.

Tuesday, on the other hand, is a chip off the old block and can be hard-nosed with the best of them. She has an incredibly sharp business brain, is ambitious and has already shown that she can do practically anything she turns her mind to. But her interests lie elsewhere. She's a great-looking girl – with the tell-tale Hines eyes – and has a fantastic personality. I have a few projects in mind that I hope I can persuade her to be involved in, and she has the advantage that most people don't have in that she knows how to handle me and get what she wants. I can see Tuesday achieving many marvellous things in the years to come and I am just so grateful that Chris Russell has given me the chance to achieve the ambition conceived when I sat shivering in that chair so many years ago.

But, in case my rivals are starting to think that Hines is writing his obituary, let me assure them they couldn't be more wrong. I've still got plans that will keep them on their toes for some years to come.

For example, I haven't done nearly enough to exploit the Zip Golf Buggies. These came about after Duncan Coulthard,

DC's father, was out on a boat with Tony Coles, the MD of La Manga Golf Club. Tony happened to say that a number of golfers had complained that their games were slowed up because buggies had to stay on the paths, so he was looking for some new, three-wheeled buggies that could go on the fairways without damaging them. Duncan said, 'I know just the man,' and put us together. We came up with a design that had a lot more flair than the old ones and worked fantastically, and we managed to make up fifty in time for La Manga's Footballers' Classic tournament. That was a couple of years ago now and they are still going strong and proving popular with the punters, so, as soon as I make enough time, I reckon we could open up that market.

There are a couple of top-secret kart projects that look as though they will come off before 2010. I'm still passionately committed to the Zip Formula and I'm convinced that will be massive in the next few years, especially in India and China. The Young Guns are as strong as ever and I'm determined to keep them at the top of the tree. And of course there's my own driving.

Oh, yes, the old man still hasn't quite hung up his helmet. Over the last couple of years, historic karting – karts produced before 1980 – has become very popular around the world. Now it just so happens that the iconic historic kart is the Zip shadow with a Yamaha TD3 engine on Bridgestone tyres in the Hermetite silver colours. That was *the* kart and I just happen to own it. I also still have my old Simpson *Star Wars* helmet, which I wore when I won the first British Grand Prix. It was the first helmet ever flown to the UK by designer Bill Simpson and was painted for me by Doug Ayres, the man who introduced painting helmets in flash colours.

I went to Monaco in 2006 to celebrate the fiftieth anniversary of karting. We drove the world-famous street track and my kart was two or three seconds faster than anything else. It will be coming out again from time to time and I still expect to win. After all, I'm going to need a big win after 2010 to keep up my record of at least one title in every decade.

Over the years people have said some nice things about me and what I have done for karting, but it's only fair to say that, no matter how much I've given the sport, karting has given me much, much more in return. The thrill of watching kids such as Luke, DC, Gary Paffett, Jason Plato, Lewis Hamilton and all the others grow up into top-class drivers would in itself be enough reward. I can't deny that I am proud that the McLaren stable now has four young drivers, including Lewis, Gary and Oliver Rowland, a trio who learned their skills in the Young Guns.

Of course, there has been some pain involved, especially with Gary, and at my age I guess it would be daft even to contemplate getting that involved again. But there are a few drivers in the Young Guns team at the moment who...

But let's leave it a year or two. Just watch this space.